"Flint details a thorough explanation of the problems that arise when celibacy is exalted in the context of an exclusively male-led, hierarchical organization. . . . Sanderson gives a brave narrative of the sexual abuses that occur in this insular unisex institution; and it is strikingly familiar to anyone who has grown up female in the greater world. This book is a fantastic summary of the reason we all need Christ's teaching of mutuality in this world without the dynamic of status."

—Jill Correnti Striebinger
Association of Roman Catholic Women Priests

"Debra Flint raises a very controversial question when she makes a link between mandatory priestly celibacy and the avalanche of historic and contemporary scandals in the Catholic Church involving clerical child sex abuse."

—Mary McAleese
Former President of Ireland

"Debra Maria Flint demonstrates how [clerical celibacy] has caused immense suffering to both adults and children. Paul Murphy Sanderson, speaking of his harrowing experience of suffering clerical sexual abuse, reveals how the institutional church has emotionally harmed victims of clerical abuse. This work describes how mandatory clerical celibacy has fostered a culture of psychosocial and psychospiritual pathology."

—Brendan A. Mooney
Psychotherapist in Hospice and Palliative Care

"This book shows the need for emotional intelligence and healthy formation training, more thorough screening for psychological issues and firm, decisive intervention from visionary leaders. And clearly, many religions need to address the prehistoric way they involve women and simply must wake up to giving them an equal place and in doing so, creating healthier communities. Clearly, too many people—from popes to parishioners—have looked the other way. Until the institutions built around mandatory celibacy become much more robust and accountable, we will continue to rely, unfairly, on the bravery of people like Paul and the courage of other distressed victims to make their voices heard.

—Alfie Joey
Actor, Artist, Presenter

The Sins of Mandatory Celibacy

The Sins of Mandatory Celibacy

The History and Consequences of Mandatory Celibacy Within Catholicism

DEBRA MARIA FLINT
and PAUL MURPHY SANDERSON

RESOURCE *Publications* · Eugene, Oregon

THE SINS OF MANDATORY CELIBACY
The History and Consequences of Mandatory Celibacy Within Catholicism

Copyright © 2025 Debra Maria Flint and Paul Murphy Sanderson. All rights reserved. Except for brief quotations in critical publications or reviews, no part of this book may be reproduced in any manner without prior written permission from the publisher. Write: Permissions, Wipf and Stock Publishers, 199 W. 8th Ave., Suite 3, Eugene, OR 97401.

Resource Publications
An Imprint of Wipf and Stock Publishers
199 W. 8th Ave., Suite 3
Eugene, OR 97401

www.wipfandstock.com

PAPERBACK ISBN: 979-8-3852-6081-2
HARDCOVER ISBN: 979-8-3852-6082-9
EBOOK ISBN: 979-8-3852-6083-6

VERSION NUMBER 120225

Scripture quotations marked (NIV) are taken from the Holy Bible, New International Version®, NIV®. Copyright © 1973, 1978, 1984, 2011 by Biblica, Inc.™ Used by permission of Zondervan. All rights reserved worldwide. www.zondervan.com The "NIV" and "New International Version" are trademarks registered in the United States Patent and Trademark Office by Biblica, Inc.™

Scripture quotations marked (KJV) are taken from The Authorized (King James) Version. Rights in the Authorized Version in the United Kingdom are vested in the Crown. Reproduced by permission of the Crown's patentee, Cambridge University Press

Dedicated by Debra Maria Flint

To the memory of the philosopher Dr Nicholas Folan, O.P. who taught me how to think.

Dedicated by Paul Murphy Sanderson

*To my parents, my family, and my friends—
but most especially to Carmel, my beloved wife.
Thank you for believing when I doubted,
for standing beside me in the dark,
and for leading me with love into the light.*

Contents

Acknowledgments | ix
Introduction | xi
  by Debra Maria Flint

PART 1: The Sins of Mandatory Celibacy
    by Debra Maria Flint

CHAPTER 1
The History and Theology of Celibacy | 3

CHAPTER 2
Mandatory Celibacy, Sexuality, and Companionship | 30

CHAPTER 3
Mandatory Celibacy and Human Rights | 43

CHAPTER 4
Mandatory Celibacy and Misogynism | 57

CHAPTER 5
Mandatory Celibacy and Sexual Abuse | 76

CHAPTER 6
Mandatory Celibacy and Fatherhood | 106

PART 2: The Sins of Mandatory Celibacy: A Personal Experience
    by Paul Murphy-Sanderson

Introduction | 119
Early Childhood and Religious Vocation | 121
Upholland College—Junior Seminary | 127
A Sexual Abuse Trial and a Suicide | 134
Castlerigg Manor, Keswick | 138
Ushaw College 1986 | 142
Years Out and More Abuse | 149

English Martyrs Church, Preston | 154
Ushaw College 1992 | 161
Mount St. Bernard Abbey | 171
Reporting Abuse to Lancaster Diocese | 182
Contacting the Police | 203
Life After the Trial | 221
The Aftereffects of Clergy Abuse | 228
From Victim to Survivor | 234

PART 3: Conclusion | 235
    by Debra Maria Flint

The Afterword | 247
  by Archbishop Jonathan Blake

Bibliography | 251

Acknowledgments

OUR GRATEFUL THANKS TO Debra's daughter, Dr Azelina Flint, for her expert copyediting.

Introduction

by Debra Maria Flint

AT THE TIME OF writing my second book, my prior work, *No Place for a Woman*, has not long been published. This book was written to highlight the spiritual abuse of women but now, in union with my friend, Paul Murphy Sanderson (a former Cistercian monk and priest), I am turning my attention to mandatory celibacy, which appears to be a major factor in the sexual abuse of children, young people, seminarians, and women, but which is also, in part, a product of the spiritual indoctrination of men who join the priesthood. I am delighted that Paul, a former Catholic priest, has joined me in writing this book. The sexual abuse scandals that have involved Roman Catholic priests have now been exposed for some decades; however, the revelations of impropriety continue. In the last few months more scandals involving the clerical sexual abuse at the Spiritan schools in Ireland have hit the headlines and the Catholic Church's dark history of sexual abuse in Belgium also cast a shadow over the late Pope Francis's last visit to that country.

The allegations against the Spiritan Fathers (formerly known as the Holy Ghost fathers) relate to incidents which began in the 1960s and continued for many decades.[1] Over 290 people have now made allegations of sexual abuse against fifty-seven abusers. Some of these priests were "serial abusers with unchecked access to children."[2] The schools concerned were Willow Park Junior School, Blackrock Primary, Rockwell College and Blackrock College, all of which were run by the Spiritans and, since these incidents were revealed, it has emerged that there was also sexual abuse at another seminary school run by them. Kimmage Manor was a formation school for young men who wanted to enter the priesthood, and eleven

---

1. All discussion of the allegations against the Spiritan Fathers refer to McGarry and McGreevy, "Blackrock College."
2. McGarry and McGreevy, "Blackrock College," para. 2.

pupils had made allegations against a priest there who has since been convicted and served his sentence.

Former Prime Minister of Belgium, Alexander De Croo, condemned the Church's "legacy of clerical sex abuse and cover-ups" and demanded "concrete steps" to show that the Church had "come clean with the past" and put victims' interests ahead of those of its own institution.[3] Historic sexual abuse by the Catholic clergy in Belgium was highlighted in 2020 after a TV documentary, *Godforsaken*, demonstrated the distress of people who had been sexually assaulted. In 2010, "the country's longest-serving bishop, Bruges Bishop Roger Vangheluwe, had been allowed to resign without punishment after he had admitted that he had sexually abused his nephew for 13 years";[4] however, he was not defrocked until 2024 shortly before the Pope's visit to Belgium. There have also been many other allegations of sexual abuse against clergy in Belgium that were revealed in this documentary, which was aired by the public broadcaster VRT in 2020. Belgian victims told their stories on camera showing "the depravity of the crimes and their systemic cover-up by the Catholic hierarchy."[5]

In France, allegations also emerged from the French bishops' conference in Lourdes. There are eleven bishops who have been named by the Church as accused of cases linked to sexual abuse.[6] Some are being investigated for sexual abuse while others are accused of failing to report it. These men face "prosecution or disciplinary action" by the Church.[7] Sadly, these alleged incidents are not the only ones to rock the Church in France in recent times. In October 2021, "an independent commission set up by the Catholic Church in France found that some 216,000 children had been abused by Catholic clergy since the 1950s."[8] France, like Ireland and Belgium, is one of many countries where sexual abuse scandals have greatly shaken the Roman Catholic Church. However, the more recent allegations are particularly sickening because they involve eleven bishops of the Church.

The sexual abuse of children and seminarians in the above examples of Ireland, Belgium and France is unfortunately not limited to these countries. It is typical of a general picture of sexual abuse by Catholic clergy which can be found in almost every country in the world. What has caused this sexual

---

3. Associated Press, "Belgium Prime Minister," para. 1.
4. Associated Press, "Belgium Prime Minister," para. 10.
5. Associated Press, "Belgium Prime Minister," para. 19.
6. All discussion of sex abuse in the French Catholic Church refers to "Cardinal Ricard," *BBC News*.
7. "Cardinal Ricard," *BBC News*, para. 4.
8. "Cardinal Ricard," *BBC News*, para. 12.

abuse? I believe one of the major causes is mandatory celibacy because, as I shall demonstrate, although sexual abuse does occur in other Christian denominations, its incidence is not as high in those denominations as it is within Roman Catholicism.

What is mandatory celibacy? The term refers to a discipline within the Roman Catholic Church that all candidates for the priesthood in the Latin West must take a vow of celibacy and will not be allowed to proceed to ordination unless they take such a vow. However, Catholic candidates for the priesthood in the Eastern rite who are also loyal to Rome do not have to take such a vow and are allowed to marry. Of the 1.3 billion Catholics in the world approximately eighteen million belong to the Eastern rite and priests in this rite are exempt from the celibacy vow. Priests from other denominations who are already married but later convert to Catholicism are also exempt from taking this vow. They are allowed to transfer over to the Catholic Church as married priests. So, mandatory celibacy is not completely universal. It is hoisted on to cradle Catholic candidates who apply to join the priesthood of the Latin rite.

In the early church celibacy was not mandated in the West until the twelfth century and many priests were married. However, the question of mandatory celibacy did come up in the West before the twelfth century due to the influence of certain theologians such as Augustine and Jerome who will be discussed later. The Eastern part of the Church, however, never liked the idea of mandatory celibacy and, as I shall illustrate, the issue of mandatory celibacy was one of several bones of contention between the East and the West up until the East–West Schism of 1054. That Schism, of course, provided the perfect opportunity for the West to mandate celibacy as, once it was free of the East, the opposition was less stringent. Therefore, the Gregorian reforms and the First Council of the Lateran which heralded in mandatory celibacy occurred in the wake of the East–West Schism. Naturally mandatory celibacy created an exclusive priesthood which was no longer representative of all humanity. By this time the female diaconate had already died out, but married priests had at least remained. Once a married priesthood was outlawed in the West the priesthood ceased to be diverse, and representative of general humanity and a separate clerical world was born. Then, through a series of ecumenical councils and the creation of Catholic canon law, celibate men in the West gave themselves more and more power. They created a world for themselves which was separate from mainstream humanity and which, to a large extent, cut them off from ordinary people. That world developed a culture of its own and, I will argue, it is that culture that has caused many clerical 'sins,' such as abuses of human rights, misogyny, and sexual abuse.

Within the Roman Catholic Church, bishops, who are of course meant to be celibate, are collectively known as the College of Bishops and can also hold additional titles such as archbishop, cardinal or pope. They are also known as 'the hierarchy' meaning that they hold the highest offices at the top of the Church. The hierarchy state that the apostles were given a special charism and office at Pentecost and that this charism and office has been transmitted to them through an unbroken succession of bishops by the laying on of hands in the sacrament of holy orders. The transmission of this charism and office is referred to as 'apostolic succession.' According to the Catholic hierarchy, this charism and office gives them special status and enables them to be exclusively responsible for teaching all Catholics, governing dioceses, discerning the workings of the Holy Spirit, sanctifying the world, and representing the Church. It also means that, in reality, all 'celibate' bishops (not only the Pope) are treated as 'infallible,' since only a bishop can grant imprimaturs (official licenses) for theological books certifying that they are free from doctrinal or moral error. Each bishop is also solely responsible for the governing of his own particular diocese. This, in effect, gives the bishops of the Roman Catholic Church absolute power, making the Catholic Church very different from any other Christian denomination. No other Christian denomination gives such power to its bishops, although several of them claim apostolic succession, and (except for the Orthodox who ordain married men but do not allow them to rise to the bishopric), no other Christian denomination ordains only 'celibate men' as bishops.

As stated, there is no other Christian denomination which gives its bishops the elevated status that the Roman Catholic Church does, and I shall demonstrate in Part One of this work, there is also no other Christian denomination that has so many incidents of sexual abuse. Some of this abuse was actually committed by bishops and, most of it (whether committed by bishops or not) was covered up by many of them for many years. Are we to take it, then, that God has chosen sexual abusers to teach and govern Catholics, discern the workings of the holy spirit, and sanctify the world? I think not, and, in this book, I will argue that sexual abuse in the ranks of the Catholic clergy is more prolific than in other professions due to the culture of enforced celibacy, which was created by the hierarchy to keep both property and power in the hands of the elite. This culture has not only led to sexual abuse; it has also created a distorted clerical world that has been inflicted on the Roman Catholic people of God, of which there are many victims. Unfortunately, the majority of people outside the Catholic Church have no idea of the extent of this distorted and disordered clerical world and how it affects many Catholics. The account of Paul, formerly Father Paul, in Part Two of this book will, however, give some inkling of it.

The distorted clerical world that has been created by the Catholic hierarchy affects all groups of people in the Roman Catholic Church, including all priests (whether in religious orders or not, since they are answerable to the hierarchy), Roman Catholic women in religious orders, Catholic married men who may wish to be priests (but are only allowed to be ordained as deacons), all Catholic women who are regarded as inferior to men and cannot be ordained at all (and were continuously told, especially by Pope Francis, that their main roles were those of wives and mothers), and, lastly, all pioneering Catholic intellectuals of either sex who seek to make great contributions to society. The source of this disordered clerical world lies in the teaching of ancient Western 'saints' such as Augustine and Aquinas who (while they may have been very good people in their own times and settings) continue to be revered by the hierarchy as examples of science par excellence and Doctors of the Church, despite the fact that their archaic theology and 'science' goes against all modern knowledge. Augustine argued that every human being is born sinful and inherits the guilt of Adam, who is supposed to have been the first man. However, it is almost certain that no such first human being called Adam ever existed, as the book of Genesis is a written myth. It was written as an attempt to put across a certain belief system and, while it may contain many spiritual insights, it is not a historical account of the creation of the world. Augustine also argued that original sin was caused by concupiscence through sexual intercourse and that this led to human beings being born utterly depraved in nature. Modern biology and psychology have now shown this theory to be complete nonsense; yet the Catholic hierarchy continue to refer to this man as a 'Doctor of the Church' i.e. a person whose teaching should be revered.

Aquinas, another 'Doctor of The Church,' taught that all women were subhuman. He stated that the female was a defective and 'misbegotten' male. Both saints were writing without the knowledge of biology and sexuality that we have today and so may be excused to a certain degree. However, the Catholic hierarchy of today, which continues to hold up these men as icons of perfection cannot be excused. They do not wish to acknowledge the biological and psychological errors that have been taught by both these men because, of course, the findings of the modern sciences turn the Roman Catholic Church's teaching concerning mandatory celibacy on its head. Modern biology and psychology would also turn the Church back towards the actual teachings of ancient Judaism and the teachings of Jesus which, in fact, were very much in line with the idea that sexuality is natural, God-given, and inherently good. Sadly, this is something that the current hierarchy do not wish to remember and, by failing to remember the practices of the early church and update their theology to reflect the developments of the biological and social sciences, the hierarchy have alienated many educated people of our times—either driving them away from their church, or damaging their mental health. The people they have driven away include the most gifted—those who could have helped them to reach out to others and make the Christian message more relevant to modern times. Some of the groups of people who have been damaged by the church, or driven away, are detailed below.

Men who would wish to be priests or who are priests are denied, not only their God-given sexuality, but also their freedom of speech, and conscience. They dare not 'rock the boat,' or say anything that is not in line with official Catholic teaching. This is because they know that if they claim they do not agree with enforced celibacy, or the ban on the ordination of women, they will either be refused ordination or disciplined (if already ordained). Priests therefore are kept silent by the threat of losing their vocations and livelihoods and exactly the same applies to women who are members of religious orders. They dare not speak out against teachings they disagree with because they know that if they do so they are likely to be expelled from their orders. For example, when Lavinia Byrne wrote *Woman at the Altar*, a book that advocates the ordination of women, she was forced to leave her religious order. The gagging of Catholic clerics and religious is an abuse of human rights and, in this work, I will argue that these abuses of human rights are due to the fact that mandatory celibacy has created a clerical 'celibate' cult.

Catholic married men who are permanent deacons are not allowed to be ordained as priests. No matter how much they feel they may be called to a priestly vocation they are not allowed to take this up and their calling is denied. As will be demonstrated in this book, this rule is rooted in the perverse teaching that the celibate state is somehow better than the married state, a bizarre concept seeing as all human beings are created in a sexualized state.

All Catholic women are denied ordination to both the diaconate and the priesthood, even though there is indisputable evidence that women were ordained to the diaconate in the early church. This evidence has been discussed in my previous book.[9] This situation has caused much suffering to many women. As stated above, some women like Lavinia Byrne, were forced to lose their homes and livelihoods as a 'punishment' for daring to state that women should be ordained.

---

9. Flint, *No Place for a Woman*.

In addition to being denied ordination, some women have also been denied consecration to vocations that are regarded as legitimate in the Church, for example the vocations of consecrated widow and consecrated virgin. Consecrated virgins and widows live independently in the community in their own homes. Some bishops have simply refused to consecrate women as virgins or widows, stating that they do not agree with consecrated women living independently in the community. It seems that, to these men, women with a vocation belong only in a veil in a convent. In their view, women should not dare to have the audacity to think that they can live independently in a house (like a priest does) while living out their vocation! In this work, I will argue that misogyny is a consequence of mandatory celibacy.

Finally, many Catholic lay people who may lead in a particular field, such as psychology, sociology, biology, and gynecology, have found that their specialist knowledge is ignored by the Catholic hierarchy. The bishops do not read or study it and most up-to-date knowledge (particularly in the spheres of psychology, biology, gynecology, and sociology) is ignored by them when they pronounce on morals or ethics. Some Catholic encyclicals show an infantile knowledge of these fields, which frustrates Catholics who have studied them. This, also, is due to the closed culture that mandatory celibacy has created. There is unwillingness to take the work and expertise of non-celibate lay people seriously. The celibate hierarchy appears to have delusions of grandeur. They believe they know everything about anything.

In this work, I will examine how mandatory celibacy came about and describe the theology underpinning it. I will then look at the effects of enforced celibacy and the culture it has produced. This book is not intended to be a criticism of Roman Catholic priests, as I will demonstrate that they, too, are often victims of abuse, which Paul's account confirms. Sadly, mandatory celibacy both creates abusers and victims of abuse. I hope that this book will give sufficient evidence to generate serious reflection about the ending of this practice. I would also like to make clear that this book is not advocating the end of celibate vocations. Both the former 'Father,' Paul, and I, are very much aware that there are men and women who feel called to live a celibate life and find such a life fulfilling. We advocate the end of *enforced* celibacy. Enforced celibacy is the demand that all candidates for the priesthood (currently male) and all priests and bishops (also currently male) abstain from sexual relationships. This barbaric practice has not only caused the suffering of many of the priests who are supposed to conform to it; it has also (due to the refusal to allow married men to be ordained as priests) created a clergy that is not representative of the vast majority of humanity, and a culture that is not normal, natural or, even (on some occasions) moral. It is a practice that needs to end.

Part 1

The Sins of Mandatory Celibacy

by Debra Maria Flint

Chapter 1

The History and Theology of Celibacy

THIS CHAPTER EXAMINES THE history of mandatory celibacy; in this chapter I will demonstrate that mandatory celibacy was not present in early Christianity. It has gradually evolved over the centuries and is a man-made creation. The topics covered in this chapter are: traditional Jewish views on celibacy, Jesus's views on marriage and celibacy as described in the New Testament, marriage as described in the New Testament, the writing of St. Clement of Alexandria on marriage and celibacy, the influence of Saints Jerome, Ambrose, and Augustine on the theology of celibacy, the East–West Schism and its effects on mandatory celibacy, the First and Second Councils of the Lateran and their effects on mandatory celibacy, St Thomas Aquinas on celibacy, the Reformation and the Protestant abandonment of mandatory celibacy, the Council of Trent and its defense of mandatory celibacy, Vatican I and Vatican II, and their effects on celibacy. I will conclude with the view that mandatory celibacy prevents the Church from developing a healthy theology of sexuality and is therefore damaging, not only to the Church, but society as a whole.

In traditional Judaism, marriage was, and still is, regarded as a contractual bond between a man and a woman in which God is involved. The husband and wife are seen as merging into one soul and a man is considered 'incomplete' if he is not married. Jewish marriage is considered holy and the sanctification of life. It is the fulfilment of God's commands. Procreation is not considered to be the sole purpose of marriage although a Jewish marriage is traditionally expected to fulfil God's commandment to have children. However, leading medieval scholars like Nachmanides also stressed the importance of friendship and sexual union in marriage. Homosexual unions were not recognized within traditional Judaism and are still not recognized today by Orthodox Jews. Reform Judaism, however, does recognize homosexual unions.

Regarding celibacy, the concept of renouncing marriage and sexuality is completely alien to Judaism. There are no references to celibates in the Old Testament, or in the Talmud, and no medieval rabbi is ever known to have lived a celibate life. Jewish theology regards celibacy as incompatible with creation (Gen 5:2) and it is seen as an impediment to personal sanctification largely because it leaves both the sexes in an incomplete state. This is because, as previously stated, a man was regarded as an incomplete being unless he married. This was due to the creation story in Genesis.

In the Old Testament, anyone who could not marry or have children was not allowed into the congregation of the children of Israel (Deut 23:1). They were often referred to as eunuchs and a eunuch could not become a priest (Lev 21: 20–21). There was also an insistence that the high priest be married and that his wife be a virgin (Lev 21:13–14). Due to this insistence on the holiness of marriage, single people were often barred from holding certain public and religious offices and were also barred as synagogue readers. Today there is not so much discrimination against single people in Judaism but there continues to be a strong emphasis on the importance of marriage. Jacobson writes that the Jewish community is "naturally and neatly organized around couples, leaving only an uncomfortable space for those who are single."[1] He also states that "'one' is still only seen as half a number" in Judaism when it comes to being single.[2]

In the New Testament, Jesus, as a Jew, reaffirms the Jewish idea that in marriage the two become one flesh (Matt 19:4). However, Jesus's teaching on divorce is slightly different to that of the traditional Judaism of his day. Jesus states that divorce is permissible on the grounds of sexual immorality, rather than just on the grounds of adultery (Matt 19:9). The Greek word πόρνεια is used and this word means any kind of sexual immorality rather than purely adultery. Therefore, most Western translations made by non-Greek speakers who simply studied Greek at university are incorrect. Any Greek speaker would confirm this and that is almost certainly why the Orthodox have always allowed divorce up to three times. Jesus also states that there is no marriage in heaven (Mark 12:25; Matt 2 23–30; Luke 20: 27–36).

Concerning celibacy, Jesus does not appear to be as harsh as his ancestors, as he does see it as an acceptable form of life; however, he is still nevertheless clear that celibacy is a gift that is meant only for the very few. The disciples ask him whether it would be better not to marry, bearing in

---

1. Jacobson, "Is Being Single Acceptable," para. 2.
2. Jacobson, "Is Being Single Acceptable," para. 5.

mind that divorce is only permissible on the grounds of sexual immorality (Matt 19: 10). The Greek text here implies that the disciples wonder whether it might be preferable not to bother with marriage, as the rules concerning it are difficult to live up to. Jesus immediately responds that not everyone can accept this (i.e., the celibate way of life) but only "those to whom it has been gifted" (Matt 19:11), which makes it quite clear that he sees celibacy as a gift. In the West this verse has often been translated as "to those to whom it has been given" (Matt 19:11).[3] This translation is not exactly correct. A better translation is "to those to whom it has been gifted."[4] To give someone something is not the same as to gift someone something. People are given things all the time, but they are not 'gifted' something as often. A person can hand to someone something of little importance such as a newspaper, but when a person 'gifts' something the implication is that something rare of special importance is given.

Jesus then goes on to describe three different types of celibate men and these are: those who were born that way, those who have been made that way by men (almost certainly those who have been castrated), and those who have renounced marriage for the sake of the Kingdom of Heaven (Matt 19:12). It should be stated here that the Greek word (ευvouχoi) used in the plural has a much broader meaning than the term 'celibates' used today. This word would be applied to men only and would cover all sorts of physical reasons for them not engaging in sexual activity and would not just refer to those who have chosen to refrain from sexual relations as a matter of choice. However, Jesus, at the end of this discourse, then goes on to state according to Western translations, "The one who *can* accept this, should accept it." (Matt 19:12, emphasis mine). This is an incorrect translation of the Greek. The text actually says, "The one who can accept this, I accept" (ὁ δυνάμενος χωρεῖν χωρείτω), and this correct translation has a very different implication to the mistranslation.

This comment of Jesus almost certainly refers to those who have renounced marriage for the sake of the Kingdom of Heaven, seeing as a person who would not be able to engage in sexual relations for physical reasons would have no choice in the matter. Jesus is making it very clear that he is aware that many people would not be able to manage the celibate state of life and that it is a gift, or a personal choice. He is also stating that he accepts those who decide to be celibate for the sake of the Kingdom of Heaven, indicating a move away from the Jewish past when celibacy was regarded as

---

3. See, for example, the King James Bible, "But he said unto them, All men cannot receive this, save they to whom it is given."

4. This is my own translation as a fluent Greek-speaker and scholar of ancient Greek.

anathema. In no way is he indicating that all his disciples should be celibate and there are no grounds whatsoever in his words for the enforced celibacy of priests. Jesus is recognizing celibacy as a legitimate vocation. He is not instigating mandatory celibacy. These words are also Jesus's only known words on the issue of celibacy and the claims by the non-Greek-speaking Cardinal Ratzinger, later Pope Benedict XVI, that these words justify enforced priestly celibacy were therefore either dishonest, or ignorant, because they result from a mistranslation of the original Greek.[5]

Some scholars have also tried to argue that Jesus's saying in Luke advocates celibacy: "I tell you most solemnly that no one who has left home or wife or brothers or parents or children for the sake of the Kingdom of God will fail to receive many times as much in this age and eternal life in the age to come" (Luke 18: 29). This is simply not the case. This saying refers to anyone who may encounter difficulties for following Jesus and it mentions leaving parents, brothers, and children, as well as a wife. Jesus was referring to the fact that many would be hostile to his message and that some of his Jewish followers might find their family relationships disrupted. It has nothing to do with mandatory celibacy at all. Quite frankly, it would appear that celibacy was not a big issue for Jesus since it is hardly mentioned in the Gospels. The question also has to be raised as to why the New Testament has been mistranslated (in regards to Matt 19:11–12) seeing as, before the East–West Schism, the use of the original Greek New Testament was widespread in Christendom and one of the causes of the Schism (from the Orthodox perspective) was the growing usage of the Latin New Testament, which was, of course, not so accurate. After this Schism, the New Testament was translated into other European languages, but how is it that these translations are inaccurate in so many places with such a different slant to that of the original Greek? The question must be asked as to whether this was deliberate.

It is generally believed that Jesus was celibate because the Gospels make no mention of him having a wife. However, there are many details in the Gospels of Jesus's encounters with women and these include: the healing of the woman with a hemorrhage (Matt 9:20–21), the healing of the widow's son (Luke 7: 11–17), the accounts of the Widow's Mite (Mark 12: 41–44; Luke 21: 1–4), the encounter with the Samaritan woman (John 4: 1–42), and the anointing at Bethany (Mark 14: 3–9; John 12: 1–11; Matt 26: 6–13). In all these accounts (and others) Jesus is both empathetic and radical in his treatment of women, often elevating their spiritual attitudes above those of the rich and powerful. For example, in the accounts of the Widow's Mite,

---

5. See Ratzinger, *Salt of the Earth*, 194–200.

Jesus states that the poor widow has given more than anyone else because she gave everything she had, whereas the others only gave of their wealth (Mark 12: 41–44).

There is evidence that women followed Jesus throughout his ministry and these women included: Mary Magdalene, Joanna, Susanna, and others (Luke 8: 2–3), and there is also evidence that his female disciples followed him to the cross and stood near him while he was crucified, whereas his male disciples run away (Mark 15: 40–41; Matt 27: 55–56; John 19: 25–27). But there is no evidence that Jesus had a sexual relationship with any of these women or that they were his wife. In fact, the Gospels refer to them all as caring for him (Mark 15: 40–41; Matt 27: 55–56), which would seem to confirm that he did not actually have a wife. Had there been one, she would presumably have been the one who cared for him.

The woman with whom Jesus almost certainly had the closest relationship was Mary Magdalene and all the canonical gospels describe her as being the first witness of the resurrection. The fact that Jesus chose to appear to her first obviously suggests that Mary was the person whom he most loved and, due to this, some biblical scholars have suggested that she may have had a sexual relationship with him. However, there is no evidence that this was the case, and, in fact, the available evidence is strongly to the contrary, not only because this kind of relationship is not mentioned in the canonical gospels, but also because of other information in the apocryphal gospels.

For example, in the gnostic Gospel of Mary, Jesus is presented as being so close to Mary that he appears to her in a vision after his death. However, it is clear that this relationship has never been a sexual one, as this gospel elevates the spirit above the flesh and encourages an ascetic lifestyle. Similarly, in the Gospel of Phillip, Mary is described as 'barren' and the 'mother of the angels' and as Jesus's spiritual companion (koivovos).[6] Like the Gospel of Mary, this Gospel defends a tradition that gives Mary Magdalene a special relationship with Jesus, and special insight into his teaching, but the contents of this Gospel would again suggest that while the two were close, their relationship was not sexual. It would therefore appear that Jesus did not have a sexual relationship with the woman with whom he had the closest friendship.

It is also interesting that Catholic theology for many centuries, until very recently, has portrayed Mary Magdalene as a prostitute when there is no evidence whatsoever, in the canonical gospels, that this was the case. The evidence from the Gospel of Mary, which is about her, would suggest that

---

6. "The Gospel of Philip," *Gnostic Society Library*.

she was a woman who valued the spiritual rather than the physical. As I demonstrated in my previous work, *No Place for a Woman*, this gospel was almost certainly suppressed by patriarchal misogynists around the second or third centuries. It is therefore even more interesting to note that the portrayal of Mary Magdalene as a prostitute did not begin until AD 591 when Pope Gregory I, without any evidence whatsoever, decided to identify her as the unnamed sinful woman who anointed Jesus's feet in Luke 7:36–50. As her Gospel had already long since been suppressed by patriarchal men who did not wish the new Christian religion to give any credence to Jesus's close friendship with a woman, it would be safe to assume that this Pope's identification of Mary Magdalen as a 'loose' woman was, in fact, a further attempt to erase her influence from the Church. There is nothing to suggest that Jesus had a sexual relationship with Mary or that she was ever a 'loose' woman.

The almost-certain fact that Jesus chose to abstain from sexual relations with the woman who was his closest friend gives no justification whatsoever for the mandatory celibacy of priests for a variety of reasons as follows: firstly, Jesus never at any time recommended that all his followers be forced to be celibate, secondly, the sayings of Jesus in both the canonical gospels and the apocrypha make it clear that Jesus recognized the Jewish ideal of marriage; thirdly Jesus would have seen marriage as personally difficult for him to combine with his nomadic ministry, and, finally, Jesus may have seen marriage as personally impossible to combine with his own status but this would not have applied to others who followed him.

The last reason above requires some clarification. In the Gospels, Jesus often refers to himself as the 'Son of Man' (although this is again a poor translation as the Greek word ανθρωπος is used which means 'person,' and so the correct translation is 'Son of the People'), and there has been much argument concerning what he meant by this. However, if he did use this term to imply that he saw himself as having some kind of divine status, it may have led to him feeling excluded from any sexual relationship. A divine being would presumably not wish to enter into that kind of relationship with a mere human. This is why the argument that the Catholic hierarchy often use for compulsory priestly celibacy is so flawed. They argue that all priests must follow Jesus's example of celibacy, but this argument doesn't make sense. If Jesus chose celibacy, he chose it because he saw himself as different to other men, not because he saw himself as the same as other men. Therefore, if he saw himself as different from other men, Jesus would certainly not have wanted other men to follow his example. Nowhere in the Gospels does Jesus ever suggest that his disciples should be celibate and it is likely that most of them were married. Peter was certainly married as we are told that Jesus healed his mother-in-law (Matt 8:14–15; Mark 1:29–31; Luke 4:38–39). There is also a reference to the son of Peter by Peter himself (or his follower/writer if he did not personally write the letter) in his first letter: "She who is in Babylon, chosen together with you sends you her greetings and so does my son Mark. Greet one another with a kiss of love" (1 Pet 5:13).

Some scholars in the West have tried to get out of this quote by stating that the Greek word used here means a spiritual son and not a blood son, but it doesn't. The Greek word 'uios' is used, and this means a blood son. This word has always been used for a blood son in the Greek for thousands of years up until today. If Peter had wanted to refer to a spiritual son, he would have used another word. It is completely shocking how some Western scholars have twisted the original Greek to suit their own ends. It has been speculated that Peter's son Mark may actually be the evangelist who wrote the Gospel of Mark.

Moving on from the Gospels to the other books of the New Testament, there is clear evidence in the New Testament that Phillip was also married and that he had four daughters (Acts 21:9). One of these daughters, St. Hermione, is officially recognized as a saint both by the Orthodox and Catholic churches. However, in the Catholic Church we rarely hear about her these days presumably because that Church does not wish to remind us of the fact that Phillip was married.

In regard to the New Testament in general, the chapter that has most commonly been used (by the Latin Church) to advocate compulsory priestly celibacy is 1 Cor 7, which was written by St Paul sometime around AD 53–55. This chapter discusses Paul's views on marriage and celibacy and is very contradictory in places.

Paul begins this chapter by saying that it is good for a man not to marry but, seeing as there is so much immorality, each man should have his own wife, and each wife a husband. He states that they should fulfil their duty to each other and that their bodies no longer belong to themselves alone, but also to their spouses and, for this reason, they should not deprive each other. He then goes on to say that he wishes all men were as he is (implying celibacy) but each has his own gift from God. He states that it is good for single people to stay unmarried but if they cannot control themselves, they should marry. He then gives various instructions on separation and divorce. Paul states that he believes each person should remain in the situation that s/he was in when s/he was called and so if a person was circumcised when he was called, he should remain circumcised. However, when Paul refers to virgins who have been called (i.e., who have accepted Christ and become Christians) he states that he has no command from the Lord, but thinks it is good that they remain as they are because of present circumstances.

Similarly, he states that a married man should remain married, and an unmarried man would be better to remain single, although, if he marries, he will be committing no sin. Paul then goes on to state that those who marry will face many troubles and he wants to spare them this. The reason for these comments of Paul becomes very clear in 1 Cor 7:29 when he states, "For this world in its current form is passing away."

All early Christians believed in the second coming of Christ, and Christians continue to hold this belief today, as it is incorporated into the Nicene Creed. This second coming of Christ would be a single instantaneous event when the world would be transfigured and the living and the dead would be judged. The idea that the second coming would occur shortly after Jesus's lifetime was probably due to words that are attributed to him in the Gospels such as, "there are some standing here who will not taste death, till they see the Son of Man coming in his Kingdom" (Matt 16:28). Similar predictions can be found in Mark 9:1; Mark 13:30; Matt 24:34; Luke 9:27 and Luke 21:32 and the historian Freeman has argued that the early Christians expected Jesus to return within a generation of his death.[7] Paul almost certainly shared this belief.

Paul lived in very turbulent times when there were many natural disasters, famines, social upheavals and disruptions in international relationships. In addition to this, the early Christian churches were under severe persecution. Christianity was not to be officially accepted as a religion until the time of the emperor Constantine who decriminalized Christian worship (AD 313) and, up until that time, Christians were often tortured and martyred for their faith. Many early Christians saw their persecutions as a sign that the second coming was imminent.

The fact that Paul believed the second coming to be imminent is very clear from his words in 1 Thess 4:17 when he describes what will happen after Christ has returned. Many Christian believers have tried to evade the fact that Paul believed that the second coming was imminent and this may be why this verse has been so frequently mistranslated in the West. This verse is usually translated as, "After that, we who are still alive and are left will be caught up together with them in the clouds to meet them in the air. And so, we will be with the Lord forever. Therefore encourage each other with these words."

Now the use of the word 'we' here already gives a strong indication that Paul believed that the second coming was imminent and that he and others would be caught up in the air to meet the Lord in his own lifetime. However, the correct translation of the Greek is even stronger than this, for

---

7. Freeman, *Closing of the Western Mind*.

Paul actually uses the Greek word, περιλειπομενοι, which actually means, "we who are sadly waiting." Therefore, the correct translation of this verse is, "After that, we who are still alive and are sadly waiting will be caught up together with them in the clouds to meet them in the air. And so, we will be with the Lord forever. Therefore encourage each other with these words."

It is therefore very clear that Paul believed that he was awaiting the second coming, which was imminent. This belief affected his entire theology. It was due to this belief that his writings on marriage were not more positive, and that he advocated no change in anyone's individual lifestyle in 1 Corinthians where he states that everyone would be better to stay in the situation in which they found themselves at the time they were called. Paul was expecting a second coming and his words must be taken in the context of the situation in which they were written. They cannot, in any way, be used as a justification for the existence of enforced priestly celibacy and indeed the Orthodox, who allow priests to marry, have never used these words in this way.

Having established Paul's views on celibacy within the First Epistle to the Corinthians, it is now possible to examine another New Testament Epistle that makes it clear that celibacy was not a norm of the times and this is the first Epistle to Timothy. Ironically, this Epistle was originally believed by many to have also been written by Paul, but in recent times many scholars have disputed this. This Epistle discusses the roles of men and women in the church, and a significant passage is 1 Tim 3:1–4:

> If anyone sets his heart on being an overseer, he desires a noble task. Now the overseer must be above reproach, the husband of but one wife, temperate, self-controlled, respectable, hospitable, able to teach, not given to drunkenness, not violent but gentle, not quarrelsome, not a lover of money. He must manage his own family well and see that his children obey him with proper respect.

Now the word that is translated as 'overseer' here is actually the Greek word επίσκοπος, which today is translated as bishop. As has already been argued in my previous book in regards to Christian ministry, and the development of a definitive Church structure, it would seem that a Church hierarchy emerged very slowly and at different times in different places.[8] In the New Testament there are three main ministries described and these are: επίσκοποι (overseers), πρεσβύτεροι (elders/presbyters known today as priests), and διάκονοι (servants/deacons). The overseers and presbyters were usually male and in the early church their roles were interchangeable,

---

8. Flint, *No Place for a Woman*.

but, eventually, by the beginning of the second century, the overseers or ἐπίσκοποι began to emerge as the leaders of their communities. It is clear from the first epistle to Timothy that these leaders were not required to be celibate. On the contrary, they were required to have one wife and manage their families well.

From the evidence examined above, it should be indisputable that there is no justification whatsoever for enforced priestly celibacy within the Greek New Testament and, for this reason, the Orthodox, who have always tried to be true to the original Greek have never enforced it.

Having illustrated that there are no grounds for enforced celibacy either in the Old Testament or in the Greek New Testament, I will now move on to examine whether there is any indication of enforced celibacy in the early Christian centuries. One of the greatest works on the history of sacerdotal celibacy was actually written in 1867 by Henry C. Lea and it could be argued that no other work has ever matched this in thoroughness.[9] In this work Lea is clear that there is no clear evidence of any general practice or obligation of priestly celibacy before the fourth century. Later scholars, such as Dennis, are in agreement with this.[10] Lea draws our attention to many things, one of them being the fact that St Petronilla was the daughter of St Peter and is specifically mentioned as such in early Christian martyrology. Her name actually means 'little Peter' or, 'of Peter,' and it was very common in Greek and Roman areas for daughters to be named after their fathers in this way.

One of the earliest Christian works is the *Stromata* of St Clement of Alexandria (AD 150–215), which is the third of a trilogy of works regarding the Christian life. Clement was a convert to Christianity, and he was familiar with Gnosticism, Greek philosophy, and literature. He is regarded as an Early Church Father and was venerated as a saint until 1586 when Pope Sixtus V removed him from the Roman Martyrology which, it will be later illustrated, is a very interesting fact.

Clement wrote three known major works and these are the *Protrepticus*, the *Paedagogus*, and the *Stromata*, which was his last work. The *Stromata* consists of seven books, and it is the third book that is of interest here. At this time, the idea of mandatory celibacy was beginning to emerge within Christian Gnosticism, which probably derived its origins from Neoplatonism. The Christian Gnostics were an early group of Christians who flourished in the second century. They believed that Christ was a divine being who had taken on human form to bring Gnosis to the world. The task

---

9. *Historical Sketch of Sarcedotal Celibacy.*
10. *The Apostolic Origins of Priestly Celibacy.*

of the individual was to unite with Christ's spiritual nature, and this led to a tendency towards asceticism and a rejection of the physical. Clement believed these ideas to be both a rejection of God's creation, and, also, contradictory to the teachings of the apostles. He therefore discusses marriage and rejects the Gnostic opposition to the married state. He argued against the idea that Christians should reject their family for an ascetic life stating that not to marry is to despise God's creation and that sex within marriage is a positive good. During the process of his advocation of marriage, Clement also gives us some very important facts, such as the fact that second marriages were permitted during his time and, also, more importantly, the fact that both Peter and Phillip were married. Of those who try to advocate mandatory celibacy, he states, "…do they also scorn the apostles? Peter and Philip had children, and Philip gave his daughters in marriage" (*Stromata*, 3:52).

There can be little doubt that it was very well known that Peter and Philip had children at this time; otherwise, Clement would not have brought this up in this very important argument for the sacredness of marriage and marital sexual relations. As has already been illustrated, the married state of Peter is referred to quite naturally in scripture when Jesus heals Peter's mother-in-law (Matt 8:14–15) and when Peter (or whichever of his followers wrote this letter) refers to his son (1 Pet 5:13). We are also told that Phillip is married in the New Testament and that he had four unmarried daughters who prophesized (Acts 21:9). How is it, then, that these facts have been evaded or swept under the carpet by the Roman Church?

Enforced celibacy has always been a very contentious issue in the Christian Church and it was a major factor both in the East/West Schism of 1054, and in the later Protestant Reformation. It would seem that the prelates in the Western Church made deliberate attempts, both in the early Christian centuries following the promulgation of the teachings of St Augustine and, post the East–West Schism, to either deny, or cover up, the marriage of these apostles. This was done by both mistranslating the Greek New Testament and, of course, through removing Clement from the Roman Martyrology, and taking away his sainthood. This happened in 1586, and the reason why this date is interesting is because it comes directly after the Reformation and the Council of Trent, which sought to counter that Reformation. Enforced celibacy had been a major issue in the Reformation, and the Protestants had dispensed with it. However, the Latin Church defended it at the Council of Trent. It was therefore highly convenient to remove Clement's saintly status at this time. This removal of his sainthood would ensure his writings were largely forgotten by the Church.

Despite Clement's attempts, during his own time, to eradicate the Gnostic idea of enforced priestly celibacy in the areas in which he travelled (namely Greece, Asia Minor, Palestine and Egypt), the idea emerged in other areas, one of which was Northern Spain. The Synod of Elvira was held there sometime around AD 305 and, unfortunately, it promulgated some teachings that had moved very far away from the teaching of the New Testament. This synod promulgated twenty-one canons, most of which were of a prohibitory nature. There was a ban on marriages between Christians and Jews, which was in stark contrast to Paul's comment that in Christ "there is no Jew or Greek, servant or free" (Gal 3:28), along with an insistence on clerical celibacy. Little is known about the origins of this church in Northern Spain and why it was antisemitic and was also gnostic in its interpretation of sexuality.

The Synod of Elvira had taken place in the West in Northern Spain where it seems that the Gnostic idea of priestly celibacy may have been growing, perhaps due to this church's proximity to Rome. This Synod had decreed that priests should be celibate. It is also reported that a Spanish Bishop tried to get a similar law given general acceptance at the Council of Nicaea (325), but this attempt failed. However, in the Eastern Church there was no such trend. The Council of Gangra (Gangra is in modern Turkey) believed to be held around AD 340 condemned all criticism of marriage and all arguments that married priests could not perform valid sacraments. It also condemned remaining celibate for any reason other than holiness. There are also a number of prominent married bishops in the East around this time. The father of the fourth century, St Gregory Nazianzus, was a married bishop. He had been converted by his wife, Nonna, and, after his conversion, was consecrated to the bishopric of Nazianzus. The fourth century St Gregory of Nyssa was also married to a woman called Theosebeia and the fourth century Spiridon of Cyprus was also a married bishop. St John Chrysostom, who was actually celibate, also wrote of married bishops stating that a married bishop must be blameless, having but one wife, and not more than one.

The idea that all priests should be forced to be celibate began to be developed after the emergence of monasticism and it was also advocated by three theologians in particular, namely, St. Jerome (c. 347–419); St. Ambrose (c. 339–397) and St. Augustine (c. 354–430). In the first three hundred years of the early church, most ministers had been lay ministers, but, by this time, the clergy were beginning to emerge as a distinctive group, and a divide between the clergy and laity was becoming more apparent. Concerns were also beginning to emerge about the dangers of church property being lost if it was passed on to a wife after the death of a priest.

Both Jerome and Augustine were converts to Christianity whereas Ambrose was born and raised into a Roman Christian family. The theology of Ambrose is also different to that of Jerome and Augustine in that Ambrose was not anti-marriage at all, even though he led a celibate life himself; he simply regarded celibacy to be the higher path. Both Jerome and Augustine, however, had lived promiscuous lives before their conversion and swung from one extreme to the other. They saw celibacy as a far superior condition to marriage and advocated that the priest needed to abstain from sexual relations in order to be 'pure.' Jerome, however, did continue to enjoy the company of women after his conversion and surrounded himself with a circle of well-born and well-educated women who either wished to consecrate themselves as virgins, or were inclined towards the monastic life. This would suggest that Jerome retained some respect for women after his conversion. He had sadly become convinced that celibacy was the higher path, but, if that was the case, he was not going to exclude women from it.

Despite Jerome's respect for certain women who wished to embrace his teachings, he had little time or respect for anyone who disagreed with him and is known for his attacks on, and persecution of, a fourth century theologian known as Jovinian. This theologian was a monk who wrote against Christian asceticism but never gave up his own personal status as a celibate. His writings praised the excellence of marriage, and he stated that virgins, widows, and married women were all of equal importance in Christianity. In actual fact, he was stating nothing different to what others such as Clement of Alexandria had stated at an earlier date. However, these views were suddenly no longer acceptable with the powers that be. Jovinian's teachings had much popular support in Rome and Milan but were condemned by both Jerome and Ambrose and he was flogged and sent into exile. The tide was beginning to turn and the once wholesome religion of the Jewish Jesus was being infiltrated by asceticism.

The theologian who was most notable in swinging the Western Church away from a married priesthood towards compulsory celibacy was undoubtably St Augustine of Hippo. Augustine was born in Algeria in AD 354 to a mother who was a devout Christian and a father who was non-Christian. Augustine's family are believed to have been heavily Romanized and to have spoken only Latin at home. He was well educated but lived a hedonistic and promiscuous lifestyle as a young man. At the age of seventeen years, he began a sexual relationship with a young woman from Carthage with whom he bore a son and this continued for at least fifteen years. However, Augustine's mother did not approve of the woman, as she was not of his class and, therefore, Augustine was unable to marry her. His mother eventually persuaded him to marry a teenaged heiress but this marriage never took place, as Augustine converted to Christianity and became a priest.

There are two often ignored factors that probably led to Augustine's later theology, and these are his inability to master the Greek language and his relationship with his mother. Augustine's inability to master the Greek language meant he could never read the New Testament in its original Greek. In regards to his relationship with his mother—this relationship has been praised throughout the centuries by the Catholic Church who have portrayed Monica as a woman of outstanding Christian virtue who prayed continuously for the conversion of her son. In actual, fact she was a mixed woman of good and bad, as are most people. She gave a lot of money to the poor but did not want her son to marry a woman who was not of his class. She prayed for Augustine's conversion to Christianity but was also clearly a dominant and overpowering woman who wanted her son to retain her mold. Her initial desire was that her son would convert to Christianity and disregard his lover and offspring (her grandchild) for a 'more suitable' woman, and she was delighted when he did so, and she supplied such a 'suitable' woman. However, the suitable woman was also later discarded by Augustine when he decided to become a priest; then, his mother did not remotely care about that woman anymore. She had no empathy for anyone other than her own son and, as will be seen, it could be argued that her overprotective attitude towards her son led him to become a man of extremes.

After his conversion, Augustine swung from being a man of the flesh to a man who hated the flesh, and his theology reflected these unbalanced extremes. He developed a concept of original sin in which human nature was damaged by concupiscence, or the libido of sexual desire. He saw sexual desire as an evil consequence of 'the fall' and all sexual acts as evil, even if carried out in marriage. He therefore advocated abstinence from marriage. However, one also has to say that his newfound theology was a very convenient way to ignore his previous lover and to take no responsibility for their son. Due to his extreme and perverse view of human sexuality it could be argued that Augustine suffered from Madonna–whore complex. This psychological complex was developed by Freud and applies to men who see woman as either saintly Madonnas, or debased prostitutes.[11] Freud wrote, "Where such men love they have no desire and where they desire, they cannot love."[12]

Freud argued that this complex usually occurred in men who had been raised by a woman who was not warm and demonstrably affectionate, but physically cold and aloof, while also being very overprotective of her son. St Monica's obsession with her son marrying into his own class, and her

---

11. Freud, *Three Essays*, 261.
12. Freud, *Three Essays*, 261.

continuous prayers for his conversion, suggest that she may have been such a woman. It could be argued that she may have been cold and aloof because her husband was unfaithful, and there are always two sides to every story; he may, also, have had his own reasons for his infidelity.

Augustine's theory of original sin and his perverse view of sexuality had a long and damaging effect on the Roman Catholic Church, which even continues to this day. Initially, however, Augustine's effect did not seem to be too great. This was because the Eastern part of the (then) universal Church rejected Augustine's views on original sin and mandatory celibacy, and most priests continued to be ordained after they were married in the East. Although the Western Church began to consistently advocate celibacy as superior to marriage, in reality, the majority of priests in the West continued to marry, and this teaching was largely ignored. Although the teaching of Augustine was initially ignored, it can be argued that it insidiously influenced Western views on sexuality in a perverse way prior to the eleventh century East–West Schism. While the Bishops of Rome (or Popes as they became post-East–West Schism) were no longer marrying, they were certainly not celibate. They, also, were beginning to view women in a dualistic 'Madonna–whore' way.

One example of a Pope with a dualistic view of women was Pope John XII (937–964). This pope came from a powerful Roman family, becoming pontiff in his early twenties. He had many mistresses including one called Joan who was said to have exercised great influence on him and whose prominence in Rome may have given rise to the legend of Pope Joan. The main event that led to the imposition of mandatory celibacy in the West was the East–West Schism of 1054. This schism resulted in the splitting of the Christian Church into two churches; these were the Christian Orthodox Church in the East, and the Roman Catholic Church in the West. The East–West Schism is often presented in the West as something that resulted from a dispute over the procession of the Holy Spirit. The laity today are usually told that the reason for the Schism was that Western theologians believed that the Holy Spirit proceeded from the Father and the Son whereas, in the East, the prevalent view was that the Holy Spirit proceeded from the Father only. However, the portrayal of this theological difference as the sole cause of this schism is not accurate. Tensions had been simmering between Eastern and Western Christianity for several hundred years from around the time of Augustine, and the schism was due to a culmination of theological differences.

Prior to the East–West schism, five patriarchs held authority in different regions and these were: the Patriarchs of Rome, Alexandria, Antioch, Constantinople, and Jerusalem. The Patriarch of Rome (now known as the pope) held the honor of 'first among equals,' but he did not possess authority over the other patriarchs. For many years the Church in the West had been pushing for the Patriarch, or Bishop, of Rome to have universal jurisdiction and authority. While the other patriarchs in the East agreed to honor the Patriarch of Rome, they believed that ecclesiastical matters should always be decided by a Council, or Synod, of all regions, and they would not grant universal jurisdiction and authority to the Bishop of Rome. The Eastern Churches would not accept that a central authoritarian figure (i.e., the Bishop of Rome) could have the absolute last word on Church doctrine; this would mean that many Latin practices would be forced on them. This was because the practices of the Eastern and Western Churches were already very far apart, due to major differences in theology. Latin thought was strongly influenced by Roman law, and an emerging scholastic theology whereas, in the East, theology was developed through philosophy and in the context of worship. Additionally, the main language of the people in the Eastern Churches was Greek and these churches developed Greek rites using the Greek language. The New Testament, of course, had been written in Greek while the Old Testament was written mostly in Hebrew. However, the Patriarchs of the East produced a Greek Septuagint translation of the Old Testament. In the Church of Rome, churches conducted their services in Latin, and their bibles were translated into Latin as per the Latin Vulgate. This led to the Churches of the East continuously stating that many practices of the Latin Church were heretical due to errors which resulted from their lack of understanding of the New Testament in its original Greek.

Aside from the dispute concerning the authority, or jurisdiction, of the Bishop (or Patriarch) of Rome, there were other theological differences between the Churches of the East and West that revolved around the following: the nature of the incarnate Christ, fasting, anointing with oil, the use of unleavened bread by the churches in the West for the Eucharist, the reverence of St. Augustine by the Latin Church (many in the Eastern Churches believed him to be bordering on heresy), the procession of the Holy Spirit and, last, but not least, clerical celibacy.

While many clergy remained married in the West, the idea that celibacy was a superior state was continually being mooted, and the number of celibate priests was growing. Contrastingly, in the East, most priests were married, and theologians saw no reason to change this. The Schism actually occurred when Norman warriors loyal to the Patriarch of Rome (Pope Leo IX) invaded Southern Italy, which was then under Byzantine rule. They replaced Greek bishops with Latin ones and tried to impose mandatory celibacy, the use of unleavened bread for the consecration, and other Latin practices. Marcus Cerularius (the Patriarch of Constantinople) responded by closing the Latin churches in Constantinople. These actions resulted in excommunications from both sides, and the Churches of the East and West eventually split.

The East–West Schism was disastrous for Christianity in the West because it left the Western hierarchy free to impose mandatory celibacy without opposition. As I will demonstrate later, this enforced denial of God-given human sexuality led to the creation of a cult of men who were perceived to be superior to the rest of humanity because of their supposed abstention from sex. It also led to the birth of a new Catholic misogynism with much discrimination against women who were now often viewed as whorish temptresses. Additionally, it led to much dishonesty about human sexuality, which the account of my co-author confirms by experience, along with the creation of a hidden and often perverse sexuality. Many clerics found it impossible to remain celibate and secretly broke their vows while keeping their sexuality 'under cover.' Other clerics obeyed the rules of abstinence from sex with a woman but found other undercover ways of fulfilling their sexual needs.

In 1122, Pope Callixtus II convoked the First Council of the Lateran, and it was then that the sins of mandatory celibacy began in full force. While this Council was called mainly for political reasons it promulgated many barbaric and misogynistic canons including: the forbidding of priests, deacons and subdeacons to associate with women, or to live with any woman other than a mother, sister or aunt, the forbidding of priests to marry, and an order that all current marriages of clergy should be immediately dissolved, and that both parties of the marriage should do penance. As canons were also passed about the disposal of 'church' properties it can be assumed that one of the reasons for the promulgations of the canons around the clergy and women was to ensure that the clergy were able to take any property that might legitimately have belonged to the wife of a cleric.

While the First Council of the Lateran made it official that all Western married clergy should abandon their wives and children, this appalling practice began under Pope Gregory VII. Now there was no turning back and many more families were broken up with abandoned wives being forcibly removed from their homes and left to homelessness, prostitution, slavery and suicide. The imposition of mandatory celibacy in the Western Church was a wicked, cruel, and ruthless affair but today we hear nothing about it. Moreover, the Church has never apologized to all the women and children who were made to endure terrible suffering due to this practice. The fact that the Western Christian Church had descended by the twelfth century to this extreme is truly shocking, especially if we remember that Jesus was a Jew and had in no way sanctioned this state of affairs. The historical Jesus had, in a revolutionary manner, removed the stigma around celibacy and recognized that a small number of people could be 'gifted' with a desire to be celibate. However, the original New Testament of the Greek koine is clear that the historical Jesus accepted the traditional version of marriage whereby marriage was seen as a contract between a man and a woman, in which God was involved, and, in which, the husband and wife became one soul. Due to the Jewish idea that men and women merged into one soul in marriage, women had always been respected in Judaism—notwithstanding the fact that they were regarded as very different to men. Now, the emerging cult of celibacy in the West was beginning to place women, who were half of humanity, on the scrapheap.

After the First Council of the Lateran, a Second Council of the Lateran was invoked by Pope Innocent II in 1139 and was attended by around a thousand clerics. This Council repeated the condemnation of marriage among the clergy, but further misogyny, and the elevation of a male celibate elite, was also beginning to creep into the Western Church. Canon 27 of this Council prohibited nuns from singing the Divine Office in the same choir as monks.

By the thirteenth century St. Thomas Aquinas had arrived on the scene. Aquinas was a Dominican Friar who became an influential philosopher and theologian. He attempted to synthetize Aristotelian philosophy with the principles of Christianity. Unfortunately, his influence on the Vatican was enormous and continues to be so. Aquinas regarded the celibate state as a higher and more perfect vocation than married life and thought it unbecoming of a cleric to lower himself to marriage. He also had an appallingly misogynistic view of women, believing them to be a source of sin, unclean due to menstruation, and inferior to men in every way. He believed that a man's sperm alone contained the whole pre-conceived child and that a woman had no active role in reproduction. He did not realize that conception involved a sperm fusing with an ovum and saw the woman's only contribution to procreation as being her womb which housed and nourished the growing child. He saw women as being misbegotten men who arose due to an accident such as weak semen or a poor diet on behalf of the mother. Only a male child was perfect; a female child was imperfect and had only one role—to help men with pro-creation. Unsurprisingly Aquinas's theology further enhanced the cult of sacerdotal celibacy and further undermined marriage.

The Catholic Church today honors Aquinas as a saint and considers him to be a model teacher for celibate men studying for the priesthood. He wrote many theological works, which include *Summa Theologiae*, *Summa Contra Gentiles*, and *Scriptum super Sententiis*. These works contain long legalistic explanations of Christian doctrine and are a very long way from the Christianity of the first three centuries of the early church. Given that Aquinas was an eminent thinker of his time, and his thoughts on women reflect the biology of his time, it is possible to understand why the Catholic Church canonized him in 1323. What is unacceptable, however, is that he has been revered as a Doctor of the Church since 1567. The term 'Doctor of the Church' is a title given to saints recognized as having made significant contributions to theology or doctrine through their studies or research. The Catholic Church today knows full well that much of Aquinas's teaching was incorrect. In particular, his 'proofs' of the existence of God are not definitive and his human biology, and concept of a woman as a 'misbegotten male,' was completely erroneous. The fact that the Church today continues to place the teachings of a man whose theology and biology has been showed to be deeply flawed on a pedestal is regrettable. This theology contributes to misogynistic attitudes worldwide.

By the thirteenth and early-fourteenth centuries, the Catholic teaching on sacerdotal celibacy had become widespread, but many clergy were not actually celibate—particularly in the British Isles and Ireland, and Lea demonstrates that many European clerics kept concubines.[13] It was not only priests who had mistresses but also more senior clergy and in 1279 the Archbishop of Canterbury (Peckham) applied for assistance in prosecuting a bishop who had refused to follow the law and whose mistress had admitted bearing him five children. Meanwhile, in Ireland, bishops had not only been keeping concubines but had also continued to marry. Even after the twelfth century reforms of St. Malachy, celibacy could still not be fully enforced in Ireland and the rule continued to be flouted.

The whole issue of mandatory celibacy in Western Europe simmered for centuries and finally came to a violent head with the Reformation. The Reformation was the second major schism within Christendom. The first major schism had, of course, been the East–West Schism where the Latin West had split from the Christian East to enforce a theology that was moving further and further away from the theology of the early church. At that time the Latin West had wanted the Bishop of Rome to be first among the five patriarchs and they had also wanted to carry out other practices that the East had found unacceptable such as universalizing the Latin Mass (when the New Testament was actually written in the Greek) and, of course, enforced celibacy for priests. Now, some of these very same issues came to the fore once again in the Western Church with the sixteenth century Reformation.

13. *Historical Sketch of Sarcedotal Celibacy.*

Martin Luther was a German Catholic monk who came to reject several teachings and practices of the Catholic Church. He disputed the view on indulgences and taught that salvation was a free gift of God's grace through faith in Jesus Christ. He taught that the bible is the only source of divinely revealed knowledge, and he opposed sacerdotalism, stating that all baptized Christians belonged to a holy priesthood. He translated the bible into the German vernacular and eventually married a former nun, Katharine Von Bora, and thus set a model for the reinstatement of clerical marriage. Eventually, when he refused to recant his writings, he was excommunicated in 1521 and, unsurprisingly, many of his fellow Catholics followed him in the creation of a new form of Christianity. Luther's marriage was reported to have been very happy, and the couple had six children.

Luther was not the only reformer to be concerned about the theological path that Rome had taken; others developed their own criticism independently, such as Zwingli in Zurich, Calvin in Geneva, and Vasa in Sweden. In England the situation was somewhat different, as the Reformation was started by King Henry VIII after the Pope refused to give him an annulment to facilitate his marriage to Anne Boleyn. Henry's theology had been Catholic in many ways, and he had initially created a Church of England that was little different to the Catholic Church, other than the fact that it did not accept the pope. Eventually, however, the Church of England developed its own theology, which was a middle way between the Catholic and emerging Protestant theologies and did, of course, incorporate a married priesthood. The Reformation spread across Europe as a whole and reached its peak in the late sixteenth century. Its greatest presence was in areas where Luther had pre-existing social relations, perhaps because he had visited these areas, or had former students there.

Of course, every time a person joined the Protestant movement they were not actually, at the time, thinking of creating a new church. The people who joined the Protestant movements were Western Catholics who were protesting against the theology and practices of the Western Latin Catholic Church just as the Eastern Orthodox had protested against the practices of the Western Latin Church in the earlier Schism of 1054. The new denomination that was eventually born took a protest name: Protest-ant. The differences, or protests, were in some ways different to the objections of the East in the earlier Schism, but there were many common factors such as the emerging idea of Papal infallibility,[14] the use of the Latin language in religious rites, the use of a Latin translation of the bible, and, of course, the enforcement of clerical celibacy. Once again, the idea that every priest

---

14. Although this had not yet been proclaimed it was, in fact, practiced.

should renounce his God-given sexuality for the sake of embracing his vocation and that, in doing so, he would become more holy, was rejected.

Although a large number of sixteenth century Catholics had protested against the (then) current practices of the Western Catholic Church, the Catholic Church of the time was not willing to take their protests on board. Had the Catholic Church of the time been willing to accommodate these protests, Church history might have been very different. The two opposing theological camps could have sat down together and worked out a middle way to prevent a further split within Christendom. Unfortunately, this did not happen and on December 13, 1545, the Roman (Latin) Catholic Church convoked the Council of Trent. This council was convened as a direct response to the protests which had resulted in the Reformation.

The Council of Trent was the nineteenth ecumenical council of the Roman Catholic Church, and it was convened in Trent for three periods between December 13, 1545, and December 4, 1563. This council was convened as a response to the Reformation. The Council of Trent embodied the ideals of what is known as the Counter-Reformation and its decrees were signed by 255 members. These members included four papal legates, two cardinals, three patriarchs, twenty-five archbishops, and 168 bishops. The council was responding to what it saw as the threats of Protestantism and the teachings of Martin Luther, in particular.

The main canons and decrees of the Council of Trent were to reaffirm the Niceno-Constantinopolitan creed; to create the canon of the New and Old Testaments, to declare that the official Bible was the Latin Vulgate and that the Church's interpretation of it was final, to reaffirm the practice of indulgences but to bring about various reforms in regards to them, to reaffirm the veneration of the saints and the Virgin Mary, to declare that justification was offered on the basis of faith and good works, and to reaffirm the seven sacraments. The council gave its greatest weight to the seven sacraments because it wanted to stress that they were necessary vehicles of grace in opposition to Luther's view that justification was by faith alone. It pronounced the eucharist as a sacrament and true propitiatory sacrifice, confirming the practice of withholding the cup from the laity.

Ordination was defined as imprinting an indelible character on the priest's soul and priestly celibacy was reaffirmed. Marriage was defined as a sacrament, but the council made it clear that celibacy was the superior state. Sadly, in the case of divorce, the council denied the right of the innocent party to marry again. This right existed pre-Trent and continues to exist in the Orthodox Church. The idea that the Catholic Church has always allowed only one marriage is fallacy.

The teaching that the ordination of a priest placed an indelible character on his soul was unfortunate because it confirmed the elevation of priests to a superior status above the rest of humanity. By reaffirming priestly celibacy, the council was, in effect, stating that ordained male celibates were superior to the rest of humanity. Both women, and married men, could not be ordained as priests; therefore, they could not access this 'indelible character' and so, in effect, became second-class citizens. The Council, through this decree, created an elite cult in which only male celibate men could belong. In doing so, it held up a way of life that is essentially unnatural and as we have seen, quite contrary to the original teachings of Jesus.

After the reformation there were now three main Christian denominations and these were: the Orthodox Church with a married priesthood that did not allow married men to become bishops, the Protestant Church who had a married priesthood that permitted married men to become bishops, and the Roman Catholic (Latin) Church with its all-male celibate clergy. None of these churches ordained women, although it can certainly be stated that some women had been ordained as priests until around the middle of the fourth century. The ordination of women to the diaconate had continued in the East until around the ninth century before it died out. One of the main roles of the female deacon had been to baptize women and, with the advent of baptizing infants, this role became redundant.

There was a major shift in the acceptance and enforcement of priestly celibacy in the Latin Church pre-, and post-, Reformation. Pre-Reformation, the acceptance and enforcement of celibacy had not been universal. The idea of celibacy as a superior state of life had grown within Latin Christendom over the centuries and the Church issued various decrees at various councils to promote this mandatory celibacy. Despite this, the practice was never universal in the pre-Reformation Latin Church. There were always a substantial number who blatantly disregarded the rules. During the reformation, however, those who did not wish to remain celibate simply left and joined the Protestant Church.

Following the Council of Trent, celibacy became universally accepted in the Latin Church and, eventually, priestly marriage became obsolete. Of course, there were those who broke their vows, but in the main it was accepted that it was no longer possible for priests in the Latin West to marry. However, the breaking of the celibate rule continued undercover and, in 1622, Pope Gregory XIV republished a Bull that had previously been promulgated in 1561. This Bull prohibited the seduction of women by their confessors, and it was made universally applicable throughout all Catholic countries, demonstrating that a significant number of priests were far from chaste, even though they accepted they could not marry. A culture grew up in which it was universally accepted that priests would be 'celibate' on paper and many of the laity took on board the idea that celibacy was the higher path and sought to persuade their sons and daughters to become priests and nuns. The problem was, however, that the book did not fit the cover and there were still many secret sexual liaisons.

By the nineteenth century, new eras were dawning with the rise of rationalism, communism, socialism, liberalism, materialism, modernism, naturalism, pantheism and secularism. The Catholic Church, however, remained stuck with the medieval philosophy of Thomas Aquinas, on the defensive against the new intellectual movements of the nineteenth century. In 1868 Pope Pius IX convoked the First Vatican Council and this Council eventually condemned all the new movements while proclaiming papal infallibility. The proclamation of Papal Infallibility was a definite departure from the ecclesiastical structure of the Early Christian Church. It invested even more power in the pyramidical hierarchical structure of the Latin Church and led to a further schism. This dogma caused considerable opposition in the Netherlands, Germany, Austria and Switzerland and a break away movement formed the Old Catholic Church when, in 1889, Old Catholics united under the Union of Utrecht. This Church still exists to this day and rejects papal infallibility while claiming apostolic succession. It also does not enforce mandatory celibacy.

By the twentieth century the Catholic Church had become increasingly anachronistic and out of touch with most modern knowledge; it was locked in the past with the flawed medieval philosophy of Thomas Aquinas. All power continued to be invested in so called 'celibate' men although, as would soon be discovered, a large number of them were not celibate at all. I do not mean to say that there is not a celibate vocation. Some people do feel called to be celibate and can manage celibacy perfectly well. The problem has always lied with enforced, or mandatory, celibacy, i.e., the refusal of the Catholic Church to allow anyone to exercise a priestly ministry unless they forsake their natural God-given sexuality. Yet, in the Catholic Church of the twentieth century, it appeared that a wind of change was blowing for the first time in many centuries, and, on January 25, 1959, Pope John XXIII gave notice of his intention to convene an ecumenical council. He expected that the Council would bring about a renewal of the Catholic Church that would incorporate modern biological, sociological and psychological knowledge into its theology, and progress towards a reunion of all Christians.

The Second Ecumenical Council of the Vatican, usually known as Vatican II, was the twenty-first ecumenical council of the Roman Catholic Church. The Council was opened on October 11, 1962, by Pope St. John XXIII, and was closed on December 8, 1965, under Pope St. Paul VI. The

Council met for four periods lasting between eight and twelve weeks in the autumn of each of the four years that it sat. The Council was, of course, comprised of bishops, and the number of bishops attending varied, but was somewhere between two and three thousand. A small number of theologians were also invited to attend, and the Orthodox and Protestant denominations were invited to send observers. There were, of course, no female attendees (other than a small number of observers) but, nevertheless, this Council was different to earlier councils such as the Council of Trent and Vatican I in that it had been called to actually look at the Church critically and to attempt to bring about reform rather than to make triumphalist declarations.

The Council's teaching is contained in sixteen documents comprising four constitutions, nine decrees, and three declarations. These documents addressed the Council's relationship with the modern world, instigated a wide variety of reforms, and reversed some of the damaging teachings of the previous Council of Trent. Throughout the period of the Council, it was made clear that its main purpose was to promote a universal call to holiness and a turning away from clericalism toward a new age of the laity.

Vatican II instigated many reforms and these included: the widespread use of the vernacular languages (instead of Latin) in the Mass, the revision of Eucharistic prayers, the abbreviation of the liturgical calendar, the ability to celebrate Mass with the priest facing the congregation, an emphasis on lay people as the 'people of God,' a new emphasis on biblical theology, a new emphasis on ecumenism, recognition of the rites of Eastern Catholics to keep their distinct liturgical practices, a new recognition of the apostolate of the laity, a call for the adaptation and renewal of the religious life, and a call for priests to become brothers as well as fathers and teachers. However, there was one issue which the Council did not address and this was the issue of compulsory celibacy for priests. On October 11, two days before the schema was to be discussed, Pope Paul VI pre-empted the debate by announcing he was withdrawing the issue of celibacy from the conciliar agenda. Bishops who wished to address the issue could send their comments in writing to him. It was expected the pope would hand the issue to a special committee. But no committee was ever set up, and in 1967 Pope Paul VI issued *Sacerdotalis caelibatus*, the encyclical maintaining clerical celibacy for Latin priests.

After the many changes of Vatican II began to settle, there was a natural expectancy among the laity that other changes would follow and, initially, there were some further changes, such as the restoration of the rite of the permanent diaconate for married men. This meant that married men could now carry out marriage, baptismal, and funeral services. However, they still could not anoint the sick, consecrate the eucharist, or hear confessions as these sacraments, could only be performed by a priest. As the presence of a married deacon became more common in the Church, there was an increased expectation that the rule of celibacy might be relaxed, perhaps to allow diocesan priests to marry while religious orders would maintain the rule of celibacy. Unfortunately, this did not happen and sadly Catholic teaching on human sexuality remained as dire and outdated as ever.

On July 26, 1968 Pope Paul VI published *Humanae Vitae*. This document reaffirmed earlier Catholic teaching on the procreative and unitive nature of conjugal relations, married love, responsible parenthood, and the rejection of artificial contraception. It had not been expected that this teaching would be reaffirmed for the following reasons: firstly, the oral contraceptive pill had actually been invented by a devout Catholic and eminent gynecologist John Rock who had believed that the contraceptive was in line with Catholic teaching and was not artificial at all, secondly, it had been hoped that the post-Vatican II Church would be much more positive in regards to human sexuality, and, finally, members of an earlier commission, the Pontifical Commission on Birth Control (1966), had voted by an overwhelming majority to allow Catholic couples to decide on birth control for themselves. The Pope had, therefore, in issuing this encyclical, gone against the findings of his own commission which had been comprised of cardinals, bishops, theologians, physicians, and even women.

Humanae Vitae was received with shock, and open dissent from the laity was voiced widely and publicly. A group of dissident theologians, led by Rev. Charles Curran, issued a statement that Catholics should decide for themselves about artificial contraception in accordance with their own consciences. The Canadian bishops also opposed this teaching in the "Winnipeg Statement," as did many theologians and several Episcopal Conferences. This teaching was widely rejected in Europe, America, and Canada, and was a factor in many people leaving the Church, as it clearly demonstrated a very poor understanding of human sexuality, and showed that (despite Vatican II) married people and women still had no say in the teachings of the Church. They had been consulted and ignored; instead, a previous teaching had been reaffirmed by a celibate Pope who, it could be argued, had little idea what it was like to be married and no real understanding of human sexuality. This encyclical stated that procreation remained the main purpose of the sexual act and failed to recognize that the sexual act is also a means of bonding, or expressing love and belonging, which is of extreme importance to the psychological well-being of humans.

Humanae Vitae was widely rejected by the laity and remains so to this day. It has undermined the credibility of the Church and it is likely that a vast number of Catholics have left as a result of it. Furthermore, the vast majority of those who have remained in the Church have ignored it. This can be evidenced when attending any Catholic Mass in the West, as it is very rare to find any family with more than three children. Yet, the hierarchy has sadly continued to endorse this encyclical in current times and to ignore the vast majority of its members. Similarly, the hierarchy has also insisted on priestly celibacy up to this day, despite the fact that priestly vocations have now plummeted in the West and it is unlikely they will ever recover. Running alongside this dearth of priestly vocations there has also been an increasing number of sexual abuse scandals. Cases of sexual abuse within the Church first began to receive attention in the late 1980s and, since then, there have been many cases all over the world that have attracted a great deal of media attention. Although the Church has officially denied any link between mandatory celibacy and sexual abuse, many Catholic theologians disagree and this book will demonstrate that there are, in fact, very strong links between the two. These links are due to, among other things, the fact that the secret elite cult of the 'celibate' few with its absence of women will be sociologically attractive to sexual deviants. In addition, Murnane has argued that some clerics are "situational abusers" who commit sexual abuse as a response to the stresses caused by a lack of positive adult relationships, social isolation, and low self-esteem.[15]

Furthermore, Paul, my co-author, confirms in Part Two of this book, the extreme distress he felt, as a man who was naturally (albeit latently) heterosexual, in finding himself in a clerical world that was disturbingly sexually active in a homosexual way during his time as a seminarian who genuinely desired to serve God in a celibate way. In making this point, I am not, in any way, condemning homosexually; what I am actually illustrating is that the Catholic hierarchy have come to represent a homosexual, rather than a diverse, world and, in doing so, have excluded married people and women from that world. This is highly disturbing. It is now almost two thousand years since Jesus walked this earth (in around AD 33) with a following of lay married men and women. He was calling for a religion of the heart and moving away from the legalistic Judaism of his time. The Catholic celibate priesthood of the twenty-first century bears no resemblance to the early Christian lay movements that began with Jesus. In addition, this celibate priesthood actually prevents the Church from being an effective leaven in the world. There are many challenges in this century regarding human sexuality. There is now, in the West, a very promiscuous culture that argues 'anything goes' with human sexuality. This culture has gone against natural law and could eventually bring about the destruction of Western society.

15. *Clerical Errors*, 63.

However, the Church is in no position to challenge this culture because it does not have a holistic and wholesome view of human sexuality. The Church, too, has a perverse view of human sexuality. The West is stuck between the Catholic false ideal of celibacy and the secular view that only extreme promiscuity is acceptable. Only when the Church embraces a healthy sexuality, which would include an ending of the celibacy rule for priests, and the blessing of long-term homosexual unions rooted in love, can it be in a position to challenge the disastrous promiscuity of modern western society.

Chapter 2

Mandatory Celibacy, Sexuality, and Companionship

THIS CHAPTER EXAMINES HUMAN sexuality and human companionship and looks at the effects that mandatory celibacy might have on priests in these areas. Firstly, a distinction will be made between companionship and sexual relationships because some psychologists argue that sex is not always necessary for self-fulfillment or self-actualization whereas companionship is always necessary. I will also briefly examine the psychology of Maslow, Rogers, and Jung relating to these areas. The Roman Catholic Church's failure to keep up with modern advances in the biological, psychological and cultural aspects of human sexuality will also be discussed, as, sadly, this Church has, in many ways, retained the ancient and disturbing teachings of St. Augustine and St. Thomas Aquinas on human sexuality. A brief history of the friendships between male 'celibate' priests and women and how these have changed throughout the centuries after mandatory celibacy was introduced will also be examined. Finally, I will look at how the denial of friendship or sex (if sex is desired) can affect a person's psyche.

The general consensus among psychologists is that it is companionship, rather than sex, that is the higher need. Companionship is sometimes referred to by psychologists as 'love and belonging' and it is stated that a person needs to feel a sense of belonging, and love, in order to be fulfilled. However, many loving relationships that may give a person a sense of belonging are not sexual relationships, for example, the relationships between family members or friends. There are a small number of people for whom these kinds of relationships are sufficient to achieve self-actualization but for the majority of people an intimate sexual relationship is a strong need in both young and middle-aged adulthood and is driven by biological, psychological, philosophical and cultural factors. This need may not be as strong in later life as it is in earlier life, but it is certainly very strong for the majority of people up until their late middle age and remains strong for some even into much later years.

The relationships that involve sexual activity are usually relationships that begin with 'romantic' attraction. However romantic attraction is a complicated phenomenon, which involves biological, psychological, philosophical and cultural factors. One person is usually sexually attracted to another person because of a combination of myriad factors such as, they find the other person physically attractive, they are drawn to the other person psychologically as reflecting their own expectations about love, care, and trust, and, finally, attraction may result from cultural similarities in moral, ethical, and spiritual areas. However, this cultural aspect of romantic sexual attraction does not always apply because sometimes a person may reject their entire upbringing and culture and therefore be attracted to another person from a very different culture.

Sexual relationships may be brief, or they may develop into deep, long-term, committed partnerships. There are no hard and fast rules about these kinds of relationships. Some may start off as purely sexual but later incorporate both sex and companionship. Others may start off as non-sexual friendships but later grow into sexual relationships only to become, still later, non-sexual friendships again. Some relationships between couples may have elements of both sex and friendship but may eventually lose the sexual element altogether. The sexual element in any relationship usually depends on the libido of the individuals concerned. The libido is a person's overall sex drive or desire for sexual activity. This also is influenced by biological, psychological, and social factors. Biologically, sex hormones regulate libido, but psychological factors such as medical conditions and stress can also affect libido, as can social factors.

It has been argued by many doctors and scientists including Charnetski and Brennan,[1] Brody,[2] and Chan,[3] that sexual activity has many positive effects on human health such as: lowering blood pressure, increasing heart health, strengthening muscles, strengthening the immune system, improving bladder control (in women), protecting against endometriosis (in women), lowering the risk of prostate cancer (in men), and improving

---

1. Charnetski and Brennan, "Sexual Frequency and Salivary Immunoglobulin A (IgA)."
2. Brody, "Relative Health Benefits of Different Sexual Activities."
3. Chan, "Why More Sex May Lower."

mental health. Nevertheless, it can be also argued that improvements in mental health might not necessarily be due to the sexual activity itself but rather from the feelings of love and belonging that have arisen from the relationship underpinning the sexual activity.

The humanist psychologist, Abraham Maslow (1908–1970), created a theory of psychological health based on fulfilling innate human needs in priority, culminating in self-actualization. Maslow believed that everyone had a strong desire to reach self-actualization (or fulfillment), but each person needed to address their basic needs before concentrating on higher needs and thereby reaching self-fulfillment. Indeed, according to Maslow, it is impossible to achieve self-fulfillment without first meeting basic needs, due to the stress of being deprived of these needs.

Maslow's hierarchy of needs is often depicted in the form of a pyramid with the physiological needs of breathing, food, water, sex, and sleep on the bottom. Once these very basic needs are met, the individual then concentrates on safety needs, such as security, employment, resources, morality, health, and property. Only after all of these needs have been met does the individual move on to 'love and belonging' (which Maslow states can be found in friendship, family, and sexual intimacy) and, finally, confidence, achievement, and respect for others and the self, which results in creative achievement and self-actualization. It is noteworthy that Maslow places sex (the innate sexual instinct) as a basic need whereas 'love and belonging' are much higher and, according to Maslow, it is only when an individual's needs concerning love and belonging are met that they can progress to self-achievement, respect for themselves and others, and finally achieve the confidence that will enable them to reach self-actualization.

Maslow defined self-actualization as the fullest use of one's talents and interests to become everything one is capable of becoming. Maslow also described the personality traits of self-actualized people as true, honest, problem-centered with a focus on problems outside of themselves, and reality-centered with a deeper insight into reality that accepts both the reality of themselves, and others, in the world. Usually, such people have faced, and overcome, many problems to achieve this state of being. In some ways, Maslow's psychological theory connects with that of the philosopher Søren Kierkegaard (1813–1855), a pioneering Danish philosopher regarded as the 'Father of Existentialist Philosophy,' who proposed that every individual is tasked with giving meaning to life and living authentically.

Many aspects of Maslow's psychological theory have been shown to be true, since it is now known how difficult it is for people who are born in chaotic or impoverished families to move beyond their basic needs. In regards to the topic of this book, mandatory celibacy, there is another question under consideration, which is this: bearing in mind that Maslow's theory states that 'love and belonging' are essential needs that must be met on the path to self-actualization, how hard will it be for a priest who undertook celibacy because it was 'part of the required package to be ordained' (rather than because he actually wanted to be celibate) to achieve self-actualization? When considering this question, it is necessary to bear in mind that when Maslow writes of self-actualization, he refers to total wholeness, and the individual's ability to become as close to this total wholeness as possible. Before considering this question, it is necessary to briefly mention two other psychologists, Carl Rogers (1902–1987) and Carl Gustav Jung (1875–1961).

Rogers was also a psychologist who lived and worked in the twentieth century at a similar time to Maslow; together, the two psychologists pioneered the movement known as humanistic psychology. Rogers' theory of the self was humanistic, existential, and phenomenological, and, again, linked to Kierkegaard, as well as the phenomenologist philosopher, Edmund Husserl (1859–1938). Rogers thought that the structure of self was developed from interaction with the environment and others, and he also believed that human beings had a basic tendency to actualize and satisfy their needs and enhance their existence. Rogers postulated that psychological adjustment exists when a person's concept of self is such that all sensory and emotional experiences can be assimilated into a consistent relationship with that concept of self. Psychological maladjustment exists when a person denies awareness of sensory and emotional experiences, and these are, resultingly, not assimilated into a consistent relationship with that person's sense of self. When this situation exists, there is psychological tension. This theory also raises a further question concerning mandatory celibacy, namely, this: does the denial and suppression of sensory and emotional experiences that arise from the mandatory celibate rule lead to psychological maladjustment in some Catholic priests?

The psychiatrist/psychoanalyst, Carl Jung, was not a humanist, but rather a psychiatrist who founded analytical psychology. His work preceded Rogers and Maslow, and its central concept was individuation, which he regarded as the lifelong psychological process of the self's differentiation out of conscious and unconscious elements. However, Santana argues that Jung developed a diverse and comprehensive body of work on sex and human sexuality because he was a victim of childhood sexual abuse. In Jung's work, there are issues concerning human sexuality that coincide with sexual issues that humanist psychologists have postulated result from the mandatory celibacy rule. This is because Jung states that all human beings are innately sexualized and their sexuality is part of their natural state of being. He states that pressures to conform to, or deny, natural instincts will create neurosis along with a psychological split between inner needs and outer demands. Therefore, while Jung may not agree with Maslow and Rogers as to the exact causes of psychological maladjustment (Jung believes it is due to denying 'natural' instincts whereas Maslow and Rogers argue that it is due to an individual being forced to deny sensory and emotional experiences that should be assimilated into a personal sense of self), the effect on a celibate priest who has taken on celibacy as a mandatory aspect of being a priest, rather than because he is drawn to celibacy, is the same. It is possible he will be a victim of psychological maladjustment and will not be able to achieve fulfilment or self-actualization.

While modern psychology sees human sexuality as a good and natural thing that is part of a person's natural state of being, it is apparent, from *The Catechism of the Catholic Church* that the Catholic hierarchy does not view human sexuality in this way at all. Unfortunately, the Catholic view of human sexuality remains with the anachronistic and dire theology of the fifth-century St. Augustine who abandoned his lover of fifteen years, and his child, to marry a wealthy woman preferred by his mother, who was subsequently abandoned for celibacy. As has been previously noted, Augustine taught that all sexual desire, even in marriage, was evil. The twenty-first century Catholic Church has moved little further forward and so we read in the Catechism: "Their mutual attraction, the Creator's own gift, changed into a relationship of domination and lust";[4] "Virginity for the sake of the Kingdom of Heaven is ... a powerful sign of the supremacy of the bond with Christ ... a sign that recalls that marriage is a reality of this present age which is passing away";[5] "Chastity includes an apprenticeship in self-mastery ... either man governs his passions and finds peace or he lets himself be dominated by them and becomes unhappy...."[6]

It is simply tragic that in the twenty-first century the Catholic Church is still stuck with a fifth-century vision of sexuality that sees our natural sex drive as flawed and needing to be conquered and virginity as a sign of the supremacy of the bond with Christ. In actuality, the original Greek of the New Testament Christ never, at any time, states that virginity, or celibacy, are superior to marriage, or that human sexuality is flawed. Christ does condemn adultery and immoral sexual acts (πορνεία) and therefore, in effect, states that sexuality can be misused (Matt 19:9) but, on no occasion, does he ever state that the sexual act itself is evil. In fact, he reaffirms traditional Jewish teaching, stating that from the very beginning people were created

---

4. "Marriage under sin," *Catechism of the Catholic Church*, 1606.
5. "Virginity for the sake of the Kingdom", *Catechism of the Catholic Church*, 1618.
6. "The integrity of the person," *Catechism of the Catholic Church*, 2239.

male and female and, in marriage, the two become one flesh (Matt 19: 4–6). Moreover, if sexuality can be misused, suppressing one's natural sexual drive is hardly the way to deal with it. Suppression is likely to lead to maladjustment and might also intensify the sexual urge.

However, the dire fifth-century view of human sexuality that continues to be used in the *Catechism of the Catholic Church* is drummed into seminarians when they train for the priesthood. They are made to feel guilty about their natural sexual urges and taught that they must 'conquer' their sexuality. To withhold modern knowledge on human sexuality from people in this way and to indoctrinate them with an ancient theory that causes them to deny their natural humanity and to loathe their God-given sexuality can actually be deemed as abusive. It is, of course, done to try and justify the official Catholic position that a candidate for the priesthood must forget that he has a penis. This kind of teaching is cruel and barbaric and will, of course, on occasion, lead to psychological damage in some priests, causing them great suffering. One example of this was the sad case of the late Fr. Sean Seddon who committed suicide at the age of thirty-eight years after falling in love with a woman.[7]

Seddon fell in love with a teacher named Jan Curry who after his death described the idea that virginity is superior to marriage as implicit in Church law. She described compulsory celibacy and priesthood as being tied together in a dualistic view of the world.[8] Women are seen as base, fleshy and corruptible, and must not be part of the life of the holy man. This view is not only misogynistic but flawed. In reality, to be human is to be in a relationship; it is an inalienable human right to marry or be in a long-term relationship. Curry described the 'sorrowing' that many priests experience when they feel strongly called both to be a priest and to marry. Seeking to suppress their sexuality often leads to despair, heartbreak, breakdown, and suicide. In regard to her lover of ten years, Fr. Seddon; he eventually threw himself under a train.

While many priests are psychologically damaged by the mandatory celibacy rule, there are, of course, some who are not. Those less likely to be damaged are either those who have a naturally low libido or those who enter the seminary with a healthy sexuality and are aware of exactly what they are giving up. These are usually mature men who think they can manage as celibates, perhaps because they have previously had sexual relationships or because they believe they have learnt to fulfill their needs for love and belonging in non-sexual relationships. "You need affection and human

---

7. Gledhill, "Doomed Love Affair Led Priest to Suicide."
8. "The Law of Celibacy Must Change."

intimacy," said one Fr Stephen Wang when interviewed by the BBC, "I've got some wonderful friends. I get home to see my family every couple of weeks. I escape to the cinema now and then. And I pray. Not to fill the gaps, because some of them can never be filled, but because the love of Christ is something very real and very consoling."[9]

So, the main areas where a celibate priest might encounter difficulties that could result in psychological maladjustment are love and belonging. Of course, not all celibate priests will encounter difficulties in this area, as is demonstrated by the above quote. Some priests will find love and belonging in their religious order or through maintaining family relationships and friendships they have formed. However, finding a sense of belonging will always be easier for: the priest who has a naturally low libido, the priest who joins as a mature candidate, or, perhaps, the priest who is homosexual. This is because a priest with a naturally low libido will obviously not have any great longing for sex, the mature priest is already well adjusted, and the homosexual priest is likely to find it much easier to make meaningful friendships with his peers than a heterosexual priest. This is because his instincts will be more likely to draw him towards friendships with men and he will be both living and working with men.

The heterosexual priest, if he is not mature and well-adjusted, will find it much more difficult to fulfil his needs of love and belonging. Firstly, he will not be living and working with women and will not come into contact with them as frequently as men, and, secondly, it would certainly be regarded as unethical for a priest to befriend a woman with whom he came into contact through his work. It is probable that such a priest would meet a woman in a position that would be regarded as having power over her, perhaps in the role of parish priest or in some other related role. This would mean that all the women he met in the course of his work would be seen as subservient to him and thus out of bounds. Homosexual priests, of course, would not be in the same position at work in regard to making and forming strong friendships, as opportunities are available for them to befriend their colleagues. These opportunities are not available to heterosexual priests due to the Catholic Church's refusal to ordain women. Heterosexual priests do not have female colleagues.

Homosexual priests can work with men who are priests on the same level as themselves and with whom, if they so desire, they can form a friendship of equals. The heterosexual priest is in no such position, and this is one of the many reasons why mature heterosexual men are no longer attracted in great numbers to the Roman Catholic priesthood. The only way in which

9. "Why I Choose to Live a Celibate Life."

a heterosexual priest could befriend a woman would be in some neutral space, i.e., if he met her on holiday or on a retreat. This greatly limits the opportunities of a heterosexual priest to form a meaningful friendship with a woman but, even if by some miracle, he did manage to form such a friendship, he would have to face the difficulty of enforced celibacy because there would be limits as to where the friendship could progress.

In the very early church nearly all priests were married but in the post-East–West Schism Church (when Latin priests had been denied the right to marry) some celibate priests did manage to form deep and meaningful non-sexual friendships with women because, in the centuries after the East–West Schism, some women held much more senior positions in the Catholic Church than today, and were thus able to meet with men on terms of equality. For example, St. Catherine of Siena (who was a spiritual director to many eminent people including two Popes) formed a close friendship with her own spiritual director, Raymond du Capua, who was Master General of the Dominican order, St. Teresa of Avila (who was a Carmelite nun) formed a close friendship with St. John of the Cross, a Carmelite Friar, and the two founded a religious order together, St. Clare of Assisi formed a spiritual bond with St. Francis of Assisi enabling her to found the Order of Poor Clares for women inspired by St. Francis's order for men, and Queen Catherine of Aragon (a member of the Third Order of St. Francis, as well as Queen of England) formed a close friendship with a Franciscan Friar, Blessed John Forrest, who was eventually martyred for his loyalty to his Queen and his Catholic faith. All these friendships were relationships between people who could, in many ways, be regarded as equals.[10]

In the Middle Ages and in the pre-Reformation Church it was considered very normal for a woman to pursue a vocation in the Church, and religious women were taken much more seriously. There were not only consecrated nuns but consecrated widows, and, in England, consecrated widows were significant in number and could be highly influential. Indeed, it is likely that the writer, spiritual director, and mystic, Julian of Norwich, was a consecrated widow. Because there were so many influential religious women, it can be argued that friendships between priests and women would have been much easier then than they are today. This is due to the fact that very few women today are consecrated as religious as this vocation no longer appeals to most modern women. The rites of consecrated widow and consecrated virgin have been restored by Rome but are not highly promoted, mainly because these women live in their own homes and wear

---

10. Even Blessed John Forrest, who was not royal, had been a very eminent theologian and Provincial of his Order before he was imprisoned for his faith.

normal attire. Some misogynistic prelates cannot bear to see consecrated women living outside a convent. In addition, the Catholic Church has failed to restore the female diaconate and refused to ordain women as priests. Therefore, those Catholic women who remain in the Church are largely lay women and this makes it much more difficult for a priest to make friends with a such a woman because they will usually not meet lay women on terms of equality. On the other hand, it should not be assumed that because there may be more opportunities for homosexual priests to make positive friendships than for heterosexual priests, that gay priests will not also struggle with the celibacy rule. Some gay priests will find celibacy difficult, and this is because mandatory celibacy differs from asexuality, or low libido, where a person feels little or no sexual attraction. Mandatory celibacy demands an active denial of sexual impulses, and this applies whatever the sexual orientation of the priest.

In July 2019, Fr. Peter Daly, writing in the *National Catholic Reporter*, argued that there could be no real reform in the Roman Catholic Church unless mandatory celibacy was done away with.[11] He stated that while there would always be a very small number of people who were attracted to the celibate life perhaps because they felt little sexual attraction, celibacy for the majority of men was simply not normal. He also stated that: it was not healthy, fostered a culture of mendacity and secrecy, was unessential to holiness, was not mandated by the Gospels, and contributed to a culture of clericalism. Daly argued that the norm for human beings was sexual intimacy and that every person needed some physical intimacy in their life. A healthy sex life, he claimed, contributed to a healthier person physically, psychologically, emotionally, and spiritually, and when men are forced to give up sexual intimacy all sorts of bad behaviors emerge. He also laid the deficit in priestly vocations very firmly at the door of enforced priestly celibacy stating, that there were fewer candidates for ordination, due to men being unwilling to take it on. Also, of those who did come forward to try their vocations, over half left—either in the seminary, or after ordination. Almost all the leavers he knew had left due to the mandatory celibacy rule. Fr. Daly was not against celibacy per se. He was against mandatory celibacy. He wrote:

> Does anyone really think that we would have so many shocking clerical sexual scandals if we did not require celibacy? The clerical scandals of the last 30 years have revealed the hidden pathologies of priestly celibacy. When men are forced to give up sexual intimacy, all sorts of bad behaviors emerge.

11. Daly, "Priesthood Is Being Crucified."

The Church would argue that priests are not "forced" into celibacy, that we chose it freely. But that is not how it is experienced. A gift must be freely given, not mandated. Celibacy in the Roman Catholic priesthood is a mandate. If you won't promise lifelong celibacy, the church won't ordain you. It is not experienced so much as a "gift", but rather as a "price" for priesthood. For many people, the price is too high.[12]

A.W. Richard Sipe was an American priest for eighteen years. He was also a trained psychotherapist. Sipe left the priesthood in 1970 because, to his shock, he had realized that just below the surface of the Church lay secrets protected by its hierarchy. In his first position as a counsellor in a high school, Sipe heard in the confessional about priests who were sexually involved with other priests, priests who had girlfriends, and, even, priests who were involved with minors. In 1967, Sipe became the director of family services at a treatment center where bishops sent 'problem priests.' Some of these stated that they had been abused by clergy themselves while others stated that the Church hierarchy was dismissive of reports of abuse. Sipe left the priesthood and later married Dr. Marianne Benkert, who was a psychiatrist. With her help, he conducted a twenty-five-year ethnographic study about the behavior of so-called 'celibates.' He found out that over half had sexual relationships. However, the Catholic hierarchy refused to listen to him, and he was blackballed.[13]

Despite criticism from the Catholic hierarchy, Sipe continued his research and, in 2002, he guided *The Boston Globe* in their investigation into the clergy of the Archdiocese of Boston. They found that 6 percent of priests there had abused minors. Later, in a 2009 study, Sipe found that there were extensive problems with the behavior of Catholic clergy in Vermont. He examined the records of 102 priests and found that twenty-three were sexually involved with children, fifteen had been involved with married women, and nineteen had sexual relationships with men. In 2008, Sipe also warned Pope Benedict XVI regarding the sexual behavior of Cardinal Theodore McCarrick who was finally defrocked in 2018 following allegations of sexual abuse towards boys and seminarians. His letter was ignored at the time.

In a foreword to Sipe's book, *Celibacy in Crisis*, Fr. Richard McBrien, Professor of Theology at Notre Dame, wrote, "Obligatory celibacy and the church's official teaching on human sexuality are at the root of the worst

---

12. Daly, "Priesthood Is Being Crucified," para. 30–31.
13. See Rodricks, "From 'Spotlight' to 'Keepers,'" para. 12.

crisis the Catholic Church has faced since the time of the Reformation."[14] In an interview he then went on to explain:

> The Eastern Orthodox do not have celibate clergy, and they have no sexual abuse crisis. When you require celibacy as a life-long commitment from any control group, you are inevitably, automatically and infallibly limiting your pool of potential recruits to one of the thinnest slices of the population.
> There are some healthy people who practice celibacy. But that requirement of the priesthood will attract a disproportionately high percentage of men who are sexually dysfunctional, sexually immature, or whose orientation will raise the question - are they attracted to the priesthood because of the ministry, or because it is a profession that forbids one to be married?[15]

Of the priests and prelates who have had the courage to criticize celibacy one, in particular, stands out. In February 2013, Cardinal Keith O'Brien spoke out strongly against clerical celibacy stating that many priests struggled to cope with it and should be allowed to marry and have children. In an interview with the BBC, he stated that Jesus had never stipulated that priests be celibate and that they had been married in the past.[16] Many were shocked by his outspokenness on the issue; there was speculation as to whether he might feel that the clerical culture enabled priests to hide their abusive behavior and a married clergy might ameliorate this. O'Brien stated that he had never considered marriage himself as when he joined the priesthood it had just been considered the norm for priests to be celibate.

A few weeks after O'Brien advocated for a relaxation of the celibacy rule, it became public that he had been accused of inappropriate sexual behavior with four men. Three of these men were serving priests at the time and one was a former priest. O'Brien stated that he accepted that his sexual conduct had sometimes fallen below the standards expected of him as a priest, archbishop and cardinal. Now, O'Brien had always been vehemently opposed to homosexuality and had referred to it as a moral degradation. In 2012, he had also criticized the government's proposals for same sex marriage, and yet, he himself had been practicing undercover as a homosexual, and was also in favor of lifting the celibacy rule for heterosexuals. This is intriguing and the question has to be asked, was O'Brien always a homosexual or did his sexual orientation change while he was a priest?

14. Richard McBrian, foreword to Sipe, *Celibacy in Crisis*, xiii.
15. See McManus, "Catholic Priests Seek End to Celibacy."
16. "Cardinal Keith O'Brien: Allow Priests to Marry."

I once had a friend who had previously been a priest in a religious order and he told me that he entered the religious order as a heterosexual man but left as a homosexual one. He told me that he had been sexually frustrated as a celibate man and had engaged in sex with other men in the order because he lived and worked with men alone and only men were available. Eventually he decided he was living a lie and left, but when he did, he found that his sexual orientation had changed, and he was no longer attracted to women. One has to ask, did the same thing happen to O'Brien? Was O'Brien originally a heterosexual who became a homosexual out of frustration? Certainly, he had a lot of sympathy for heterosexual celibate priests who do not wish to be celibate, and he was also, sadly, very clearly homophobic. Did O'Brien loathe himself because he had become homosexual and did he believe that if he been allowed to marry, he would not have become homosexual?

We will never know the reasons for O'Brien's sexual misconduct, but we do know he was not a happy man, and he came to believe that the celibacy rule should be relaxed. He was as much a victim as the men whom he had abused. He was a victim of a church and a system that denied priests their God-given sexuality. O'Brien was almost certainly what Murnane describes as a "situational abuser" because, he would almost certainly not have spoken out against mandatory celibacy if this wasn't so.[17] Murnane describes situational abusers as those who did not enter the priesthood with any inclination to abuse but later became abusive in responses to stresses, lack of positive adult relationships, or social isolation.

O'Brien was a cardinal of the church, but he was certainly not the first of senior prelates to fall due to the celibacy rule. In 1992 the resignation of Bishop Eamonn Casey of the Diocese of Galway, Kilmacduagh and Kilfenora was a pivotal moment which shook the Catholic Church in the West.[18] It was revealed that Casey had engaged in an affair with an American woman, Annie Murphy, and fathered a child. Casey had made covert payments for the upbringing of his son but had refused to engage in a relationship with him as, had he done so, he would have been made to resign his office. Eventually his former lover whistle-blew on him because he would not have a relationship with their son. Casey was then ordered by the Vatican to leave Ireland and become a missionary in Ecuador and later took on a position as a priest in England. Casey has since had several other sexual allegations made against him that related to his time as a bishop in Galway and it is clear that he was in no way celibate as a bishop and that he lived a lie. But

---

17. Murnane, *Clerical Errors*, 63.
18. For more information on the Eamonn Casey scandal see Prone, "Eamon Casey."

why? What caused him to become so perverse? That is the question. And, if he had been allowed to marry, would he ever have become so perverse? Since then, there has been a substantial number of sexual allegations made against prelates at the top of the Church including, more recently, eleven prelates in France. If anyone has any doubt that celibacy isn't working and that some prelates are maladjusted, one has only to look at the number of sexual allegations made against prelates to dispel these doubts. The sins of celibacy are everywhere and, as Murnane states, if the demand that priests maintain lifelong celibacy has been based on the distorted suspicion of sexuality founded in the writings of Jerome and Augustine, then this demand is a clerical error that betrays the Gospel of Jesus.

CHAPTER 3

Mandatory Celibacy and Human Rights

THIS CHAPTER WILL EXAMINE human rights and will argue that mandatory celibacy is an abuse of human rights. I will first define what human rights are and will then illustrate how enforced celibacy is an abuse of these rights. I will also examine other abuses of human rights that priests experience as a result of their celibate state. For example, many priests are threatened with, or have experienced, a loss of their homes, jobs and incomes when they have dared to challenge the Vatican on issues such as enforced celibacy and female ordination. Finally, I will examine the laws that allow the Catholic Church to exempt itself from discrimination and thereby actually practice discrimination. I will argue that the Catholic Church should not be exempt from international equality and discriminatory law and the fact that the Vatican is recognized as a state is a contributory factor in its ability to exempt itself. Geoffrey Robertson QC has argued that the recognition of the Vatican as a state, which did not occur until 1929, has enabled it to carry out abuses of human rights and I will discuss why this is the case.

    Supposedly, the purpose of religion is to make the world a better place. There is no point in a religion that makes the world a worse place nor is there any point in assisting a religion to have lower standards than those held in the secular world. Of course, there was a time when, for Europe, the teachings of the Catholic Church represented the general moral consensus of both Church and many states. However, that time has now long since passed and, as will be demonstrated, the Catholic Church's interpretation and implementation of certain human rights in some (not all) areas is far worse than the interpretation and implementation of these rights in many modern national states. Yet, despite this, although Catholic Canon Law should not technically be binding outside of the Vatican state, the Catholic

Church seeks to bind all practicing Catholics anywhere in the world to its own Canon Law and, in particular, to use this law to discriminate against all its priests the world over. These priests are allowed no freedom of conscience. The way celibate priests are discriminated against is completely shameful and the Vatican would do well to upgrade its theology and its Canon Law to incorporate the internationally recognized human rights that most other Western states try to uphold. The Catholic hierarchy often refers to secular European states as 'worldly,' implying that only the Vatican is true to the teachings of Christ where European secular states are not. The reverse is often true, as many European states honor human rights that the Vatican does not. In this chapter, I will demonstrate that forcing a person to give up their natural God-given sexuality to become a priest is a cruel, perverse, and barbaric breach of natural God-given human rights. As has already been noted, it has nothing to do with the teachings of Jesus.

The belief in the sanctity of human rights has ancient precedents in some religions of the world and in ancient Greek philosophy. Both Aristotle and Aquinas wrote of the theory of 'natural law' which stated that all people have inherent rights conferred by God, nature, or reason. Aquinas argued that because human beings have reason, and reason is a spark of the divine, all human beings are sacred and of infinite value. He stated that all human beings are intrinsically equal and invested with an intrinsic set of rights that no one can remove. Unfortunately, however, when Aquinas spoke of human beings, he did not really mean all human beings at all, since he believed that women were imperfect 'misbegotten' males who, due to their inferiority, were subordinate to men and thus almost sub-human.

During the seventeenth century the philosopher, John Locke (1643–1704), developed a more egalitarian conceptualization of human rights. He believed that all people are naturally free and equal and that they have natural rights that are divine in origin, since humans are created by God. Locke's thinking was very influential and led to the creation of the English Bill of Rights. This bill was a landmark moment in British political history because it limited the monarch's powers and set out the rights of parliament. It established the freedom to petition the monarch, the freedom from cruel and unusual punishments and the freedom from being fined without trial.

In the eighteenth century there was a major revolution in the United States and, as a result of this, *The Virginia Declaration of Rights* (1776), set up a number of fundamental rights and freedoms. This was followed by the *United States Declaration of Independence* (1776), which incorporates the concept of natural rights, stating that all people are created equal and endowed by the creator with inalienable rights, such as, the right to life, liberty, and the pursuit of happiness. Similarly, in the eighteenth century, there was also a revolution in France that resulted in a declaration of human rights. The French *Declaration of the Rights of Man and of the Citizen* (1789) defines a set of individual and collective rights belonging to the people. The term 'man' in this document referred to all people, and not just men.

After these revolutions, there were other humanitarian movements such as the foundation of the International Committee of the Red Cross (1863), the first of the Geneva Conventions (1864) laying the foundations of international humanitarian law, as well as movements to suppress and abolish slavery. The Catholic Church also began its official Catholic Social Teaching with the Apostolic Exhortation *Rerum Novarum* (1891). This document was largely concerned with workers' and citizens' rights against state intrusion.

The main drive towards the establishment of what we now call human rights occurred after the two World Wars. The League of Nations was established in 1919 at the negotiations of the Treaty of Versailles that followed World War I. The goals of this charter were disarmament and the prevention of future wars through collective security, negotiation, and diplomacy. Also enshrined in this charter was a mandate to promote many of the rights that were later included in the Universal Declaration of Human Rights. Despite this charter, another World War occurred, and it was actually following World War II that the Universal Declaration of Human Rights was adopted by the United Nations General Assembly in 1948.

The Universal Declaration of Human Rights is a milestone document in the history of human rights. This document enshrines the rights and freedoms of all human beings. It is a non-binding declaration that was drafted by a UN committee chaired by Eleanor Roosevelt. This committee was comprised of representatives with different legal and cultural backgrounds from all regions of the world. It was proclaimed by the UN General assembly as Resolution 217 on December 10, 1948, and it sets out a common standard for all peoples and nations. The declaration commits nations to recognize all human beings as being born 'free and equal in dignity and rights' regardless of nationality, place of residence, sex, national, or ethnic, origin, color, religion, language or any other status. It consists of thirty articles that detail these basic rights and fundamental freedoms, which are affirmed as inherent, inalienable, and applicable to all human beings. There are two articles in this document that are continuously and persistently breached by the Roman Catholic Church. The first is Article 16, which states:

1. Men and women of full age, without any limitation due to race, nationality or religion, have the right to marry and to found a family.

They are entitled to equal rights as to marriage, during marriage and at its dissolution.

2. Marriage shall be entered into only with the free and full consent of the intending spouses.

3. The family is the natural and fundamental group unit of society and is entitled to protection by society and the State.

The Roman Catholic Church continuously breaches this Article in regard to priests in the Latin Church because it will not allow the majority of them either to marry or be ordained as married men. Any man in the Latin Church who wishes to become a priest is coerced into giving up his right to marry because the Roman Catholic Church will not allow him to carry out this vocation in the married state. This is particularly disturbing because the same Roman Catholic Church does not deny its priests in the Eastern rite this same human right. Priests in the Eastern rite *are* allowed to be ordained as married men. Additionally, the Roman Catholic Church does not deny married priests who convert this same human right. Married priests from other denominations *are* allowed to be ordained in their married state if they convert to Catholicism. They *are* allowed to serve the Roman Catholic Church as married priests.

It surely cannot be right that men who are ordained Roman Catholic priests in one part of the world are allowed to be ordained as married men whereas men who are ordained as Roman Catholic priests in another part of the world are not. Neither can it be right that married priests who convert from another Christian denomination to Roman Catholicism are allowed to serve as married priests in the Western Roman Catholic Church while those who were ordained as single men are forced into mandatory celibacy. If there is a theological reason why married men cannot be ordained, which there is not, then that reason should be applied to *all* candidates for the priesthood shouldn't it? What the Church implies by its actions is that there is no actual theological reason for mandating priests to be celibate (some priests are allowed to be married). This is an inequitable breach of Article 16 and therefore an inequitable breach of a human right. I would postulate that the reason for this may very well be the Vatican's preoccupation with its power rather than any legitimate moral or theological concern. The Vatican wants to keep power in the hands of a male celibate cult, which has been created since the time of the East–West Schism. It is possible to maintain this cult if only a few married men are ordained but allowing many married men to be ordained would, of course, bring an end to this cult. This male celibate cult has nothing to do with the Jesus of the New Testament.

The other Article of the Universal Declaration of Human Rights that the Church continually breaches is Article 19, which states, "Everyone has the right to freedom of opinion and expression; this right includes freedom to hold opinions without interference and to seek, receive and impart information and ideas through any media and regardless of frontiers." Sadly, this human right has been continuously abused by the Vatican since its creation in 1948 and particularly in the wake of the Second Vatican Council (Vatican II). Some very strange things have happened since Vatican II as per below.

The main theologians at the Second Vatican Council who were in favor of the reform of the Roman Catholic Church were: Marie-Dominque Chenu OP, Henri de Lubac SJ, Yves Congar OP, Karl Rahner SJ, John Courtney Murray SJ, Berhard Haring CSsR, Edward Schillebeeckx OP, Joseph Ratzinger, and Hans Kung. These theologians formulated and drove through the reforms of Vatican II. Following the closure of the council, one of these theologians, namely Joseph Ratzinger (later Pope Benedict XVI), who described himself as an admirer of Rahner and Schillebeeckx, suddenly turned coat and decided that he was not in favor of the reforms he had helped to bring about after all! This turning of the coat is believed to have happened sometime around 1970 and, from that time onwards, Ratzinger began to swing further and further to the so-called 'traditionalist' right. (These right wing 'traditionalists' are, of course, not really traditionalists at all since they derive their interpretation of the Church from the declarations of the Council of Trent, rather than from the practices of the early church.)

Later, in 1981, Ratzinger was named the Prefect of the Sacred Congregation for the Doctrine of the Faith under Pope John Paul II and took a stance that opposed the views of some of those with whom he had originally worked. On April 19, 2005, he was elected as Pope and took the name of Benedict XVI. As Pope he continued in his conservative stance. Some of the theologians whom Ratzinger either undermined or persecuted during his time as Prefect or as Pope, included Hans Kung, Karl Rahner, Leonardo Boff, Matthew Fox, Anthony de Gustavo Gutierrez, Edward Schillebeeckx, Eugen Drewermann, and Tony Flannery. He was almost certainly behind the persecution of Lavinia Byrne, a female religious sister, whose case will not be examined here as this book concentrates on the plight of celibate men. None of these individuals were allowed the right of freedom of expression without interference, as detailed below.

Hans Kung had worked with Ratzinger during the Second Vatican Council but began to question Papal Infallibility in 1971. Later, he criticized mandatory celibacy and wanted to restore the female diaconate, and he also called the ban on dispensations for priests who wanted to leave the priesthood a violation of human rights. He was stripped of his license to teach as a Catholic theologian before Ratzinger became Prefect for the Sacred Congregation for the Doctrine of the Faith but Ratzinger, during his tenure, did nothing to help him and continued to ensure that Kung was both penalized for his views and denied his freedom of expression. In 2010, Kung published a letter in which he criticized Pope Benedict's handling of liturgical, collegial, and inter-religious issues, as well as the Church's sexual abuse scandals. He also objected to the canonization of Pope John Paul II on the grounds that his was "an authoritarian pontificate which suppressed the rights of both women and theologians."[1]

Karl Rahner was a German Jesuit priest who had also worked with Ratzinger during the Second Vatican Council. At that time, Ratzinger had declared that he was a great admirer of Rahner. The influence of Rahner at the time of the Second Vatican Council, and in the following decade, was enormous. He is linked to the council's receptiveness towards other religious traditions due to his theory that all human beings have a latent experience of God or proto revelation. His theology led to a drive towards ecumenism but unfortunately this was turned back by *Dominus Iesus* produced by Ratzinger during the tenure of Pope John Paul II. This document stated that the Catholic Church is the sole true Church founded by Jesus Christ.

Leonardo Boff was a Catholic Franciscan priest and a liberation theologian. He criticized the Catholic hierarchy for being fundamentalist and power driven and stated that the Church should promote social justice and environmental stewardship. In 1985, Ratzinger silenced him for his book *Church: Charism and Power* and he was almost silenced again in 1992 when he was prevented from participating in the Eco-92 Earth Summit. This led to him leaving his religious order and priestly ministry. He later accused Ratzinger of religious terrorism. Once again Ratzinger had breached Article 19 of the Universal Declaration of Human Rights by denying freedom of expression and forcing a priest, who would not conform to Ratzinger's version of theology, out of a job.

Matthew Fox was a renowned Dominican theologian who had masters' degrees in both philosophy and theology and a Doctorate of Spiritual Theology from the Institut Catholique de Paris. In 1984, Ratzinger told the Dominican order to investigate Fox's writings; however, the three Dominican theologians who investigated did not find his books heretical. Later, due to Fox's questioning of original sin, Ratzinger forbade Fox from teaching or lecturing for a year. Fox wrote a "Pastoral Letter to Cardinal Ratzinger and the Whole Church" in which he called the Catholic Church a "dysfunctional

---

1. Qtd. in Fox, "Hans Kung on John II Beatification," taken, and translated, from an interview with the German daily newspaper, the *Frankfurter Rundschau*, para. 1.

family."[2] In 1998, Fox was ordered to leave the Institute of Culture and Creation Spirituality. This was an institute that Fox himself founded. He refused to do so, and, in 1993, he was expelled from the Dominican Order to become yet another theologian who had been denied freedom of expression in the course of his work. Like many others, he was stripped of everything he possessed when he failed to conform to Ratzinger's version of theology.

Anthony de Gustavo Gutiérrez was a Catholic theologian and Dominican priest. His theological focus was connecting salvation and liberation through the 'preferential option for the poor.' In 1971, he published *A Theology of Liberation* under the name Gustavo Gutiérrez. However, in 1984 Ratzinger ordered the Peruvian bishops to examine Gutiérrez's writings. He and other liberation theologians were subjected to a thirty-six-page Vatican Report that declared Marxism to be incompatible with Catholic teachings and sent the message to 'comply with what we believe or else.' The Catholic Church in Peru then held a vote to rebuke Gutiérrez's ordination, which ended in a tie. Gutierrez escaped censorship by the skin of his teeth, and he was better treated under Pope Francis.

Edward Schillebeeckx was a Belgian theologian who was born in Antwerp and a member of the Dominican Order. He was highly influential during the Second Vatican Council but, over the course of his life, he had to defend his theological positions against the Roman authorities on three occasions. His natural human right to freedom of opinion and expression was not honored and the Vatican tried continuously to meddle with his ideas. He was challenged on his Christology, his writings on ministry, and his views on the sacramental nature of office. Of course, once again, one of the main opponents to his theology was the turncoat, Ratzinger, who had worked with Schillebeeckx at the Second Vatican Council when he had expressed similar views. It is interesting to note that of all the theologians at the Second Vatican Council, Ratzinger achieved the highest office and then went on to suppress not only those who had worked with him at the Council, but many others. In the end, Schillebeeckx's work was never officially condemned but his theology did fall out of favor under Ratzinger when he was Prefect of the Sacred Congregation for the Doctrine of the Faith and, later, when he was Pope.

Eugen Drewermann is a German who was formerly a Catholic priest. Sadly, he was not allowed freedom of opinion and expression and was driven out of the Church by Ratzinger and other leading Catholic prelates. Drewermann is both a psychologist and a philosopher, as well as a theologian, and, unfortunately, it is pretty normal for the Catholic Church to drive

---

2. Qtd. in Hyer, "Priest Agrees to Stop Teaching Spirituality."

out its most intelligent thinkers when their thinking threatens the power of the cult of the celibate priesthood. Drewermann has criticized the Roman Catholic Church's literal interpretation of miracles and events such as the virgin birth, the ascension, and the resurrection. He has accused the Catholic church of being medieval and has called on Rome to understand biblical stories symbolically in such a way that they can be relevant and healing to modern Christians. In 1989, Drewermann published a critique of the Vatican's clerical ideal, which he described as psychologically cruel and resulting in mental enslavement, due to, among other things, mandatory celibacy. He had dared to challenge the cultish status of the Vatican, which will not be challenged, and his days were immediately numbered. As a result of this, on October 7, 1991, Archbishop Degenhardt of Paderborn disallowed him to teach at the Catholic Seminary of Paderborn. His license to preach was revoked in 1992. Another great mind was silenced and Drewermann eventually left the Catholic Church in 2005.

Tony Flannery is an Irish Redemptorist priest who was suspended by the Vatican in 2012. At this time, Ratzinger was Pope Benedict XVI. Ratzinger later resigned as Pope in 2013. On September 1, 2010, Flannery founded The Association of Catholic Priests as an independent voluntary association of Catholic priests in Ireland. The group was founded to discuss theological issues and to fight for the rights of priests, defending them in situations where their bishops did not support them. Flannery was suspended for founding the organization and advised to go to a monastery where he might pray and reflect. Three other priests were also silenced, and these were Fr Sean Fagan, Fr Owen O'Sullivan, and Fr Brian D'Arcy. Flannery has been told that he will only be allowed to return to ministry if he agrees to write, sign, and publish a statement agreeing that women can never be ordained and that he will adhere to church orthodoxy on matters such as contraception and homosexuality.

Flannery has stated that he will not be terrorized into submission. The Association of Catholic Priests continues in Ireland, but its initial impetus has been curbed by fear. This is due to the Vatican's continuous refusal to allow priests any freedom of expression, or opinion, in direct breach of Article 19 of the Universal Declaration of Human Rights. Any healthy organization will always allow discussion and debate because it is only through the modes of discussion and debate that our knowledge can grow. However, the official view of the Vatican is that the Catholic Church is the sole true Church founded by Jesus Christ and that nothing can be added to or taken from its dogma.[3] The problem is, of course, the Church's interpretation of

---

3. See Ratzinger, *Dominus Iesus*.

the scriptures and the writings of the Early Church Fathers. The Roman Catholic Church has declared its interpretation of these ancient documents as the definitive and 'true' interpretation but other Christian denominations such as the Orthodox, and various protestant congregations, disagree. The course of Christian history suggests they are right to do so. This triumphalist declaration allows no possibility for the reinterpretation of ancient documents via the medium of other Christian denominations, or the human development of knowledge, which is never static.

Of course, such a triumphalist document was made possible by the 1870 declaration of Papal Infallibility, many hundreds of years after the birth of Christ. Prior to this ridiculous declaration, this triumphalist assertion may have been made, but many Catholics would have been free to disagree with it. Now, they are not supposed to. The Pope has spoken 'ex cathedra' and is preserved from the possibility of error on doctrine! The teachings of the Catholic Church are, according to that document, absolutely true, and all other Christian denominations and religions are inferior. Unfortunately, this kind of triumphalist dogma is revered by a significant number of prelates who derive their thought from the teachings of the Council of Trent (1563) and the First Vatican Council (Vatican I), which had declared the infallibility of the Pope in 1870. Both Trent and Vatican I are a million miles from the Early Christian Church founded by Jesus. As has been noted, the Early Christian Church consisted of married apostles, and the vast majority of priests were also married. Nonetheless, both the Council of Trent and Vatican I promoted an elite celibate cult that presides at the top of a hierarchical Church.

In addition to the case of Tony Flannery, there are some other prominent cases of dissent in Ireland by well-known clerics. Michael Cox has set up an independent Catholic movement through the foundation of the Irish Orthodox Catholic and Apostolic Church. He claims apostolic succession because those who consecrated him claimed lineage from the Catholic Archbishop, Ngo Dinh Thuc. This archbishop was excommunicated by the Roman Catholic Church for consecrating a number of bishops without the Vatican's approval. One of those bishops was Pat Buckley, also an Irish Independent Catholic Bishop. He was suspended from the priesthood in 1986 following theological disagreements on all the usual subjects that the Vatican refused to discuss under Ratzinger as Prefect for the Congregation for the Doctrine of the Faith. These subjects included the ordination of women and gay marriage. Later, Buckley was ordained as an independent Catholic bishop by Michael Cox and subsequently excommunicated by the Roman Catholic Church. Sadly, he is recently deceased.

According to data from the Irish Census and the European Social Survey, mass attendance within the Roman Catholic Church in Ireland has declined from around 91 percent in 1973 to around 30 to 40 percent at present, depending on which statistics are used.[4] One therefore must raise the question as to what these suppressions of freedom of speech actually achieve. They certainly do not seem to be building up the Irish Roman Catholic Church. On the contrary, the reverse would appear to be the case. The laity are leaving the official Church en masse and, in addition, a new independent Catholic movement is on the rise. The Open Episcopal Church has several clergy serving there and there are also other independent bishops who have been consecrated in Ireland.

All the cases I have described above have been about men whose freedom of expression was denied in some way under Cardinal Ratzinger (later Pope Benedict XVI); therefore, it could be hypothesized by the reader that all might be well in the Church because Pope Benedict XVI resigned and was succeeded by Pope Francis and, more recently, Pope Leo XIV. Rumors have been circulating that prior to his resignation Pope Benedict XVI regretted leading the Church in such a coercive way. It has been said that one of the reasons for his resignation was that he felt unable to 'about-turn' again so late in life and office and, therefore, decided to remove himself, so that a more progressive pope could be elected. Pope Benedict XVI has now passed away.

However, all is certainly still not well. There are an increasing number of prelates within the Roman Catholic Church who call themselves 'traditionalists' and believe that this gives them the right to suppress the freedom of expression of their priests. Many Catholic priests I have spoken to have advised me that they continue to fear for their freedom of expression and, when they preach, they do not preach as they would like because they know if they preach what they truly think they are likely to be suspended from preaching and/or teaching. There was also some concern about the leadership of Pope Francis who often appeared to promise reform on many issues and then backtracked on his promises. For example, he called the recent Synod on Synodality to supposedly 'consult' the laity but when the laity spoke in favor of removing of mandatory celibacy and reinstating the ordination of women as deacons, these items were immediately removed from the synod agenda. The fact that this denial of freedom of expression continues to occur can also be seen in the following description of events.

A new bishop was appointed to the Roman Catholic Diocese of Ferns on June 11, 2021. His name was Gerard Nash. Shortly after his appointment

---

4. See McGarry, "Irish Figures for Mass Attendance," para. 8–9.

he gave an interview with the press. When asked about whether he agreed with women priests, Nash stated that the lack of women priests had been a bone of contention for many people in the diocese for decades. He then went on to claim that the full ministry of the Church should be open to all baptized people. He asserted, "When is that going to happen, I don't know. I am in favor of this. Most of the Irish Bishops are on record as striving to make ministry as inclusive as it should be. I think the idea of ministry and governance of the church being entirely male is completely wrong. I will be advocating for change. We must move forward."[5]

However, a few days later on June 24, 2021, another article appeared in *The Irish Catholic* in which the new bishop elect did a complete about-turn of his previous views. This article stated that he completely agreed with the rulings of Pope St. John Paul II and Pope Francis that the Church has no authority to introduce ordination of women. He stated, "It's way outside my area of competence all together, I suppose what I was coming at there, the work I've done over the past few years is supporting women in ministry. You know, those roles—to get roles for men and women, to develop a whole sense of room for women to minister within the Church. Ordination is a separate issue which is not in our Church and I fully accept that."[6]

This incident was extremely disturbing because it clearly illustrated that within a few days of becoming the Bishop Elect of The Roman Catholic Diocese of the Ferns, Gerard Nash was coerced to change his view on the ordination of women. Clearly, he must have been told that if he did not change his view his consecration as a bishop would not go ahead. Why else would he change his view? And this is always the problem, isn't it? When Catholic priests or potential bishops speak out, they are threatened with obstructed promotions, or expulsion, if they do not align their views with those of the Vatican. This makes their lives very difficult. What else would they do if they were not priests? Where else would they go? Many of them joined the Church as young seminarians at a very young age. They have never known anything else. It takes a very strong person to give up everything they have ever known for the sake of personal conscience.

The above examples are just a very tiny percentage of a large number of cases in which priests have been denied their freedom of expression in breach of Article 19 of the Universal Declaration of Human Rights. I have chosen to describe the cases of some very high-profile individuals. However, there are numerous other cases, many of which involve clerics with lower profiles. Why does the Vatican get away with this? Why is it not challenged

---

5. Danaher, "Clare Bishop," para. 5.
6. Jones, "New Bishop of Ferns 'Daunted,'" para. 12.

about its abuses of human rights in the way that other religions and states are? The reason would seem to be that the Vatican is not only the headquarters of a major religion. The Vatican is also a European state.

Vatican City was established in 1929 as an independent state by the Lateran Treaty. This treaty made it independent from Italy. The Vatican state is the smallest state in the world consisting of only 121 acres and a population of around 770. It is a sacerdotal-monarchical state and is governed by the Pope who is an absolute monarch and its head. In addition to being head of the Vatican state the Pope is also titled, Bishop of Rome and Head of the Catholic Church, Vicar of Jesus Christ, Successor of the Prince of the Apostles, Supreme Pontiff of the Universal Church, Patriarch of the Latin Church, Primate of Italy, Archbishop and Metropolitan of the Roman Province, and Servant of the Servants of God.

While the law of the Vatican City state consists of many treatises, the most important is the *Canon Law of the Catholic Church*. This is highly disturbing in itself because the Canon Law is twelfth century (i.e., medieval) in origin, and predates much later philosophy and learning, as well as all laws regarding human rights. Although the *Code of Canon Law* has been revised over the centuries, the purpose of the revisions has always seemed to be to increase the power of the clergy and enhance their hierarchical status, rather than to update Canon Law according to wider international developments and understandings of international law that have incorporated growing knowledge across the biological and social sciences, as well as other disciplines in the humanities.

For example, in the 1917 Code of Canon Law, the Vatican did away with the rights of lay people to become cardinals and it was decreed that only those who were priests or bishops could become cardinals. Originally there was no requirement that cardinals be ordained, and the status of cardinal was an honorary one that could be bestowed on lay people. During this revision of the *Code of Canon Law*, the power of lay Catholics was diminished, and no attempt was made to consider modern philosophical knowledge. In fact, the purpose of this revision of Canon Law was to incorporate the decrees of Vatican I that had been convened to condemn schools of modern thinking, such as rationalism, socialism, communism, liberalism, modernism, naturalism, and pantheism.

Furthermore, when the *Code of Canon Law* was revised in 1983 no attempts were made to take on board, or incorporate, the articles of the Universal Declaration of Human Rights. Instead, a Synod of Bishops was created as an advisory body to the pope. The purpose of this body was to "meet together at fixed times to foster closer unity between the Roman Pontiff and bishops, to assist the Roman Pontiff with their counsel in the preservation and growth of faith and morals and in the observance and strengthening of ecclesiastical discipline, and to consider questions pertaining to the activity of the Church in the world."[7]

So, the synodality of the Church now rested with the celibate bishops and with the Pope whereas, in the early church, synods had been attended not only by bishops but also by lay people, including women. Of course, a small number of lay people and women were invited to attend the fairly recent Synod on Synodality convened by Pope Francis and were even given a vote there, but the overall power in Church governance at that synod still rested with the celibate bishops. The right of a few women to vote made no difference whatsoever. Women had no real voice there. They did not have an influence like that of St Hilda at the Synod of Whitby.

In 2008, the Vatican, under Pope Benedict XVI, announced that it would not automatically adopt new Italian laws, which conveniently enabled it to escape the growing trend of all European nations adopting concepts of equality and diversity into law. Geoffrey Robertson QC has argued that the Vatican should never have been given a status as a national state because this gives the Catholic Church many advantages denied to other religions. The Holy See's status as a UN 'non-member state' means that it can do all that a state member can do, except vote. Robertson states that the Vatican's army of diplomats exploit this privileged status relentlessly in UN conferences to promote their archaic dogmas to the diminishment of women, divorced couples, and homosexuals.

In my view, the Vatican also exploits its privileged status to the diminishment of its own priests. These privileges have enabled it to avoid challenges on mandatory celibacy and mandatory celibacy is abusive. Its privileges have also enabled it to avoid challenges concerning its denial of freedom of speech for its priests, which is, again, abusive. This is because many secular priests feel trapped and torn apart. They are not happy with the Church's teaching on issues like celibacy and the ordination of women and they want to denounce these teachings, but they know that if they do, they could lose their ministries and their livelihoods. They love their ministries, and they need a livelihood. What can they do? Staying silent seems the only option for diocesan priests, as every attempt to speak out by eminent theologians and other priests has always failed since Ratzinger held office.

Concerning the medieval Catholic dogma that is abusive in the sense that it does not conform with the Universal Declaration of Human Rights, Robertson would argue that the Catholic Church is entitled to advance its views, which are usually similar to the views of Libya and Iran at UN

---

7. *Code of Canon Law*, Can. 342.

meetings, but it would have no right for preferential treatment in doing so if it was not a state and it should never have been made one. How can an area of land that is comprised of 121 acres and a population of between seven hundred and eight hundred people be regarded as a national state on a par with other larger countries that have a higher populace of many more ordinary citizens? The statehood of the Vatican seems to be preposterous, bearing in mind that most of its residents are ecclesiastics and not ordinary citizens at all. Robertson has also argued that this statehood has enabled the Vatican to cover up child abuse by use of its own laws, which are far less severe. This allegation will be examined in a later chapter.

Finally, in many countries, anti-discriminatory law does not apply to religious organizations. For example, in the UK, the 2010 Equality Act does not apply to religious positions, such as being a priest, bishop, imam, or rabbi. These positions have apparently been exempted to protect freedom of belief. The question I would like to raise is whether we should be protecting freedom of belief when doing so legitimizes abuse. For example, the Roman Catholic Church does not allow women to be priests because it claims that its interpretation of history, which declares that women were never priests, is true.

However, in my book, *No Place for a Woman*, I demonstrated that there is strong evidence that women were actually priests in the Early Christian Church and the evidence that they were deacons is irrefutable. The majority of scholars and academics would agree with me. Similarly, the Roman Catholic Church has defended its position on mandatory celibacy for priests but admitted that this is actually just a discipline and there are no theological grounds to refuse ordination to married men. For that reason, the Church *does* ordain a few married men. Since there are no definitive theological arguments to exempt married men from ordination, I would argue that this position is abusive, and I would raise the question as to why European law sanctions abuses of human rights. In my view, no religion should be exempt from equality law. The purpose of a religion is to encourage worship of a supreme being and enlighten and guide all people in good practice in their daily living. If a religion is not actually doing these things but is, instead, promoting abusive non-egalitarian practices, then surely the state has a right to force that religion to ensure the equal treatment of all people. Why has this not happened? It is perhaps because many nation states contain a significant number of Catholics and politicians who court power and the Catholic vote, even though they know that the Catholic hierarchy has a long history of abusing human rights.

Chapter 4

Mandatory Celibacy and Misogynism

This chapter will look at the relationship between mandatory celibacy and misogynism in Roman Catholicism. It will be demonstrated from the New Testament accounts that Jesus was not a misogynist and that the very early church was not initially misogynistic. The development of misogynism in Christianity can be seen in the writings of some early church fathers and, also, in some early church councils, and so it cannot be laid completely at the feet of male celibacy or male mandatory celibacy.

However, disturbing misogynistic trends began to develop in the West as male celibacy became more prominent through the writings of ascetic theologians like Augustine, Jerome, and Ambrose. The East always resisted the elevation of male celibacy above marriage, and, due to this, celibacy did not become mandatory in the West until after the East–West Schism in 1054. Celibacy has never been mandated in the East. Sadly, once the East–West Schism took place, the Western Catholic Church immediately began to mandate celibacy initially through the Gregorian reforms and later at the First Council of the Lateran. It will be demonstrated that after the inauguration of mandatory celibacy in the twelfth century, misogynism grew rapidly and there is a very strong relationship between mandatory celibacy and misogynism.

The Gospel accounts within the New Testament are clear that many women followed Jesus on his travels through towns and villages where he preached the "Good News of the Kingdom of God." (Luke 8:2–3; Mark 5:24–25) and they also followed him to the place of his crucifixion while the male disciples run away (Mark 15:40; Luke 23:27–30; Matt 27:55–56; John 19:25–26). These four gospel accounts also give many incidents of Jesus dealing with women in positive and non-discriminatory ways and their accounts of Jesus's earthly ministry mention more women than virtually any other secular writing of that era.

The New Testament narratives of Jesus's ministry are clear that Jesus was radical in the way he dealt with women and that he was, on occasions, challenged by outside forces and his own disciples for being so. However, since the earliest Gospel (Mark), was written at least thirty years after the death of Jesus, we cannot be sure of the accuracy of any of the gospels—but we can be sure that there is a pattern concerning Jesus's treatment of women that was ground-breaking. The way Jesus treated and interacted with women was counter to the culture of the time. He chatted with women, healed them, and allowed himself to be touched by them.

Some examples are, the healing of a woman with an issue of blood (Luke 8:43–48; Mark 5:25–34; Matt 9:20–22); the healing of Peter's mother-in-law (Luke 4:38–39; Matt 8:14–15; Mark 1:29–31) and the accounts of Jesus being anointed by a woman (Matt 26:6–13; Mark 14:3–9; John 12:2–9). The accounts of the anointing at Bethany are very interesting, as they have echoes of the preparation for a major ministry. Jesus says the woman is preparing him for his burial which of course will ultimately lead to the resurrection, and we would do well to remember that anointing is now used in sacramental rites such as baptism, confirmation, ordination, and anointing of the sick. Jesus's anointing is a sacramental act, and he was happy for a woman to do it. However, Jesus did not only heal women and allow them to touch him and minister to him; he also defended women.

For example, in the account of the woman caught in adultery (John 8:1–11), the pharisees challenge Jesus, asking whether she should be stoned. Jesus states (John 8:7), "If anyone is without sin, let him be the first to throw a stone at her" and, after he states this, all the pharisees (who would have been men) begin to go away one-by-one until Jesus is left alone with the woman. Jesus then tells her that, since no one has condemned her, he, too, does not condemn her and she should go and live a life free from sin. This passage is interesting because it is more complicated than it initially might seem to those of us living in the twenty-first century. Someone else would have committed adultery with this woman, a man, but there is no mention of any man being pursued for sin because the men escaped all punishment while the women were stoned. It is quite possible that some of the men who wished to condemn this woman may also have committed adultery at some point. They are certainly quick to disappear when Jesus suggests that he who is without sin should throw the first stone. What Jesus was actually doing here was challenging misogyny and hypocrisy. He was challenging the fact that men who commit adultery were treated differently to women who did the same thing.

Jesus liked women and he developed a rapport with them and there is some evidence that his male disciples found this strange and even unacceptable, for example, in the accounts of the anointing at Bethany (Matt 26:6–13; Mark 14:3–9; John 12:2–9) and, also, in the accounts of his interaction with the Samaritan woman at the well (John 4:1–7). However, later, during the passion, Jesus's male disciples are nowhere to be seen. It is his female disciples who follow him to the cross. There are some differences in the Gospel accounts as to which women are there (Mark 15:40–41; Matt 27:55–56; John 19:25–27) but what we can be sure of, from all accounts, is that Mary Magdalene was definitely there.

After the death of Jesus, all the gospel accounts have Mary Magdalene as the first witness of the resurrection although there are some differences in the descriptions of these events (Mark 16:1–11; Matt 28:1–10; Luke 24:111; John 20:1–18) but it's interesting, isn't it, that Jesus chose a woman as the first witness of the resurrection and not a man? And isn't it also interesting that men wrote the canonical gospels,[1] yet all of them adhere to the fact that the first witness of the resurrection was a woman! So, after the death of Jesus, it was a woman chosen by him, who initiated the first movement towards establishing a new Christian religion. Why did Jesus choose a woman to be the first witness of the resurrection? There can only be one answer, and, that is, because Mary Magdalene was the person to whom he had been the closest in his earthly life. Some might argue that he only appeared to her because she was the first to go to the tomb. Such an argument is complete nonsense. If Jesus was truly risen from the dead, he would have appeared to the person who was most important to him wherever they were. It is therefore likely that he chose to appear to Mary Magdalene because she was the person to whom he had been closest during his earthly life and that was why she went to the tomb. Why, then, is Roman Catholic Christianity now patriarchal rather than respectful of both sexes? Jesus had been countercultural regarding women but the attempted eradication of women from his ministry began almost immediately after his death and insidiously grew. The most rapid acceleration of this misogyny in the West, however, occurred after the East–West Schism of 1054 when the Latin Church began to mandate celibacy.

During the early church there is strong evidence that women were ordained as both deacons and priests but the ordination of women as deacons appears to have been more widespread than the ordination of women as priests. Evidence of the ordination of women as deacons is found not only

---

1. The men to whom the gospels are ascribed are not necessarily the men who wrote them; some of these gospels may have been written by members of communities who formed around an original witness of the events.

in the New Testament (Rom 16:1–3), but also in a letter written by Pliny the Younger (AD 61–113) who was a lawyer, author, and magistrate of ancient Rome, and appears in the writings of the early church fathers. Some of the ancient sources that refer to women deacons are: St. Epiphanius of Salamis, *The Epistle of Ignatius to the Antiochians*, and *The Apostolic Constitutions of the Holy Apostles* attributed to Clement. It is clear from the writings of the early church fathers that they approved the ordination of women as deacons but were not so enamored with the ordination of women as priests. The ordination of women as priests was opposed by Tertullian in AD 200 in a very unpleasant and spiritually abusive way,[2] and, later, by the Council of Laodicea—the exact date of which is unknown but is believed to be mid-fourth century.

However, at the time that this council opposed the ordination of women as priests, they were still clearly being ordained since the women are referred to by the council as per the following: "That the so-called presbyter-esses or presidentesses are not to be ordained in the Church."[3] This would suggest that these women were currently being ordained but the Council was suppressing their ordinations. There is also evidence that the *Gospel of Mary*, which may have been dictated by Mary Magdalene herself, or written by her later followers, was also suppressed.

The *Gospel of Mary* was rediscovered in 1896 (by Carl Rienhardt) after been lost for over fifteen-hundred-years and, when it was rediscovered, the fragment that Rienhardt purchased contained only half of the original Gospel. This Codex dates back to the fifth century. Since then, two more Greek fragments of the same Gospel have been discovered that date back to the third century. While there was initially some debate as to whether the *Gospel of Mary* was about Mary Magdalene or some other Mary (some stating that this was Mary the mother of Jesus) the consensus of most scholars is that this Gospel was written by followers of Mary Magdalene. The style of the written codex would also strongly suggest that this 'Mary' was a close spiritual friend of Jesus rather than his mother.

Karen King has stated that it is unusual for several early fragments to have survived and therefore it is likely that the *Gospel of Mary* is a very early Christian work.[4] However, there are no known fragments of this gospel after the fifth century, and this would strongly suggest that it was almost certainly suppressed. The very fact that the Gospel was lost for so many years confirms its suppression. Had the Gospel been approved, it would not

2. Tertullian, *Prescription Against the Heretics*.
3. Council of Laodicea, Canon 11.
4. King, *Gospel of Mary of Magdala*.

have been lost. Why was it suppressed? Well, already, in the *Gospel of Mary*, there is evidence that Mary is being challenged about her right to speak on behalf of Jesus. Of course, this Gospel was probably written quite a few years after her death but, even so, the fact that the disciples are presented as challenging her authority cannot be ignored. For example, Peter is presented as saying, "Did he really speak secretly with a woman and not openly so that we could all hear? Are we just going to turn around and listen to her? Did he really choose her and prefer her to us? Surely, he wouldn't have wanted to show that she is more worthy than we are?" (Gospel of Mary 9:4–6). This excerpt is significant because it demonstrates a developing early split between Mary Magdalene and the disciples.

However, the suppression of Mary's Gospel may not have been entirely due to the fact of her close relationship with Jesus. This gospel is also clearly a gnostic gospel. Gnosticism flourished until the second century after which it was suppressed by both St. Irenaeus and St. Hippolytus of Rome. It portrayed Jesus as an embodiment of the Supreme Being who became incarnate, in order to bring spiritual enlightenment to earth, and this brand of Christianity was eventually rejected. It is very interesting that Mary was almost certainly a gnostic as gnostics had a very negative view of the flesh and a much higher view of the spirit, and, in this Gospel, Mary is presented as a visionary and a mystic. There is no evidence whatsoever that Mary was ever a prostitute in this gospel, or the canonical gospels. This idea was put around by Pope Gregory the Great in the sixth century when he merged an anonymous 'sinner' in Luke's Gospel with Mary Magdalene and it would almost certainly have been done to discredit her. Why would he have wanted to discredit her? Almost certainly because Mary's version of Christianity was the main opposition to a growing patriarchal version of Christianity, since she was the first witness of the resurrection.

While the ordination of women as priests was suppressed by the fourth century, the ordination of women as deacons continued for hundreds of years. However, in AD 517 the Synod of Epaone determined (in Canon 21) that the ministry of women deacons should be revoked in its area, and this may have been the beginning of the decline of this ministry, even though women deacons flourished in other areas of the Byzantine Church until well into the eighth and ninth centuries. There are thus many women deacon saints venerated in the calendar of the Orthodox Church which, in fact, has never (unlike the Western Catholic Church) abrogated the female diaconate. In the East the female diaconate fell into disuse for hundreds of years but was never abolished. Due to this, a small number of women have again been ordained in the Orthodox Church as deacons in both the twentieth and twenty-first century.[5]

The main function of the women deacons in the early church was to baptize women (although they also guarded the holy gates or iconostasis) and to anoint them when they were sick. It may be that they eventually died out in the East due to the decline in the baptism of adults. They had been revoked in the West at an earlier stage and this was probably due to the movement towards priestly celibacy there which had begun with ascetic theologians such as Augustine and Ambrose. These theologians put a strong emphasis on both virginity and celibacy and this led to more priests attempting to lead a celibate life in the West than in the East. As will be demonstrated below it was the imposition of celibacy on priests in the West which led to an escalation of misogyny.

For several hundred years before the East–West Schism of 1054 the churches of the East and the West were developing very strong theological and cultural differences. At the time of the schism, five patriarchs held authority in different regions, but for many years the Western Church had been pushing for the Patriarch, or Bishop, of Rome to have universal jurisdiction and authority. The other patriarchs believed that ecclesiastical matters should be decided by a council or synod of all regions and would not grant universal jurisdiction and authority to the Bishop of Rome.

In the West, a Latin rite had developed that was strongly influenced by Roman law and a developing scholastic theology; however, in the East, theology was comprehended through philosophy and the context of worship. The Eastern churches had also developed Greek rites using the Greek language in their religious ceremonies. Some of the other theological differences between the East and the West revolved around: the nature of the incarnate Christ, clerical celibacy, fasting, anointing with oil, the use of unleavened bread for the Eucharist in the Western churches, the reverence of St Augustine in the Latin Church, and the procession of the Holy Spirit.

The Eastern Church's rejection of Augustinian thinking is particularly interesting due to Augustine's perverse and unhealthy view of sexuality, which, of course, ignited the Western Church's progression towards celibacy and increased misogynism. Augustine of Hippo (AD 350–430) would be seen by modern psychologists as an unbalanced man who suffered from what is now known as the Madonna–whore complex. Men who suffer from this complex see women either as saintly madonnas or debased prostitutes. They also see love as being either sacred, or profane, and they categorize women into two groups: women they can admire or women they find

5. Flint, "East and West."

sexually attractive. There can be, for these men, no integration between the two. These men are unable to have a healthy sexual relationship with a woman because ultimately, they see sex as being something dirty and disgusting rather than something that is beautiful and God-given. They are therefore unable to develop a holistic long-term sexual relationship of mutual enjoyment and love with any woman but instead seek a series of sexual thrills that they perceive to be cheap, exciting, and dirty. This perverse sexuality is thought to be caused by the male having been raised by an overprotective mother.

Augustine did have an overprotective mother and, in rebellion against her continuous warnings concerning the sins of the flesh, he began to lead a very hedonistic lifestyle. Augustine was involved in many sexual exploits before becoming involved for many years with a woman of a much lower status than his own. She had an illegitimate child who was known to be Augustine's son. Eventually Augustine ended this relationship and promised his mother that he would marry someone 'more suitable', but, in the meantime, he took another mistress. Eventually, at the age of thirty-one, Augustine converted to Christianity, and, following this conversion, his thought swung from extreme hedonism to extreme puritanism. He became a celibate and developed a perverse theology of sexuality, stating that sex could not be a beautiful act of love, but instead was a dirty evil result of 'the fall.' He argued that the only way to avoid the evil caused by sexual intercourse was to take the 'better' way of abstaining from marriage and becoming a celibate. Sadly, Augustine's theology of sexuality was embraced by the Latin Church, which seemed to have forgotten both the words of Genesis "and the two shall become one flesh" (Gen 2:24), and, also, the Jewish view of marriage as the ideal state where two halves become one, completing each other—an ideal that Jesus had upheld.

By the time of the East–West Schism, Augustine's views on sexuality had grown in the West, and some priests were pursuing celibacy. However, in the East, the sexual views of Augustine were, in the main, rejected, and priests continued to marry. The Eastern churches, of course, did not reject celibacy per se. They recognized that celibacy could be a good thing for a very small number of people but only if it was voluntary. They rejected enforced celibacy. Priests were allowed to marry prior to ordination in the East. This issue was one of several festering bones of contention in the relationships between the Eastern and Western churches. The 1054 Schism resulted from a stand-off between the Patriarch of Constantinople and the Patriarch of Rome (now referred to as Pope Leo IX) when Norman warriors loyal to the Patriarch of Rome tried to replace Greek bishops with Latin ones in southern Italy, which was part of the Byzantine Empire at the time.

The Patriarch of Constantinople responded by shutting down the Latin churches in Constantinople and the Schism was sealed.

After the East–West Schism, the former Patriarch of Rome was now a Pope over the Western Church while the Eastern Church went its own way. There were four popes between Pope St Leo, who died shortly after the Schism, and Pope Gregory VII who initiated the 'Gregorian Reforms.' The so-called 'reforms' of Pope Gregory VII instigated a culture of misogyny. While there had always been celibate priests in the Latin Church from the time of Augustine, this Pope took up the mantle of championing compulsory celibacy for all priests with great energy. In 1074, he published an encyclical absolving the people from their obedience to bishops who allowed married priests, and he encouraged them to take action against the married priests and deprive them of their revenues. Many priests tried to resist these reforms while those that caved in left their wives and families destitute. Many women were forced into prostitution to survive. Sadly, the Church has never apologized for what it did to these women and their families. These 'reforms' not only left women destitute; they also began to create a cult of celibate men who were seen as separate, elite, 'special,' and above the rest of humanity. Women began to be seen as temptresses who threatened the pure celibate status of the priests and also, they came to be seen as a second sex to be avoided at all costs by the clergy. Now, women were not only refused ordination; they were also barred from marrying priests. They were confirmed as the inferior half of the human race.

In 1122, almost seventy years after the East–West Schism, Pope Callixtus II convoked the First Council of the Lateran and this council not only forbade priests to marry; it also stated that all marriages to priests that had already been contracted must be dissolved. Women could now officially be discarded by the 'special' cultish cleric. Later, in 1139 the Second Council of the Lateran was convoked by Pope Innocent II, and inevitably, this council made matters even worse. This council confirmed the condemnation of marriage among priests, subdeacons and deacons, as well as introducing other sexist practices that confirmed the superior status of celibate men over 'inferior' women. For example, the council prohibited nuns from singing the Divine Office in the same choir as monks.

While the official celibate status of priests led to the growth of a misogynistic Christian culture that was far removed from the teachings of Jesus, it would not be balanced for me to state that this was the only factor that led to the demise of women in Catholicism. Of course, there were other factors. For example, Anglo-Saxon Britain was a matriarchal society where abbesses ruled over double monasteries of men and women, and those abbesses had great powers of governance. These monasteries were destroyed by the Viking raids and, once they were gone, the influence of these women was never recovered. It became very rare to find double monasteries of men and women that were presided over by an abbess after the ninth century.

However, one of the reasons why these matriarchal abbesses did not reappear in later centuries would have been the increased influence of Rome with its male celibate governance. Overall, it would be true to say that the official celibate status of priests was an overriding factor in the escalation of misogyny in Catholicism because it created a culture that had no roots in Judaism or the teachings of Jesus. Its roots were in the theology of Augustine which, at the time, had been regarded as highly suspicious by the Eastern Church. Modern psychology would also regard the sexuality of Augustine as the sexuality of an unbalanced man who had some very serious personal issues. As previously stated, the founder of psychoanalysis, Sigmund Freud, would have regarded Augustine as a sufferer of Madonna-whore syndrome with an extremely unhealthy attitude towards women. Later psychologists like Rogers and Maslow stated that the fulfilment of sexual needs is essential to the development of a fully rounded person, and to achieve self-actualization, but, sadly, the Church has not pursued a vision of a healthy sexuality. Instead, it has pursued a version of sexuality that has, until very recently, assigned all women to either the status of madonnas or whores.

After the effects of the East–West Schism, and the First and Second Councils of the Lateran on women, the ministerial roles of women tended to be confined to the consecrated life. Most women who desired a ministry in the church were consecrated as nuns, but these nuns did not live in, or preside, over double monasteries. They lived in all female houses, which, generally speaking, did not have the same status as the double houses that had died out, or the all-male monasteries. Between the time of the East–West Schism and the Protestant reformation, there were some other forms of consecrated life available to women, such as the vocation of consecrated widow, and the vocation of anchoress. The vocation of consecrated widow was very popular in England where the women were known as 'vowesses.' They took vows of chastity alone and did not share in the monastic vows of poverty and obedience. They lived in their own homes and were answerable to their diocesan bishops. Generally speaking, they did a lot of good community work at their own expense. The anchoresses led the anchorite way of life, which was one of the earliest forms of Christian consecrated life. They flourished between the eleventh and sixteenth centuries in England, as well as in some other European countries.

The English anchoresses followed the *Ancrene Riwle* of 1229. They lived in single cells that were built against the walls of a church. These cells had windows through which the anchoress could view the altar or provide spiritual counsel. Margery Kempe, who was a minor female mystic, claimed in her writings that one of these anchoresses, Julian of Norwich, was particularly known for her wise counsel. Julian also wrote the *Revelations of Divine Love*, which is believed to be the first book to be written in English by a woman. While both vowesses and anchoresses had considerable influence, they did not share in the high status of governance previously held by the abbesses of the double monasteries. Sadly, both of these vocations were eventually suppressed by the Reformation.

The Reformation had a detrimental effect on women but, as will be seen, the effects of the Council of Trent (the Catholic Church's answer to the Reformation) were even worse. In England, the Reformation resulted from Henry VIII's desire to marry Anne Boleyn. He had grown tired of his first wife, Catherine of Aragon, and he was disappointed she had not given him a son. Henry argued that his marriage to Catherine of Aragon was invalid because it had been arranged for political reasons. He claimed there had been immense pressure for him to marry Catherine, his deceased brother's wife. He claimed that the marriage was invalid and, in 1527, he requested an annulment from the pope. The pope was not convinced of Henry's case, and the king became increasingly angry. In 1531 he publicly separated from Catherine of Aragon and, in 1533, when an annulment had still not been granted, Henry went through a private form of marriage with Anne Boleyn. This marriage was later solemnized publicly in April of the same year and, in June, Thomas Cramner, Archbishop of Canterbury, granted Henry the annulment, independent of Rome. Pope Clement VII promptly declared the union of Henry invalid. Henry was furious, and, in 1534, the Act of Supremacy was passed. This Act declared the King and his successors head of the English Church and the split from Rome was definitive.

While the Reformation in England occurred due to Henry VIII' s desire to divorce and marry Anne Boleyn, there was, at the same time in Europe, a protestant theological movement that posed a religious and political challenge to the papacy and the authority of the Catholic Church. This movement is usually considered to have started with the publication of the *Ninety-Five Theses* written by Martin Luther in 1517. Later, other reformers like Huldrych Zwingli and John Calvin appeared. Generally, the Reformation dominated Northern Europe while Spain and Italy became seats for the Catholic Counter-Reformation.

The Reformation was not good for women because one of the results of it (particularly in countries such as England) was the complete eradication of the female consecrated life. King Henry VIII dissolved all the monasteries and religious houses and transferred all their wealth to himself. Plate and silver were sent to the royal treasury and the furniture was auctioned. Lead, woodwork, benches, grates, locks, and other things were sold on the spot or sent to London. A significant part of English heritage disappeared and all forms of religious life, including the female consecrated life, were eradicated. It was not only the consecrated life of those women who were living in religious houses that was destroyed. There were a significant number of vowesses (consecrated widows) and anchoresses whose way of life was destroyed. The religious profession of widows and the cells of the anchoresses were eradicated. The Reformation had thus created a society in which the only option available to women was marriage. From the female point of view, there was only one positive benefit that came out of the Reformation, which was that priests were, again, allowed to marry; now, at least, a woman was considered worthy to marry a priest. In Catholicism, of course, the celibacy rule for priests remained.

One of the most unfortunate results of the Reformation for women was that it caused the destruction of many church records, leading to a legacy of lost history. Previously, monasteries had been large centers of learning and would have held many ancient records concerning the practice of religion in Britain; all these were burned and destroyed. Of course, this did not only happen in Britain, but also in other European countries. Significant shrines were looted, pillaged and plundered. In England, the famous shrine of Walsingham was destroyed. This meant that the majority of records concerning the visionary who had established the shrine were lost and to this day her identity remains a mystery. This is, of course, a great pity as she would have been one of the last influential Anglo-Saxon women if the shrine was indeed, as some believe, founded in 1061.

The destruction of past church records by the protestants was a significant factor in the development of Catholic misogyny because it allowed the church to begin again with a clean slate and to conveniently forget the history of women in the earlier church. Since the Reformation, Catholic women have lost most of their influence and status, which has never been recovered. The situation in Protestantism is somewhat different because in modern times various ministries have been restored or opened to women although the female consecrated life was completely eradicated at the time of the Reformation. For example, in Anglicanism, the female diaconate was restored in the nineteenth century and, later, in the late twentieth century, women were admitted to priestly ordination. There was a similar opening up of ministries to women in all other protestant countries but, in Catholicism, the church has never moved forward from restoring the female religious life post-Reformation and, in many ways, modern consecrated women have far less influence than women of the early church. One of the main causes of the demise of women and their influence was the Council of Trent, which immediately followed the Reformation.

The Reformation was seen by the Catholic hierarchy as a threat to its very existence and therefore, with this in mind, they responded with the Council of Trent, which was the Catholic answer to the reformation. This council was the nineteenth ecumenical council of the Roman Catholic Church and was convened in Trent for three periods between December 13, 1545, and December 4, 1563. The council responded to the new protestant theology, particularly the teachings of Martin Luther. Of course, Luther, like everyone else who participated in the Reformation, was a Catholic who was protesting against the corruption of the Catholic Church and that is why these protesters became known as *protest*ants. There was, in the Latin West, no religion other than Catholicism.

Luther was an Augustinian priest who disputed various tenets of the theology of his time. He argued that salvation was not earned by good works but was entirely received as a free gift of grace. He challenged the authority and office of the pope and taught that the bible was the only source of divinely revealed knowledge. He believed that the bible should be studied in its original languages of Hebrew and Greek and translated into the vernacular languages of the people. Additionally, he disagreed with the Catholic Church on the books to be included in the Canon of Scripture. He rejected the elevation of priests to a superior status (known as sacerdotalism) and believed all Christians to be part of a holy priesthood. He also rejected the Catholic Church's teaching on indulgences. Unfortunately, while Luther may have raised many very valid points regarding the Catholic Church of his times, he was sadly extremely anti-Semitic.

The main canons and decrees of the Council of Trent (formulated in opposition to Luther's theology) were to reaffirm the Niceno-Constantinopolitan Creed, to create the canon of the New and Old Testaments, to declare that the official Bible as the Latin Vulgate, to affirm the Church's interpretation of the Bible as final, to reaffirm the practice of indulgences but to bring about various reforms in regards to them, to reaffirm the veneration of the saints, and the Virgin Mary, to declare that justification was offered on the basis of faith and good works, and to reaffirm the seven sacraments.

Naturally, whether one agrees with Luther or not, there were major problems in regards to the decrees of the Council of Trent. For example, how could a Latin translation of the Hebrew Old Testament and the Greek New Testament become the official bible when the original works had been written in the vernacular to ensure that they reached the people? And how could the Catholic Church's translation and interpretation of these documents be final? Surely it could be possible that other more gifted linguists could appear and translate these documents better than anyone in the Catholic Church had managed to do? But in any case, why would there be a desire to have a Latin bible in a language which by that time was a dead language unless there was a desire to keep the bible from the ordinary people and create an elite cultish church which was available only to its educated clergy? Moving on from there, the council's reaffirmation of the sacraments, particularly its revision of the theology of the priesthood, is more relevant to my examination of history and my assertion that the Council of Trent enshrined misogyny in Catholicism.

The Council gave its greatest weight to the seven sacraments because it wanted to stress that they were necessary vehicles of grace in opposition to Luther's view that justification was by faith alone. It pronounced the Eucharist to be a true propitiatory sacrifice as well as a sacrament and confirmed the practice of withholding the cup from the laity. Furthermore, ordination was redefined as imprinting an 'indelible character' on the priest's soul and priestly celibacy was reaffirmed. Even though marriage was defined as a sacrament, the Council made clear that celibacy was a higher state and priests had a superior status above the rest of humanity. These teachings demeaned the status of women and confirmed the creation of an inferior second sex because women could not be priests and therefore had no access to the 'indelible character' that was supposedly imprinted on the priest's soul at the time of ordination. In addition, a woman could not marry a priest and so she was completely cut off from this elite group who were supposedly the most holy people in Christendom. A woman could access the inferior sacrament of marriage but not with a priest.

The decrees of the Council of Trent on the sacraments were completely contrary both to the teachings of Jesus in the gospels and to the letters of St Peter and St Paul in the New Testament. New Testament scholars agree that Mark is the earliest Gospel, and throughout this gospel, Jesus is presented as being against the so-called superiority of the 'clerics' of his day. For example, we read, "Beware of the scribes who like to walk around in long robes, to be greeted respectfully in market squares, to take the front seats in the synagogues and the places of honor at banquets; these are the men that devour the property of widows and for show offer long prayers. The more severe will be the sentence they receive." (Mark 12:38–40).

The writer of St Peter's letters, whom some scholars argue was not St Peter, also does not favor an elite priestly caste, and presents every Christian as part of the priesthood. He wrote, "But you are a chosen race, a kingdom of priests, a holy nation, a people to be a personal possession to sing the praises of God who called you out of the darkness into his wonderful light.

Once you were a non-people and now you are the people of God; once you were outside his pity; now you have received his pity" (1 Pet 2:9–10).

Of course, women were very much included in this definition of the priesthood but, in the Council's definition, they were not. The spiritual status of women had been very much demeaned by both the Reformation and the Council of Trent, and, within Catholicism, women have been regarded as 'lowly' ever since. A few Catholic women have tried to break through the Catholic 'spiritual glass ceiling' and failed to do so and, in fact, over the past few hundred years, the situation for Catholic women has become even worse rather than better. Some of the women who have tried to achieve change are described below.

Mary Ward was born in 1586 to a well-off northern Catholic recusant family in England and, apparently, two of her relatives were involved in the Gunpowder Plot. In 1595, her family home was burned down in an anti-Catholic riot and the children were saved by their father. She later developed the desire to enter a religious order and, as there were no religious orders left in England, she fled to the low countries. Mary tested her vocation in two separate convents but found that the contemplative life was not for her. She returned to England in 1609 and soon realized that what she was really seeking was an active religious life rather than a contemplative one. She developed the idea of an active religious order for women which, like the Jesuit order for men, would teach and perform charitable works. Mary obtained the consent of her local bishop and opened a branch of what was to be later known as the Mary Ward Institute in London before founding a second branch at Fountains Abbey.

However, Mary's new congregation was initially persecuted by Protestants and later by the Roman Catholic Church. In 1629, the Congregation of the Propaganda suppressed Mary's institute, stating that religious women should be enclosed and not active. Not for the inferior sex the status of priests with indelible marks on their souls! Mary was imprisoned but eventually managed to acquire permission for some of her sisters to continue their apostolate in England. Sadly, this was under the condition they lived private vows which, of course, meant that they had no official recognition. In actual fact Mary's institute did not receive any recognition during her lifetime and was not given formal approval until 1877 by Pope Pius IX. This was 232 years after Mary's death and, even then, it was hardly breaking the 'glass ceiling.' Religious women could finally be active but they still could not be ordained, and they did not have the powers of governance that women in the early church had once held.

At this time, the active religious life began to flourish both in England and in Europe and many different religious orders sprung up. The women concerned provided a great service in the spheres of education (for girls in particular) and in social care. They made available for girls an education that had not previously existed except for female children of the aristocracy through offering a huge selection of convent schools for girls that were the envy of mainstream England. Some orders also specialized in helping children with special needs and paved the way in the process of informing society of the value of disabled people. These religious orders opened schools for children who were deaf, speechless, and blind, as well as for children with learning difficulties. There were also other female religious orders that established teacher training colleges, and this enabled women to become teachers without becoming religious sisters. Yet, despite all these achievements and their beneficial impact on women, and humanity, these religious sisters were still regarded as inferior to their priestly counterparts.

Women were regarded as second-class citizens in the Catholic Church itself and this is evidenced by the fact that the Catholic female religious orders received no support with the funding of their teacher training colleges and had to raise money for themselves where the established Church of England aided and funded the establishment of teacher training colleges for men. So, at this time, the female active religious life was thriving, but these sisters were still regarded as inferior to their priestly male counterparts. They also did not have the synodal vote which religious women in Anglo-Saxon Britain and Ireland had certainly exercised up until around the ninth century.

On December 8, 1869, Pope Pius IX convoked the First Vatican Council. This Council pronounced that the Pope was infallible. The dogmatic constitution stated that the Pope had "full and supreme power of jurisdiction over the whole Church" and that when he "speaks ex cathedra, that is, when, in the exercise of his office as shepherd and teacher of all Christians, in virtue of his supreme apostolic authority, he defines a doctrine concerning faith or morals to be held by the whole Church, he possesses, by the divine assistance promised to him in blessed Peter, that infallibility which the divine Redeemer willed his Church to enjoy in defining doctrine concerning faith or morals."[6]

This declaration of infallibility had been something that the Western Church had been wanting to declare for hundreds of years as a means of universalizing its power. However, no previous declaration of infallibility had ever been made and it was simply not credible for a pope to suddenly be declared so in 1870 when continuous opposition from the Eastern Orthodox during, and before, the East–West Schism, and further opposition from

---

6. Pius IX, *Decrees of the First Vatican Council*, 3.9.

the Protestants (who did not deem the pope to be infallible and rejected certain strands of the Catholic theology) during the Reformation, prevented him from previously being declared as 'infallible.'

Unfortunately, this declaration has also done women no good whatsoever as they have never been consulted about the Pope's pronouncements. It is impossible to understand how any figure can be infallible when defining a doctrine of faith that is to be held by the whole church when half of the church, namely women, have not, since the seventh century, and, until very recently, been allowed to sit on or speak at synods or ecumenical councils. In recent years, the late Pope Francis made some attempts to involve some women, giving a small number of them the vote at the Synod on Synodality. But there were thirty-five women in a synod directed and governed by the pope and approximately three thousand male bishops and, thus, these women had little influence.

In the mid-twentieth century the Catholic hierarchy seemed to begin to realize that the Church was becoming out of touch with the modern world and the Second Ecumenical Council of the Vatican was opened on October 11, 1962, by Pope St. John XXIII. This Council met for four periods before it was closed by Pope St. Paul XI on December 8, 1965. The Council was, of course, composed of celibate bishops and there were no female attendees other than twenty-three women auditors who were not allowed to speak.

Nevertheless, the council did strive to bring about reform rather than to make triumphalist statements. The council's teaching was contained in four constitutions, nine decrees and three declarations. It was made clear that its main purpose was to promote a universal call to holiness and a turning away from clericalism. The council did instigate many reforms, which included: the widespread use of the vernacular languages (instead of Latin) in the Mass, the revision of Eucharistic prayers, the abbreviation of the liturgical calendar, the ability to celebrate Mass with the priest facing the congregation, an emphasis on laypeople as the 'people of God,' a new emphasis on biblical theology, a new emphasis on ecumenism, recognition of the rites of Eastern Catholics to keep their distinct liturgical practices, a new recognition of the apostolate of the laity, a call for the adaptation and renewal of the religious life, and a call for priests to become brothers as well as fathers and teachers.

Vatican II was initially greeted with enthusiasm by the vast majority of clergy and laypeople, and a new era of hope dawned in the Catholic Church. There were also, in its wake, some further reforms, such as the restoration of the permanent diaconate for married men. However, the priesthood remained celibate. There had been plans to discuss mandatory celibacy at the council, but it was dropped from the agenda with a proviso that it would be discussed later. (It was never discussed.)

Nevertheless, at the time, lay Catholics remained hopeful that the Church would do away with mandatory celibacy relatively quickly and that the female diaconate would also be restored. Unfortunately, neither of these things happened and during the 1970s vocations to the priesthood and the female consecrated life started to decline. There still remained, for some time, however, an expectation of reform, with many people thinking that the reform process was just taking longer than expected. With that in mind some respected theologians, such as Sr. Lavinia Byrne, continued to promote the ordination of women. But, not long after the Second Vatican Council, in July 1968, Pope. St Paul VI had written *Humanae Vitae* which should have served as a warning that the Church's view of women had never really changed and continued to reflect the views of misogynistic celibate men.

Humanae Vitae had reaffirmed earlier Catholic teaching on the procreative and unitive nature of conjugal relations, married love, responsible parenthood, and the rejection of artificial contraception. This teaching had not been expected to be reaffirmed for the following reasons: firstly, and foremostly, the oral contraceptive pill had actually been invented by a devout Catholic and eminent gynecologist, John Rock.[7] He had seen the terrible suffering caused by the collapsed wombs, and premature deaths, of mothers who gave birth to numerous children. Due to this, he had spent years working on the creation of a pill that he believed was in line with Catholic teaching, as it gave women a little more of a natural hormone that was already in their bodies and extended the 'safe period.' Secondly, the Vatican II church had seemed to be so much more positive in regard to sexuality than it had been for hundreds of years. Finally, members of an earlier commission, the Pontifical Commission on Birth Control, which had been set up by the Pope himself, had voted by an overwhelming majority (in 1966) to allow Catholic couples to decide for themselves about birth control. It had therefore been assumed that the pope would go along with his own commission, but, in writing this encyclical, he had gone against the findings of the cardinals, bishops, theologians, physicians, and women that he had appointed to research these issues. Of course, if he was going to do that, he may as well have not set up a commission at all.

Sadly, the misogynistic idea that the whole purpose of the existence of women is to bear children remained entrenched in Catholic theology.

---

7. For further information on John Rock, see American Experience, "Dr John Rock (1890–1984)."

Of course, women are physiologically designed in a way that enables them to carry and bear children if they so wish but that does not mean that they *have* to choose to bear children, does it? Nor does it mean that they *have* to be enslaved to being childbearing machines. Men are also physiologically designed to ejaculate sperm to enable procreation but that doesn't mean they have to ejaculate inside every woman they happen to meet, does it? The Pope's issuing of *Humanae Vitae* was an ominous sign that women would continue to be brushed aside and ill- treated in Catholicism.

In 1993, Sr. Lavinia Byrne published her famous and renowned book, *Woman at the Altar*, which outlined her arguments for women priests.[8] She also wrote about contraception. Sadly, Byrne and others, were immediately suppressed by Pope St. John Paul II who, in 1994, issued his apostolic letter, *Ordinatio Sacerdotalis*. This letter stated that the Church had no authority whatsoever to confer priestly ordination on women and that this judgement was to be held definitively by all the Church's faithful. Of course, the Pope would never have been able to issue such an encyclical had not a previous pope of the Roman Catholic Church declared himself, and all future popes, to be infallible at the First Vatican Council. This was a highly spurious claim that was not rooted in history. Sr. Lavinia Byrne was a member of the Institute of the Blessed Virgin Mary and enormous pressure was put upon her, and her superior, by the Vatican to recant her book, or leave her order. The Vatican refused to converse with Sr.. Byrne directly and would only converse with her superior. Of course, such pressure was tantamount to spiritual and political power abuse and eventually Sr. Byrne left her religious order to protect both the order, and her conscience.

At that time, she stated, "What I'm concerned about now is not so much the debate about the ordination of women, because if it's God's will, it's going to happen anyway. My concern is the way people in the Congregation for the Doctrine of the Faith deal with dissenters. The rightful and necessary administration of the church becomes a faceless bureaucracy condemning individuals without hearing their story or point of view."[9]

Sr. Byrne told *The Guardian* that despite her high profile as a broadcaster in England and Wales, the fate of religious women was to become an invisible sub-species. She stated that the 'lot' of most Catholic women today is to be deeply devout, to pray, to attend church on Sunday, and simply not count. The way this manifested was through selecting men only to represent Christ. She also said that there had been a time when some of the

---

8. For more on the history of Sr. Lavinia Byrne, see Flannery, "Story of Lavinia Byrne."

9. Meek, "Nun Quits over Ordination."

most original thinking in the Church had come from women religious, but this was no more. Cardinal Joseph Ratzinger (later Pope Benedict XVI) was behind Sr. Byrne's demise.

Nothing has changed since Lavinia Byrne left her religious order. The woman herself went on to become a respected lay woman and to write many more books. However, the Catholic hierarchy have continued to demean women and to allow them no say in Church matters. I, myself, after five years in formation for the consecrated life, became another victim of the same misogynism. The Roman Catholic Church maintains a misogynism that is unbiblical and in no way aligns with either the teachings of Jesus, or with the practices of the early Christian Church. This misogynism has arisen largely because of the Catholic all male celibate cult. Catholic priests have no real contact with women, as they are not allowed to be priests, and so male priests therefore have no female colleagues. They are also not allowed to marry women. This lack of contact with women means that they have no understanding whatsoever of the female of the species. They are also inculcated with an instruction to distance themselves from women. Yet, despite all this distancing from women, the Catholic hierarchy has the audacity to believe that it can control women and advise them how they must behave.

Chapter 5

Mandatory Celibacy and Sexual Abuse

THIS CHAPTER EXPLORES HOW mandatory celibacy may have impacted the sexual abuse of both adults and minors in Catholicism. This is an enormous subject which would warrant a book in itself, and, clearly, only some key points and issues can be discussed. The areas under discussion will be: the history of sexual abuse in Christianity and Roman Catholicism in particular, the twentieth- and twenty-first- century exposure of sexual abuse in the Roman Catholic Church and the shockwaves that followed, the geographical areas in which sexual abuse has occurred, various reports, commissions, and studies into sexual abuse in the Roman Catholic Church, the prevalence of sexual abuse in Roman Catholicism, the question of whether this abuse is higher in the Roman Catholic celibate clergy than in other institutions, and, finally, the possible causes of sexual abuse in Roman Catholicism. In these areas, the works of A.W. Richard Sipe and Peter Murnane are foundational and will be discussed at length. Both are Roman Catholic priests who researched into sexual abuse in the Roman Catholic clergy, and, as priests themselves, they are closer to this topic than other researchers. Sipe left the priesthood and married a former nun. Murnane has remained a priest all his life.

The sexual abuse of individuals and minors in particular is not a recent problem in Catholicism and history shows it is almost as old as Christianity itself. One of the earliest Christian documents, *The Didache* of The Twelve Apostles, states, "Thou shalt not corrupt youth" (2:2). Tertullian also spoke about the enslavement, prostitution, and sexual exploitation of children as did The Council of Elvira in Spain (AD 305). Canon 71 of the council specifically condemns anyone who sexually abuses boys and states they should be permanently excommunicated. Murnane states that there was an increase in the sexual abuse of young boys after the establishment of monasteries.[1] Boys were viewed as both innocent virgins and tempters, and the abusing older monks were seen as more important than the boys with a few exceptions such as *The Spanish Rules of St Isidore of Seville* (AD 636), which recognized grooming as a concept. In AD 693 one of the Councils of Toledo (there were around thirty) ordered that any clerics who committed acts 'against nature' should be degraded, exiled, and debarred from Holy Communion.

However, Murnane states that by the mid eighth century, a large body of clerical privilege had built up, based on Patristic writings, papal decrees, and acts of councils, and this led to clerical corruption eventually becoming widespread by the eleventh century. St Peter Damian (Bishop of Ostia) sent Pope Leo IX the *Book of Gomorrah*. This book lamented the problem of the clergy abusing young boys and adolescents and denounced the failure to address these abuses. It was later suppressed by Pope Alexander II. Sadly, during the twelfth century, the Church became much more interested in stamping out clerical marriage than it was in stamping out child sexual abuse, and of course, celibacy was eventually made mandatory at the First Council of the Lateran.

It is clear from the above history that sexual abuse had existed alongside clerical marriage in the early Christian centuries although, interestingly, there seems to be more evidence for its existence in the West than in the East. In the West, of course, there had been a drive towards mandatory celibacy long before the First Council of the Lateran and, indeed, the issue of mandatory celibacy had been a contributing factor of the East–West Schism because the East would not accept mandatory celibacy and has always regarded it as unbiblical.

The imposition of mandatory celibacy in the West did not improve sexual morality in the clergy, and sexual abuses and indiscretions continued- becoming an issue, yet again, at the Protestant Reformation. The Protestant churches once again refuted mandatory celibacy and Luther, himself, married in 1525. However, the Catholic Counter-Reformation (an alternative to the Protestant Reformation embodied in the Council of Trent (1545–1563)) was, for some of its sessions, led by a sexual abuser. These sessions were the twelfth to the fifteenth sessions which were led by Pope Julius III. In 1550, Pope Julius III embarked on a sexual relationship with his nephew Innocenzo (the adopted son of his brother) who was fifteen years of age. The Pope created him a cardinal and showered him with benefices including the commendatario of the Abbeys of Mont Saint Michel in Normandy and Saint

---

1. Murnane, *Clerical Errors*, 19.

Zeno in Verona. The Venetian ambassador reported that the boy shared the pope's bed and the pope, himself, boasted of the boy's prowess in bed.

The sixteenth century which was, of course, the century of the Reformation was also a time when sexual abuse among the clergy was particularly high both before and (bearing in mind Pope Julian III's antics) after the Reformation. The Dutch scholar, Erasmus, lamented that many priests committed acts "too abominable to mention" under the pretense of confession.[2] This practice had been going on for some time and became fodder for protestant critics of the Roman Catholic Church. In these cases, it often involved the abuse of women, as confession was one of the few accepted occasions when respectable women could meet with men outside their families unsupervised. These encounters were fertile ground for improper relations, and the problem did not cease after the reformation. Between 1561 and 1741 four popes decreed that any priest trying to commit abuse during the sacrament of confession must be reported.

There are also other historical examples of sexual abuse outside the confessional, particularly during the eighteenth century. For example, Fr Johann Gauch of Furstenburg, Germany exposed himself to girls and molested boys in the town. He was eventually imprisoned. Also, at a similar time, Johannes Figules of Prum, abused two ten-year-old boys and was condemned to perpetual imprisonment. The eighteenth-century philosopher Denis Diderot, who had, as a young man, briefly considered joining the clergy, wrote a novel *La Religieuse* about a young nun who was sexually molested in a convent. There has been much speculation as to where he found the inspiration to write the novel, including the idea that some of the information may have been given to him by his own sister who was actually a nun. Whatever the inspiration, it is clear from the fact that Diderot chose the abuse of a nun as a storyline that clerical abuse must have been a live issue during the eighteenth century.

There is evidence that the sexual abuse of women through the vehicle of the confessional continued through the nineteenth and twentieth centuries and there is also some evidence of the abuse of boys through means other than the confessional during the same period. Murnane states that in Kapunda, South Australia, sisters in Mary McKillop's new congregation reported in 1870 that the Franciscan priest Patrick Keating was committing sexual offenses through the confessional.[3] He was found guilty and ordered to return to Ireland. He later tried to take revenge on the sisters through a priest friend but ultimately did not succeed.

2. Qtd. in Tracy, *Erasmus of the Low Countries*, 141.
3. Murnane, *Clerical Errors*, 35.

Concerning the sexual abuse of boys, the nineteenth century Australian bishop John Bede Polding received allegations that a deacon, John Caldwell, was sexually abusing boys but did little about it other than to move him elsewhere. Another member of Polding's clergy, Fr. Dom Garroni, was also reported as being, "habitually unchaste; very dangerous among young men" but very little was also done about him.[4] Despite these nineteenth century examples, nothing much was generally reported on the sexual abuse of women and children within Catholicism until the twentieth century. This lack of such reporting was mainly due to the Catholic hierarchy's attempts to cover up all such abuse.

The accusations of abuse and cover-ups in the Catholic Church began to receive significant media and public attention during the 1980s and many of these cases alleged decades of abuse because they were frequently made by adults many years after the abuse occurred. Cases were also brought against the Catholic hierarchy due to their covering up of sexual abuse allegations and their moving of abusive priests to other locations or ministries where the abuse continued. There were also cases where seminarians or priests themselves had made allegations of sexual abuse because they had joined the Catholic Church with high visions of self-sacrifice and high expectations of service but later found themselves to be victims of sexual abuse by their own superiors.

One such example was reported more recently by the former priest Brian Devlin in his book, *Cardinal Sin*, and, as we will see, the co-author of this book also had a similar experience. The earliest reports of sexual abuse, however, were in the 1980s in both the US and Ireland. In Ireland, these abuses were associated with Catholic institutions. In the US, child sexual abuse was first publicized in 1985 when a Louisiana priest pleaded guilty to eleven counts of molestation of boys. By the 1990s, cases of sexual abuse by Roman Catholic clergy began to receive significant media attention not only in the US and Ireland, but also in other countries such as Canada, Chile, Australia, South America, and much of Europe. It soon became clear that this was a universal phenomenon, and a brief summary of its prevalence will be detailed below. In this summary I largely use Murnane's overview because his work is very recent and, as a Dominican priest, he has researched this subject in depth with accuracy. Please note that this is only a summary of some of the very worst cases and there are far more cases than those listed. Notable in these cases is the prevalence of offenders in the hierarchy. The hierarchy did not only cover up sexual abuse; they perpetrated it. Indeed, Murnane states that more than a hundred cardinals and bishops

---

4. Royal Commission, *Final Report*, 142.

from many countries have been credibly accused of sexual crimes against children and adults.[5]

AFRICA

Tanzania

In the 1960's Fr Kit Cunningham, a priest of The Institute of Charity (known as the Rosminians) and several other priests abused many pupils in a school in Soni. This was not officially known at the time, and he returned to London to become a popular priest. After he died in 2010 one of his victims noticed his obituary and many victims spoke out. Pupils stated that he had made the school "a loveless, violent and sad hellhole."[6] They recalled being hauled out of bed at night and having their genitals fondled and other sexual abuse. The Rosminians later awarded twenty survivors of sexual abuse two million UK pounds in compensation.

ASIA

India

In 2002, Mathew N. Schmalz, an academic who is the founder of the *Journal of Global Catholicism*, stated that the Catholic Church sexual abuse cases in India are generally not spoken about openly. He said, "you would have gossip and rumors, but it never reaches the level of former charges."[7] In 2014, Raju Kokkan, a priest in Kerala, was arrested on charges of raping a nine-year-old girl. After escaping his captivity following his arrest, he was removed from his position in the Church. Later, in the same year, three other priests in Kerala were arrested on charges of raping minors. In 2017, Fr. Robin Vadakkumchery of St Sebastian church in Kannur was arrested in Kochi on the charge of repeatedly raping a fifteen-year-old girl who later gave birth to a child. He was sentenced to twenty years in prison. In 2018, five religious sisters accused Bishop Mulakkal of raping the former leader of

---

5. Royal Commission, *Final Report*, 58.
6. Lotty, *Abused: Breaking the Silence*.
7. Qtd. in Paulson, "World Doesn't Share US View of Scandal," para. 23.

their congregation. Her complaints had been ignored by both the Bishops' Conferences of Kerala and India and by the Vatican. Mulakkal responded aggressively and was acquitted but the sisters launched an appeal.

Japan

Murnane states there are reports of abuse by overseas missionaries that have been ignored.[8]

Philippines

In July 2002, archbishop Quevedo, president of the Catholic Bishop's Conference, apologized for sexual conduct including child abuse, homosexuality, and affairs by various priest offenders over the past two decades.

Singapore

A psychotherapist and author, Jane Leigh, alleged in her autobiography, *My Nine Lives*, that she was sexually abused by Roman Catholic priests as a teenager. In 2022, a Catholic priest was jailed for five years for sexually abusing two teenaged boys on several occasions. The court imposed a gag preventing his identity and that of his victims being released.

AMERICAS (SOUTH AND CENTRAL)

El Salvador

In 2015, Fr. Jesus Delgado, secretary to Archbishop Oscar Romero, was dismissed by the archdiocese after investigations revealed he had molested a girl when she was between the ages of nine and seventeen years. In December 2016, a canonical court, convicted Delgado and two other El Salvador priests of committing acts of sexual abuse between 1980 and 2000 and they were laicized. Another El Salvador priest, Jose Adonay Chicas Campos, was laicized in 2019 after pleading guilty to sexual abuse in a criminal trial at the Vatican and was sentenced to 16 years in prison.

---

8. Murnane, *Clerical Errors*, 29.

Costa Rica

In 2019, Fr. Mauricio Viquez (Episcopal Conference spokesman and professor at the University of Costa Rica) was dismissed from the clerical state by the Holy See and the process of the removal of his tenure was started due to allegations against him. He fled overseas and an international arrest warrant was issued against him. Eventually he was captured in Mexico and was later convicted in 2022 of the rape and abuse of an eleven-year-old boy. Another priest wanted for sexual abuse, Jorge Arturo Morales Salazar, also tried to escape when allegations were made against him but was arrested at the Panama border.

Dominican Republic

In 2014, a Papal Nuncio was laicized due to allegations of the sexual abuse of minors during his tenure as a Vatican Ambassador in Santo Domingo (2008–2013). Unfortunately, the cleric concerned (Josef Wesolowski who was of Polish origins) died before a trial could be held.

Honduras

In 2018, Bishop Juan Hoses Pineda, an auxiliary bishop, resigned following revelations of the sexual abuse of seminarians.

Argentina

In 2009, Julio Cesar Grassi was sentenced to fifteen years imprisonment for sexually abusing two minors during his time at a foundation for children in need. In 2019, two priests were sentenced to forty years in prison for sexually abusing deaf children at the Antonio Provolo Institute.

Bolivia

A former priest confessed to having abused eighty-five children in Bolivia during the 1970s and 1980s in his personal diary prior to his death in 2009.

Chile

An enquiry found that Jesuit priest Renato Poblete had sexually abused at least twenty-two women over forty years. Another priest, Fernando Karadima, was exposed as a serial abuser in 2010. Pope Francis initially did not believe the allegations against him but later admitted his mistake. The Pope also laicized two retired bishops for abusing minors. The laicizing of bishops as a punishment for sexual abuse is an insult to lay people. It suggests that they are reduced to the lay level because they have committed these crimes and implies that lay people are somehow beneath the clergy in their moral norms, but, as we will see, there are more sexual abusers in the Catholic priesthood than there are in the Catholic general population.

Columbia

Cardinal Alfonso Lopez Trujillo was found to have been seducing seminarians and using prostitutes. There is also an on-going investigation involving a network of pederasty which includes at least thirty-eight abusive priests. In 2020, the Constitutional Court ordered the Columbian Catholic Church to reveal its secret file of complaints to journalists or citizens on request, but the hierarchy have still not fully complied with that instruction.

NORTH AMERICA

Canada

In the 1980s, allegations of physical and sexual abuse were made against members of the Christian Brothers who operated the Mount Cashel Orphanage in Newfoundland. Eventually more than three hundred former pupils came forward with allegations of abuse at the orphanage. There were also many incidents of abuse among the children who had passed through Canada's Residential Schools. Murnane states that, by 2015, almost forty-thousand former students had made allegations of physical or sexual abuse.[9] In addition, abuse was found to have been committed at Canada's training schools between 1930 and 1974, and twenty-eight De La Salle brothers were charged with offences. C$8.5 million was paid out in compensation.

9. Murnane, *Clerical Errors*, 23.

United States

In the United States bishops have reported over three thousand lawsuits against the Catholic Church, many of which have resulted in multi-million-dollar settlements. Clerical sex abuse in the US first came to the attention of the media in 1984 when the Louisiana priest, Gilbert Gauthe, was sentenced to twenty years imprisonment for abusing altar boys. Later, in 2002, the *Boston Globe* published evidence that led to one Fr. Geoghan being sentenced to ten years in jail. He had raped more than a hundred and thirty children in six different parishes. More than a thousand victims of other priests then came forward and this demonstrated that child sexual abuse among clergy in Boston was widespread. The hierarchy had attempted to cover up this abuse and Cardinal Bernard Francis Law fled to the Vatican where Pope St. John Paul II later appointed him Archpriest of the Basilica di Santa Maria Maggiore in Rome in 2004.

Meanwhile, at around the same time, a Grand Jury in Philadelphia exposed many cases of abuse against children. This abuse had also been concealed by Cardinals Krol and Bevilacqua. Finally, in 2018, Cardinal Theodore McCarrick was himself accused of sexual abuse. Evidence later materialized that showed that this abuse had been going on for years, but no one had ever done anything about it. He resigned from the College of Cardinals in 2018 but allegations against him had first began in 1994 when a priest wrote a letter to the Bishop of Metuchen saying that McCarrick had inappropriately touched him. Allegations were also made against him in 1994 concerning his conduct towards seminarians in Newark, and, in 2005 and 2007, the Diocese of Metuchen and the Archdiocese of Newark paid compensation to two priests who had accused McCarrick of abuse. Many more allegations were made against the cardinal, and more lawsuits were filed against him. He was eventually laicized in 2019 but was later charged with the criminal offence of sexual abuse for an incident that occurred in 1974. In 2023 McCarrick's lawyers stated that he had experienced significant mental decline and was not fit to stand trial. The court ruled that he was mentally incompetent to stand trial and so no trial ever took place.

Mexico

One of the most scandalous cases of sexual abuse was that of Fr Marciel Maciel who founded the *Legion of Christ* in the 1970s. He was found to have fathered six children with three women and to have abused at least sixty minors. He was forced to retire from ministry by Pope Benedict XVI in 2006.

EUROPE

Austria

In 2010, an independent group that operated a hotline to help people exit the Catholic Church, released a report documenting physical, sexual, and emotional abuse perpetrated by Austrian priests, nuns, and religious officials. In 1995, a Benedictine, Cardinal Hans Goer, had also been forced to step down as archbishop following allegations that he had sexually abused seminarians and priests.

Belgium

From the 1990s, there were a number of priests who were convicted and imprisoned for raping minors. In 2006, several clerics and ex-clerics were arrested through Operation Falcon, a worldwide investigation of internet child pornography. Later, in 2010, Bruges' bishop Roger Vangheluwe resigned after admitting that he had been abusing his nephews for thirteen years. In 2023, a TV documentary *Godforsaken* was aired by the public broadcaster VRT. Belgian victims told their stories on camera showing the depravity of many crimes and their systemic cover-up by the Catholic hierarchy.

Croatia

In 2000, Ivan Cucek was convicted of the sexual abuse of thirty-seven young girls. Later, in 2007, Drago Lubicic was sentenced to three years imprisonment for molesting five teenage boys.

France

On October 3, 2021, an independent commission set up by the Bishops' Conference of France released a report estimating that three thousand clerics had abused children since the 1950s and that 216,000 children had been abused by Catholic priests between 1950 and 2020. Around 80% of the victims were boys. One of the most prominent cases was that of the priest Bernard Preynat who, in 2020, was sentenced to five years' imprisonment for sexually abusing seventy-five boy scouts but was alleged to have also committed many other sexual offences which had happened too long ago to enable prosecution. Allegations have also emerged against eleven bishops who have been named by the Church linked to sexual abuse allegations. Some are being investigated for sexual abuse while others are accused of failing to report it. These men face prosecution and/or disciplinary action by the Church. Sadly, these alleged incidents are not the only ones to rock the Church in France in recent times.

Germany

A report by the German Catholic Church in 2018 found that 3,677 children in Germany had been sexually abused by Catholic clergy between 1946 and 2014. In 1979, Archbishop Joseph Ratzinger (later Pope Benedict XVI) accepted the priest Peter Hullermann into his Munich archdiocese for 'therapy'. Ratzinger knew that Hullermann had admitted demanding oral sex from an eleven-year-old boy but assigned the priest to pastoral work after giving him warnings. The priest again abused minors and was eventually sentenced in 2020.

In 2015, it was claimed that 547 members of the Regensburg boys' choir were physically or sexually abused between 1945 and 1992. From 1964, the choir's conductor had been Georg Ratzinger, the brother of Joseph Ratzinger, or Pope Benedict XVI. It was alleged that Cardinal Muller blocked an investigation into the abuse. While Georg Ratzinger was not one of the forty-nine abusers it was alleged that he knew of the abuse and turned a blind eye to it. Georg Ratzinger denied this was the case.

Ireland

In August 2018, a list was published which revealed that over thirteen hundred Catholic clergy had been accused of sexual abuse. At that time, eighty-two of them had been convicted. On June 12, 2024, the *Irish Independent* published an article stating that there had been 252 abuse allegations made against members of the Catholic Church in Ireland in the last year.[10] Most of the cases were historic but there was one recent allegation.

10. Mac Donald, "252 Abuse Allegations."

There have been a number of government reports about clerical sexual abuse in Ireland that will be examined later. Some of the most infamous cases include the priests Sean Fortune and Brendan Smyth who, from 1945–1989, indecently assaulted or raped over one hundred children. The Dominican Friar, Vincent Mercer, former headmaster of Newbridge College, was jailed for assaulting 13 boys in their dormitories and in 2012 faced thirteen other charges.

As stated in the introduction, more recent cases relate to the Spiritan Fathers (formerly known as the Holy Ghost fathers) with whom incidents began in the 1960s and continued for many decades. Over 290 people have now made allegations of sexual abuse against fifty-seven abusers within the Spiritans. Some of these priests were serial abusers with unchecked access to children. The schools concerned were Willow Park Junior School, Blackrock Primary, Rockwell College and Blackrock College, all of which were run by the Spiritans and since these incidents were revealed, it has emerged that there was also sexual abuse at another seminary school run by them. Kimmage Manor was a formation school for young men who wanted to enter the priesthood, and eleven pupils had made allegations against a priest there who has since been convicted and served his sentence.

Italy

Murnane alleges that in Italy the issue of clerical sex abuse has been largely buried and that of those found guilty, even by an Italian civil court, few are imprisoned.[11] A group of religious and lay associations are now apparently calling for an independent enquiry into sexual abuse, but some bishops are resisting this.

Norway

The Catholic Church in Norway along with the Vatican acknowledged in 2010 that Georg Müller had resigned from his position of Bishop of Trondheim (1997–2009) because of the discovery of his abuse of an altar boy twenty years earlier. Norwegian law did not allow a criminal prosecution so long after the event.

---

11. Murnane, *Clerical Errors*, 33.

Poland

On May 11, 2019, a TV documentary, *Tell No One*, went viral. This documentary reached 8.1 million viewers on You Tube by May 13. It exposed decades of official concealment of clerical child abuse, especially under Pope St. John Paul II, whom the Vatican have had the audacity to canonize. The writer believes this canonization should be revoked. Why are those who covered up child abuse revered as saints by the Vatican?[12] On November 6, 2020, the Holy See's Nuncio to Poland announced that following an investigation into allegations of sexual abuse Cardinal Henryk Gulbinowicz was now barred from using his episcopal insignia and attending any kind of celebration or public meeting. He was also denied the right to a Catholic funeral and burial.

Portugal

In 1993, a Catholic priest, Frederico Cunha, was convicted of the murder of a young teen named Luis Correia. During the trial four witnesses told the court how they also had been sexually abused by the priest. In 1998, Cunha escaped to Rio de Janeiro where he continues to live. A report published in February 2023 revealed that at least 4,815 children had been sexually abused by clergy in the Catholic Church in Portugal since 1950.

The Netherlands

In 2011, a comprehensive investigation identified eight hundred Catholic clergy and other church employees who had sexually abused children since 1945. A newspaper claimed that twenty Dutch cardinals and bishops had been involved in concealing these crimes. Four senior clerics were also found to be abusers.

United Kingdom

In 2013, Cardinal Keith O'Brien, the Archbishop of St Andrew's and Edinburgh, resigned following publication of allegations of predatory sexual conduct with priests and seminarians under his jurisdiction.

---

12. There has been some public controversy concerning Pope St. John Paul II's canonization. See, for example, Matranga, "Saint John Paul II Accused of Protecting Pedophiles."

In 2020, the Independent Inquiry into Child Sexual Abuse released a report which stated that the Catholic Church of England and Wales had swept allegations of child sex abuse by numerous Catholic clergy under the carpet. Many of these incidents occurred in schools run by the Benedictine Order. In Northern Ireland, the De La Salle Brothers and the Sisters of Nazareth admitted, during another inquiry there, to the physical and sexual abuse of children in Northern Ireland in institutions that they had overseen.

Cases of sexual abuse by Catholic clergy, or former Catholic clergy, in the UK, keep coming to the fore. For example, Timothy Gardner has recently been jailed after engaging in online chats encouraging the abuse of children. Timothy Gardner is a former member of the Dominican order, and he was originally convicted of downloading pornography (in 2014) while he was a member of that order and teaching religious education at a Catholic school. He was sentenced and laicized by the Catholic hierarchy and his bishop (Robert Byrne of Hexham and Newcastle) resigned in 2022 due to (among other reasons) his former associations with Gardner (they were reputed to be great friends).

However, the Vatican were also looking at other inappropriate behavior by Bishop Byrne, such as a sex party that took place at St. Mary's Cathedral. Additionally, the Dean of the Cathedral was under suspicion and killed himself after finding out that he was also being investigated for child sex abuse. Bishop Byrne, after the laicization of Gardner, continued to associate with him until his own resignation in 2022. Since then, the laicized Gardner has gone on to commit further sexual offences and has now been sentenced to eight and a half years in prison for assisting or encouraging the abuse of a child.

The Vatican

Murnane states that Martel's book *Closet* has confirmed that, in the Vatican, there is a clerical closet of secretly homosexual clergy who do not keep to their vows of celibacy and are both "active and influential."[13]

---

13. Murnane, *Clerical Errors*, 34.

OCEANA

Australia

Early nineteenth-century examples of Australia's bishop, John Bede Polding, ignoring allegations of sexual abuse against one of his deacons (Caldwell) and one of his priests (Dom Garonni) have already been discussed. Since then, the hierarchy of the Catholic Church in Australia has been greatly criticized for both developing, and leading, a culture that repeatedly covered up sexual abuse.

Mystery surrounds, and opinions are greatly divided about, Australia's Cardinal Pell (1941–2023) who was convicted of child sexual abuse in 2018 but had the conviction quashed on appeal. Whether one believes Pell was innocent, or guilty, there can be little doubt that he did cover up a great deal of sexual abuse. According to findings released by Australia's *Royal Commission into Institutional Responses to Child Sexual Abuse* (2020), Pell knew about the sexual abuse in the Australian Catholic Church as early as 1973, ignored or punished child victims, did not investigate allegations, allowed documents to be destroyed, and failed to prevent abuse by clergy who had been reported of sexual abuse. He did this by transferring them to new parishes or dioceses which did not know of their history.

Cardinal Pell, however, was not the only prelate to behave in this way. The commission also named prelates in Ballarat, Maitland-Newcastle, Melbourne, Sydney, and Wollongong who had covered up sexual abuse. Moreover, there were large religious orders that had carried out the same coverups such as: the Christian Brothers, the Marist Brothers, the Salesians, the Dominicans, and the Jesuits.

This commission also found that around 7 percent of Catholic priests in Australia were alleged perpetrators of child sexual abuse and the average age of victims was eleven and a half years for girls and ten and a half years for boys. It also found that 46 percent of Catholic churches had child sexual abuse cases. This level of sexual abuse among the Catholic clergy was five times higher than in other religious institutions. In September 2020, the state of Queensland passed legislation to ensure that priests of the Roman Catholic Church would no longer be able to use the 'sanctity' of confession as a defense against failing to report information about the sexual abuse of children. Clergy who failed to report confessions of sexual abuse would also face up to three years imprisonment.

New Zealand

In 1958, Dunedin priest, Magnus Murray, won the trust of a Catholic couple and often visited their home. He abused their son for fourteen years, starting at the age of seven. Unfortunately, the child did not realize for many years that he was being abused and so did not report it. Later, while ministering in Woollahra, Murray groomed a seventeen-year-old girl called Paula. They initially had a friendship that later became sexual, and he kept in touch with her after she married. He baptized one of her three sons and, while staying with her family in Dunedin, had sex with her husband. Murray was not allowed by his bishop, Bishop Kavanagh, to continue to work in Dunedin and was moved to Auckland under the jurisdiction of Bishop Mackey. He worked in five parishes there before moving to the Hamilton diocese. After four years the police prompted Bishop Gaines to retire Murray and the families of two boys who he was alleged to have abused in that diocese were paid compensation. Murray was eventually jailed for three years and laicized in 2019.

The above is a brief summary of some of the incidents of sexual abuse in the worldwide Roman Catholic Church. I will now examine some of the reports and studies concerning Catholic child sex abuse. I will concentrate on three reports in particular; these are: *The John Jay Report* (2004) from the US, *The Commission to Inquire into Child Abuse* (2009) from Ireland, and *The Independent Inquiry into Child Sexual Abuse* (2022) from the UK. The British report looked at abuse in all institutions, not just Catholic ones.

The John Jay Report was originally known as *The Nature and Scope of the Problem of Sexual Abuse of Minors by Catholic Priests and Deacons in the United States*. It was commissioned by the US Conference of Catholic Bishops and carried out by the John Jay College of Criminal Justice. It is based on surveys completed by the Roman Catholic Dioceses in the United States and was finally published, after various corrections, in June 2004. The period covered by the report began in 1950 and ended in 2002.

On August 23, 2025, the summary of this report on Wikipedia reads:

> The report determined that, during the period from 1950 to 2002, a total of 10,667 individuals had made allegations of child sexual abuse. Of these, the dioceses had been able to identify 6,700 unique accusations against 4,392 clergy over that period in the US, which is about 4 percent of all 109,694 ordained clergy, i.e., priests or deacons or members of religious orders, active in the USA during the time covered by the study. However, of these 4392 accused, 252 (5.7 percent of those accused or less

than 0.1 percent of total clergy) were convicted. The number of alleged abuses increased in the 1960s, peaked in the 1970s, declined in the 1980s, and by the 1990s had returned to the levels of the 1950s.[14]

In actual fact, the statistics provided by Wikipedia are challenged by the scholarship of A.W. Richard Sipe and other authorities who found that the true percentage of clergy against whom there were accusations of sexual abuse was more likely to be between 6 and 9 percent, with some dioceses reaching as much as 20 percent.[15] Murnane has also criticized the John Jay survey for relying on the integrity of the US dioceses in providing accurate information.[16] He states that many bishops had strongly resisted any investigations into clerical sexual abuse and therefore could not be relied upon to provide accurate information. He also states that not enough allowance was made for the fact that many victims do not expose their abuse to authorities until up to thirty years after the event.

The Commission to Inquire into Child Sexual Abuse was set up by the Irish Government in 1999 to investigate the extent of the abuse of children in Irish institutions from 1936 onwards.[17] Most of these institutions had been operated by the Catholic Church but were funded and supervised by the Irish Department of Education. The Commission was initially known as the Laffoy Commission after its chair, Justice Mary Laffoy. It later became known as the Ryan Commission and published its final report, known as the Ryan Report, in 2009. The report dealt with allegations collected over a period of nine years from 2000 to 2008. These related to experiences ranging from 1914 up until the opening of the commission in 1999. The victims were compensated but the perpetrators were not prosecuted. The commission's report stated that testimony had demonstrated beyond a doubt that the entire system treated children like prison inmates and slaves and completely ignored their human rights. Some religious officials had encouraged ritual beatings and had shielded their religious orders from any investigation amid a culture of self-serving secrecy. There was also evidence of very serious sexual abuse including rapes, naked beatings in public, and children being forced into oral sex. The abuse was said to be particularly endemic in

---

14. Wikipedia, "John Jay Report."
15. Sipe, *Celibacy in Crisis*, 52,
16. Murnane, *Clerical Errors*, 58.
17. All discussion of *The Commission to Inquire into Child Sexual Abuse* refers to O'Fatharta, "Ryan Report."

the institutions that dealt with boys and has been described as "systematic, pervasive, chronic, excessive, arbitrary, and endemic."[18]

The then Irish president, Mary McAleese, called the abuse "an atrocious betrayal of love"[19] and, since the cessation of her presidency, McAleese has spent much of her time campaigning for the reform of the Catholic Church. Cardinal Sean Brady (the then leader of the Catholic Church in Ireland) said he was "profoundly sorry and deeply ashamed that children had suffered in such awful ways in these institutions."[20]

While the report uncovered the true extent of child abuse in Ireland, it was criticized because of an indemnity deal that had secretly been signed in 2002 between representatives of the Conference of Religious in Ireland and the minister, Michael Woods. This deal indemnified the religious orders from legal action and meant that the perpetrators could not be prosecuted although the victims were paid compensation. The religious orders had initially paid the state around €128 million in cash and property in exchange for their indemnity. In the event the amount of money required fell short of this and they were asked to pay further amounts. The report caused shock and outrage across the Irish Republic, and it would be fair to say that the exposure of such terrible child abuse perpetrated by Catholic religious is one of the main factors in the decline of the Catholic faith in Ireland.

In 1975, mass attendance in Ireland was 91 percent. A survey conducted by the Association of Catholic Priests in 2021 found that Mass attendance in Ireland had dropped by two thirds since 1975 and then stood at 30 percent. This was not the only report to follow investigations into abuse in Ireland. There was also an investigation into the Magdalene laundries, institutions also run by the Roman Catholic Religious Orders, which led to *The McAleese Report* being published in 2013. Senator Martin McAleese had chaired the committee that conducted this inquiry. The purpose of the Magdalene laundries was to house 'fallen' women who had become pregnant outside wedlock. Both the women and their children were abused, and many died and were buried in mass graves.

There is currently a further state investigation into abuse at schools in Ireland. This investigation is ongoing and will eventually produce another report. Preliminary findings, which include the allegations at schools run by the Spiritan Fathers, have already been published.

The Independent Inquiry into Child Sexual Abuse (IICSA) in England and Wales was an inquiry examining how the country's institutions handled

18. Bunting, "An Abuse Too Far," para. 1.
19. Rutherford, "Devasting Account of Abuse," para. 10.
20. Brady, *Statement by Cardinal Seán Brady*, para. 3.

their duty of care to protect children from sexual abuse. It was announced by the (then) British Home, Secretary Theresa May, on July 17, 2014. It had initially been set up following investigations into the Jimmy Saville sexual abuse scandal and was intended to be a Panel Inquiry supported by experts. However, it was reconstructed in February 2015 as a statutory inquiry under the Inquiries Act 2005. This gave it greatly increased powers to compel sworn testimony and to examine classified information. The IICSA published nineteen reports in all, the last of which was on October 20, 2022. The relevant report here is the one concerning child sexual abuse in the Roman Catholic Church.

The IICSA investigated institutional failures in the Roman Catholic Church regarding child protection with a focus on the failings of the Roman Catholic Church to protect children from sexual abuse. It considered the impact of previous reviews on the church's policy and practice. There were specific case studies conducted that included the English Benedictine Congregation and the Archdiocese of Birmingham. In November 2020 the IICSA published a 144-page report of its findings, which is known as *Safeguarding in the Roman Catholic Church in England and Wales*.

The IICSA report into safeguarding in the Roman Catholic Church in England and Wales is extremely damning. Between 1970 and 2015 the Church had received more than nine hundred complaints involving over three thousand incidences of child sexual abuse against individuals connected to the Church. The report found that the Church had put its own reputation above the welfare of children for many decades. It stated that the Church's moral purpose had been betrayed by those who sexually abused children and those who turned a blind eye to such abuse. It found that the Church repeatedly failed to support victims and survivors and instead took positive action to protect abusers through moving them to different parishes and ignoring the abuse in schools.

In regard to the English Benedictine congregation, it was found that for decades the monks tried to avoid giving any information about child sexual abuse to the police and social services. Ten monks were later convicted or cautioned in relation to offences involving sadistic sexual activity with a large number of children, as well as pornography. Sadly, the inquiry had also received numerous reports of systematic and sadistic sexual abuse perpetrated by other monks who were deceased at the time. The Chair and Panel made recommendations to better protect children from sexual abuse that arose directly from their findings. Regarding the Benedictine congregations, it was advised that the monks no longer have any involvement in the management of the schools and that the schools be completely separated from the abbeys.

There have been many debates about the prevalence of sexual abuse within the Roman Catholic clergy and whether it is higher than in other groups. The consensus usually seems to be that 4 percent of Catholic clergy sexually abused a minor during the last half of the twentieth century with the rate dropping off dramatically in the twenty-first century due to increased awareness of these matters and the implementation of safeguarding policies and procedures. This rate, if it is accurate, would not be any different to other professions in the rest of the population and the argument often used by the church hierarchy is that it is not higher than in other professions as if that makes it alright. But it does not make it alright bearing in mind that the Roman Catholic hierarchy has the audacity to set itself up as the guardian of morality. If it wants to be a guardian of morality it should be setting itself up as an example in practice and it should be doing much better than other organizations in regard to the prevalence of sexual abuse among its clergy. Moreover, there are many statistics that would suggest that sexual abuse among the Roman Catholic clergy is actually higher than in other professions. For example, *The New York Times* survey found that the levels of sexual abuse were 6.2 percent in Baltimore; 7.7 percent in Manchester, New Hampshire; and 5.3 percent in Boston,[21] and William R Stayton, a professor at Widener University in Chester, Pennsylvania, stated that this was not a true picture and only the tip of the iceberg, "You really don't have a true picture. I have worked with many clergy sexual abuse cases over the years, and very, very few of them were reported."[22]

A.W. Richard Sipe (the former Benedictine monk who had left the priesthood) also found that the percentage was much higher. For example, in May 2009 while conducting a survey of the sexual behavior of clergy in Burlington, Vermont, Sipe found that out of 102 priests there were twenty-three who were sexually involved with children under the age of thirteen years. This amounted to higher than 20 percent of the clergy.

A finding by the Australian *Royal Commission into Institutional Responses to Child Sex Abuse* (2013–2017) also supported a higher rate of sexual abuse amongst clergy in comparison to laity. Of 4029 survivors of sexual abuse, it found that 52.9 percent alleged abuse by priests in ministry in comparison to 29 percent who alleged abuse by lay people.[23] The Commission also detailed the number of abuse claims against ten religious orders from 1950 to 2010 and found that four religious orders had allegations of abuse amongst more than 20 percent of their members. It produced

---

21. Goodstein, "Trail of Pain."
22. Zoll, "More Than 1,200 US Priests Accused," para. 7.
23. Royal Commission, *Final Report*, 31.

a report on child sexual abuse in the Diocese of Ballarat between 1980 and 2015 and found that seventeen of the 21 percent of alleged perpetrators were priests—8.7 percent of the total number of priests who ministered during this period.

Numerous studies have been conducted into child sexual abuse in the Catholic Church over the last twenty years and most of these studies agree that, in recent years, the level of abuse among minors has fallen dramatically due to the implementation of new diocesan policies and procedures to prevent and manage child sex abuse, which have raised greater awareness. Yet (as already noted) child sexual abuse is not the only form of sexual abuse. There are also other forms of sexual abuse, such as the sexual abuse of women and the sexual abuse of seminarians and priests by other priests. These forms of abuse are much easier for the church to cover up and much more difficult to quantify because there is not the same level of outrage concerning these forms of abuse as there is with child abuse. The circumstances around these forms of abuse are much more complicated.

The sexual abuse of women by Catholic clergy is difficult to quantify. There are some who would argue that any sexual activity between a priest and a woman who comes under his jurisdiction due to being a parishioner of his or, perhaps a nun, is always abusive. They would argue that this is always the case because of the imbalance of power between the priest and the woman. This is clearly not the case because some of these relationships have resulted in the priest leaving the priesthood and marrying the woman in question. A famous example was that of the Jesuit, Peter Hebblethwaite, who left his Jesuit ministry of sixteen years in 1974, in order to marry Margaret Speaight. There have been numerous other less famous examples of priests leaving to marry the women they met in ministry. These are relationships that were clearly not abusive. They were relationships of mutual consent regardless of how they started.

Nevertheless, it is clear that many priests have sexually abused women, especially nuns, on occasions where there has been an imbalance of power. Even Pope Francis admitted the same in response to a question on a papal plane in February 2019.[24] He stated that there had been priests and bishops who had committed sexual abuse against nuns and that it was continuing and the Church needed to do more. But his comments were very vague and disappointed those who were advocating for nuns who had been abused by priests. The Associated Press spoke to Karlijn Demasure about the matter.[25] Demasure confirmed that there was no data on how widespread the problem

---

24. AP, "Pope Acknowledges Scandal of Priests Sexually Abusing Nuns."
25. Winfield and Muhumuza, "Vatican Meets #MeToo."

is but stated that anecdotal evidence suggested it wasn't exceptional. She stated that the abuse often occurred in a relationship of spiritual guidance with the priest grooming the victim over time.

Therein, of course, lies the problem. While many of these spiritual guidance relationships between priests and women have resulted in sexual abuse, some have ended in genuine relationships of mutual love and marriage. The other problem is that the Vatican will never be transparent enough to release data to enable the abuse to be quantified and, even if it did release this data, it is unlikely that even the Vatican would have sufficient information on this matter as many cases of sexual abuse are simply not reported by women.

Investigations into the sexual abuse of women by priests have been few and far between because this matter has largely been eclipsed by the abuse of children and minors. However, some religious sisters have written reports about the abuse of nuns and tried to draw attention to this matter including Sr. Maura O'Donohue ("Urgent Concerns for the Church in the Context of HIV/AIDS", 1994), Sr. Marie McDonald ("The Problem of the Sexual Abuse of African Religious in Africa and in Rome," 1998), and Sr. Esther Fangman ("Address to the Congress of Benedictine Abbots," 2000)[26]. They alleged that the sexual abuse of nuns by priests was a serious problem—especially in Africa and other parts of the developing world. They also claimed that Catholic clergy exploited their financial and spiritual authority to gain sexual favors from religious women who had been culturally conditioned to be subservient to men.

Another form of abuse that has received little attention is the sexual abuse of seminarians and priests by other Catholic priests. This matter was finally hurled into the limelight in 2021 when Brian Devlin published his book, *Cardinal Sin*. Devlin and three other serving priests had made claims against the Archbishop of St Andrews and Edinburgh (Cardinal Keith O'Brien) alleging that he had groomed and sexually abused them while they were seminarians under his direction. The Cardinal later apologized and resigned. There were also numerous reports between 1994 and 2008 of the US Cardinal Theodore McCarrick abusing seminarians. This kind of abuse seems to have been pretty widespread in seminaries around the world with reports of abuse occurring in many European countries including Italy, Scotland, and Ireland; the co-author of this book is such a survivor.

What is particularly disturbing about this form of abuse is the fact that the hierarchy appear to have persecuted the priests or seminarians who tried to report it. For example, in the US, two seminarians, Stephen Parisi

---

26. Degeorge, "Women Religious Leaders."

and Matthew Bojowoski, stated that they were bullied by superiors and shunned by their fellow seminarians when they tried to go public on sexual abuse.[27] There are also disturbing reports of priests being both persecuted and suspended for reporting other priests for abuse, especially in Scotland. For example, it was reported that one Fr. Matthew Despard was suspended after he wrote a book claiming that he was approached inappropriately for sex as a seminarian and stating that trainee priests who spurned the advances of higher clergy were bullied.[28] Parishioners were very supportive of Fr. Despard but were thrown out of the church by a new priest who has, many years later, been highly promoted by the Vatican. Fr. Despard had refused to leave his parish home but was eventually evicted. Ten years later it was reported by the BBC that Fr. Despard was living in a flat that was paid for by the Church, but he had no ministry. He had been forced to withdraw his book but would not be allowed to minister unless he apologized for telling the truth. He would not apologize. Similarly, again in Scotland, there are reports of another priest, Fr. Lawson, being persecuted after speaking out about another abusive priest, Fr. Paul Moore.[29] Fr. Lawson was wrongly dismissed, and the case was eventually settled out of court.

It is extremely disturbing to read of such cases, for the priest whistleblowers often state that they have are treated like traitors who have betrayed the Church by calling out abuse. They are often told that they have broken their vow of obedience and brought the Church into disrepute by reporting abusers. Paul, who authored the second part of this book was not told this directly, but we will see that he was certainly made to feel that by exposing the abuse he had experienced he was somehow betraying the Church.

The hierarchy has tried to keep these cases of abuse hidden and certainly, most cases concerning the abuse of seminarians has been covered up. On January 13, 2019, *The Sunday Post* reported that 126 allegations against priests in Scotland had gone unreported for years and only a fraction were ever prosecuted.[30] Today it would be reasonable to assume that the number of cases of sexual abuse among minors has dropped significantly because there are now policies and procedures in place to encourage the reporting of such abuse; however, it is not reasonable to assume that the same applies to the abuse of seminarians. This kind of abuse is an internal abuse that can easily be covered up because seminarians are supposed to be 'obedient' to

---

27. Boorstein, "Catholic Seminarians Are Speaking Out."
28. Braiden, "Priest to Sue Fellow Cleric."
29. McLaughlin, "Catholic Priest 'Dismissed' over Abuse Claims."
30. Scott and Mullen, "Investigation."

their diocesan bishops. In the past, whistleblowers have been bullied into silence by those same bishops.

The Catholic vow of obedience is a convenient way of ensuring that abuse is covered up and kept in the system. No one should ever feel compelled to be obedient to an abuser. The fact that the Catholic Church still has no internal policies and procedures in place to acknowledge that a bishop could be an abuser or could be covering up abuse and to advise seminarians (and others) what to do on these occasions is highly disturbing. The co-author of this book was a victim of abuse while a seminarian/priest. You will later read of his harrowing experiences.

Finally, having briefly detailed the history of sexual abuse in the Catholic Church and examined its occurrence around the world, it is now time to consider the possible causes. Some of the causes that have been suggested are: causes of the person, institutional causes, clericalism, mandatory celibacy, the training of seminarians, and the failure of canon law. I will briefly look at these causes along with misogynism, which plays a part in sexual abuse committed by clergy. In my view, culture is the main overriding factor for Catholic sexual abuse. I will argue that this culture stems from mandatory celibacy.

Concerning causes in the person, it is a very well-known fact that around 90 percent of child abuse is committed by men. There are many authorities who confirm this, one of them being the UK Office for National Statistics (ONS).[31] Therefore, if an organization is comprised only of men, it is already likely to have a much higher rate of child sexual abuse than any other organization comprised of both sexes, especially if the men concerned are forced to profess celibacy.

Murnane has also noted that research has confirmed that many priests who abused children have grown up in families where relationships were cold and the father was emotionally absent while the mother may have been dependent on the absent male.[32] In such a family, sex might have been a taboo subject around which there was much suppression, guilt, and very poor knowledge. According to Murnane, those who later became offenders lacked experience of intimacy and continued to be deprived of it in their seminary training.[33] Because many of them joined the priesthood at a young age and had never discussed their sexuality in the seminary or elsewhere, they were later hit by their sexual drives and need for intimacy. As such,

---

31. See, for example, ONS, "Child Sexual Abuse in England and Wales" (March 2019).

32. Murnane, *Clerical Errors*, 61.

33. Murnane, *Clerical Errors*, 76.

they may have tried to find such intimacy with children in their care, and this could become habitual in communities where they were surrounded, only, by celibate priests. If this hypothesis is correct, a reason why these men became stuck and were unable to discern the problems inherited from their dysfunctional backgrounds, or to understand their own sexuality, is that they were mandated to be celibate from a young age.

Another cause of the person could be narcissism. Being ordained a Catholic priest gives a person an honored status that can lead to adulation. Both Sipe and Murnane define a type of narcissistic spirituality. Narcissistic priests have a need to be admired and loved. They are grandiose and feel entitled to attention, therefore seeking power. Sexual abuse is as much about power as twisted pleasure. In fact, many victims recall being told by their abusers that no one would ever believe them because their abuser was so important and well respected. Murnane states that seminary formation has been unable to identify and eradicate the narcissistic traits that are prominent in clergy who abuse children.[34]

Moving on to seminary formation, Marie Keenan stated that sexual abuse is inevitable given the "meaning system" that is taught by the Catholic Church to which many priests adhere.[35] Keenan's research involved in-depth research with clerics who had abused and their experience of being priests prior to, during and after the times they had abused. She stated:

> Celibacy is seen as a gift from God, for which the individual must pray. Sex and sexual expression are construed as a set of 'acts,' and the list of sexual sins is based on lists of rules and regulations regarding the sex 'acts.' Sexual desire and emotional intimacy are seen as less relevant for priests and religious brothers than they are for other individuals. Women and girls are seen as a threat to the celibate commitment. Intimacy with men is also construed as threat, in particular because of underlying Church policy on homosexuality ... Clergy are seen as set apart and set above ... Human perfection is the aim in serving God, and failing to achieve perfection is interpreted as personal failure and must be covered up...[36]

The consequences of the model of 'Perfect Celibate Clerical Masculinity' are clear: it is a model that it is impossible to live up to. It fosters an environment in which "sexual abuse is inevitable" and in which "abuse and

---

34. Murnane, *Clerical Errors*, 63–65.
35. Keenan, *Child Sexual Abuse*, 245.
36. Keenan, *Child Sexual Abuse*, 245.

violence become 'normal practice.'"[37] Keenan argued that it was clear that seminary training, and theology, needed to change to enable this model of the priesthood to lose its position of dominance and its grip over the lives of many priests. She questioned the distinction between clergy and laity and called for a synod in the Irish Church and a Third Vatican Council to bring about changes to the institution of the priesthood itself, as well as clerical culture and the Catholic understanding of sexuality. Neither of these things have happened, but Pope Francis did instigate the Synod on Synodality in October 2021. Unfortunately, this synod failed to take on board the views of both lay people and priests about the ordination of women and the relaxation of the priestly celibacy vow. It therefore continued the closed hierarchical culture of the Roman Catholic Church, brought about no major change, and achieved absolutely nothing.[38]

Regarding the institutional causes of sexual abuse, Murnane argues that the church creates many situational and contextual factors that interact with a person's personal weaknesses, thereby increasing their tendency to abuse. He connects the sexual abuse of women, children, and seminarians to the power that is given to the cleric by the institution of the Church, i.e., the teaching that the priest is a channel through which all can access the transcendent. He also states that church structures are flawed because they expect clerics to be accountable only to those above them and not to the people that they serve.

The institutional causes of clerical abuse go hand in hand with clericalism, which Murnane describes as the attitudes of a culture that excessively idealizes the role of clerics and gives them preference as persons who are superior to other members of the church.[39] Murnane states that clericalism derives from the clerics' claim that "they alone" have the power to celebrate the eucharist. Of course, "they alone" are now all celibate men.[40] As I have already demonstrated, married men were originally ordained up to the Gregorian reforms and the twelfth century First Lateran Council. As I have argued in *No Place for a Woman*, it is highly likely that women were ordained as deacons until the ninth century and as priests until ca. AD 350.

Therefore, in earlier centuries clerical ministry was much more diverse. There was also no claim in earlier centuries that priests were marked with an 'indelible character' via ordination and it is this claim (invented by the Council of Trent at the time of the Reformation) that has created a

---

37. Keenan, *Child Sexual Abuse*, 255.
38. See Reese, "Synod on Synodality Report Is Disappointing."
39. Keenan, *Child Sexual Abuse*, 69.
40. Keenan, *Child Sexual Abuse*, 69.

power structure that gives all power to celibate males alone. Murnane declares that this is an unbiblical clerical error because it creates inequality between church members and is in conflict with the New Testament.[41] The deference given to priests and bishops not only enabled them to commit sexual abuse, it enabled them to cover it up for years because that they were seen as 'beyond reproach.' Therefore, clericalism was a factor that enabled sexual abuse to thrive among Catholic clergy.

However, Keenan goes even further than this and argues that clerical offenders in the church should not be labelled sexual deviants or moral degenerates. She states that the structures and practices of the institution of the Catholic Church have created the perfect climate in which to both grow and nurture such offenders. For these reasons, we should not individualize the problem to one of 'evil priests' but instead seek major reform of the church at multiple levels through new theologies, ecclesiologies, and structures.

Many scholars have also postulated that the failure of Canon Law has contributed towards a culture of sexual abuse. Murnane has stated that Canon Law has made the pope and papal curia gradually become more powerful over the centuries; they govern the church with a high degree of central control.[42] In my previous work, *No Place for a Woman*, I argued that since the 1054 East–West Schism the Roman Catholic Church has used a series of ecumenical councils to promote a white European male celibate elite who stifle all debate. The only exception to this system of power was Vatican II, which attempted reform, but unfortunately failed. The other ecumenical councils have been concerned with creating some kind of priestly celibate caste who keep all power and influence in the hands of the celibate few. This is usually done under some kind of pretext. For example, the First and Second Councils of the Lateran supposedly denied priests the right to marry because some of them were having affairs. But the real reason for enforcing celibacy was to enable the church to seize and keep control of property. It certainly didn't stop priests having affairs and probably resulted in priests having many more illicit affairs than they did when they were married.

The later declarations of the Council of Trent rendered the clergy a separate and elitist cult with divine status. This council stated that ordination gave priests a sacerdotal power and imprinted an 'indelible character' on their souls. Later, in Vatican I, the Church went even further by declaring the pope infallible. Then, in 1917, all these theological changes were incorporated into a new Code of Canon Law. Murnane claims it was this code of

---

41. Keenan, *Child Sexual Abuse*, 71.
42. Murnane, *Clerical Errors*, 86.

Canon Law that enabled the church to cover up child sexual abuse.[43] This code discarded many old decrees that had stated that priests guilty of sexual abuse should be handed over to the state, instead allowing the church to investigate the abuse 'in house'. Then, in 1922, five years after the code was introduced, the Holy Office issued the instruction, *Crimen Sollicitationis*, stating that once an investigation into abuse has begun all participants (including victims) are bound to secrecy and, if they breach this secrecy, they will be excommunicated. This effectively prevents victims from contacting the state police and keeps clerical crimes from public view.

The 1917 Code of Canon Law was revised in 1983 under Pope St. John Paul II with the new code's language about priests who commit sexual crimes being much milder than the 1917 code. Some scholars have stated that the Vatican was clearly reluctant to submit priests to justice, and it has now materialized that much child sexual abuse took place under the pontificate of Pope St. John Paul II. This pope was made a saint within nine years of his death which is disgraceful due to his terrible legacy concerning child sexual abuse. Some of his actions include: allowing three priests to continue to work in the 1970s despite knowing they had been accused of abusing minors, refusing to believe accusations against Fr. Marcial Maciel Degollado beginning in the 1970s and continuing for decades,[44] appointing a disgraced Boston child abuser, Bernard Law, to a prestigious post in Rome, and ignoring warnings concerning Cardinal Theodore McCarrick, and, instead, raising him to the powerful position of Archbishop of Washington.[45] The Code of Canon Law that Pope St. John Paul II produced in 1983 favored the abusing priest rather than the victims with Canon 1341 commanding clerics to repair the scandal of a cleric's crime against a minor firstly by "fraternal correction, reproof or methods of pastoral care." The code contained no command that the bishop give pastoral care to the victims of abuse or to their families. The code also made no mention of reporting a cleric's crimes to the civil authorities.

In 2001, Cardinal Castrillon Hoyos congratulated the French Bishop Pecan for not reporting a priest's abuse to the police, stating that the relationship between a bishop and priest was a sacramental relationship and a very special bond of spiritual paternity. Other cardinals have also claimed that bishops should not report accused priests to authorities. Canon 1362 also introduced a new law that automatically extinguished all crimes of sexual

---

43. Murnane, *Clerical Errors*, 89.

44. Degollado was eventually found to have sexually abused minors and seminarians and fathered several children (Thavis, "Legion of Christ").

45. McCarrick was later defrocked for abusing minors (Harlan, "Ex-Cardinal McCarrick Defrocked.").

abuse of minors if they had not been reported within five years. As the average victim does not disclose abuse until years later, this law effectively silenced victims permanently and left the predator free to commit other crimes. It is not surprising that I regard the pontificate of Pope St. John Paul II as an era of licensed abuse, and his canonization absolutely appalling.[46]

The same use of this flawed canon law continued under Pope Benedict XVI with the same covering up of abuse. It was not until 2021 that Pope Francis changed church canon laws to criminalize sexual abuse and to take away the discretionary power that had previously allowed high ranking clergy to ignore, or cover up, allegations of abuse against priests. Does this now mean that the Church is taking sexual abuse seriously? Before we celebrate, it would be wise to consider that Canon 1398 classes the sexual abuse of a minor as a crime *on the same level as ordaining a woman*. This is an insult to half the human race and indicates that the Church does not understand the gravity of sexual abuse and is disturbingly misogynistic. It is one thing for the church to refuse the ordination of women, but to regard it as a criminal offence on the level of child abuse demonstrates a culture that has no respect for women.

In chapter 4, I described how women were gradually erased from influence in the church. Initially, they were treated as equals by Jesus and in the early church they were ordained as both deacons and priests, but these ordinations were suppressed by the ninth century. Later, after the East–West Schism, the Church prohibited priests from marrying women in the First and Second Councils of the Lateran. This, in effect, prevented priests from having any contact with women and enabled the Church to become increasingly misogynistic in its practice. Does eliminating women from the clergy and forbidding their close association with the clergy, such as through marriage, effect the scale of child abuse in Catholicism? The answer is yes because child abuse is much less prevalent among women than it is among men!

Finally, I pose the question: is mandatory celibacy the main cause of sexual abuse in Catholicism? I answer that there are many causes of sexual abuse in Catholicism, such as causes in the person, institutionalization, clericalism, the failure of canon law, misogyny, and mandatory celibacy. With the exception of causes within the person, all these causes are found in the clerical culture of the Catholic Church.

However, the clerical culture of the Catholic Church has arisen from two main factors: misogyny and mandatory celibacy. It is fair to say that

---

46. There has been some public controversy concerning Pope St. John Paul II's canonization. See, for example, Matranga, "Saint John Paul II Accused of Protecting Pedophiles."

misogyny came first because the ordination of women was suppressed before priests were prohibited from marrying women. The prohibition of priests from marriage was a direct consequence of misogyny. Moreover, removing women from the priest's world made sexual abuse more likely. (Statistically, it is known that men are much more likely to commit sexual abuse than women). Once celibacy was mandated, an elite priestly 'celibate' sect and a culture of priestly adulation was created. This sect gave rise to a practice of 'secret sex' because priests were not allowed to express their normal and natural sexuality like other human beings, even while continuing to have normal sexual desires. This suppression led to a culture in which sex had to be conducted in secret and hidden from public view. This need to hide all sexual activity in turn gave rise to a climate in which the vulnerable could be secretly pressurized for sex and, due to the culture of priestly adulation, bullied into submission. All of this, cumulatively, resulted in prolific sexual abuse and the covering up of such abuse. Therefore, the root causes of sexual abuse in Catholicism are misogyny and mandatory celibacy.

Chapter 6

Mandatory Celibacy and Fatherhood

THIS CHAPTER WILL EXAMINE the issue of 'celibate' priests who father children. In the past, there has been a lot of secrecy surrounding this issue and, though the Vatican now professes to be more transparent, much secrecy still remains. The current canon law dealing with this matter will be discussed along with the pressure upon priests who father a child to 'step aside.' Some prominent cases will be brought to the fore and the psychological welfare of the clerics' offspring will be considered. Since the twelfth century (when celibacy was made compulsory by the Latin Church) many priests have fathered children. Until very recently, these relationships were covered up by the church and many Catholics had little idea that they were going on. One of the first scandals to lead to a greater awareness of these relationships among the general public was the case of Bishop Eamon Casey. This case has been described as a pivotal moment within Ireland's relationship with the Catholic Church.

Eamon Casey was an Irish Catholic priest who served as Bishop of Galway and Kilmacduagh in Ireland from 1976 to 1992. Casey was a very popular bishop who was loved by the Irish people. He seemed to personify a move away from dogmatism to a generalized goodwill towards all people and this led to his popularity. He resigned as a bishop in 1992 when it was revealed that, in the 1970s, he had been in a relationship with an American woman, Annie Murphy, with whom he had fathered a child. Apparently, Casey had made covert payments to Murphy to support their son for many years but had refused to develop a relationship with him or to acknowledge him. Murphy became increasingly upset and angry about this and contacted *The Irish Times* to tell the truth about their affair in the early 1990s. Casey was forced to resign as bishop and fled the country under a cloud of scandal while Murphy published a book, *Forbidden Fruit*, which revealed the truth about their previous relationship and their son.

Meanwhile, Casey was ordered by the Vatican to become a missionary in Ecuador and, after his tenure was completed, he took up a position as a parish priest in the UK. Eamon Casey died in March 2017, but, prior to his death, many other women made allegations to the Catholic Church that they were sexually abused by him. One of these women was his own niece who alleged that she had been repeatedly sexually assaulted by him as a child. When Casey's affair was initially discovered, the idea that a Catholic bishop (supposedly an epitome of the celibacy rule), who was so popular, could have fathered a child simply shocked the Irish Catholic laity, especially when it was later revealed that Bishop Casey had been great friends with one Fr. Michael Cleary.

Fr. Michael Cleary was an Irish Catholic priest who became very popular to the extent that he was a radio and TV personality. After his death in 1993, it was revealed that Phyllis Hamilton, who had worked as his housekeeper, had actually been his secret partner and he had fathered two children with her—one of whom was adopted. The other son remained with them, and they lived as a family in secret. Although there are no statistics on the number of priests who have had relationships with their housekeepers or secretaries that result in children, it is highly likely that there have been many such cases. In fact, the writer has heard of one such ongoing relationship between a priest and a secretary.

There have also been other cases of fairly well-known and/or eminent clergy fathering children and these have included: a Los Angeles Auxiliary Bishop, Gabino Zavala, who resigned after disclosing to superiors that he was the father of two children, and the former Bishop of San Pedro, Fernando Lugo, who resigned in 2005, but was not laicized until 2008. Lugo's child, a boy, was born in May 2007. Another example of this sad state of affairs is the case of Marcial Maciel—the founder of the Congregation of the Legionaries of Christ who, in 2005, was forced to step down due to sexual scandals. Maciel was found to have abused at least sixty children and seminarians and to have fathered three children with two different women.

Obviously, the antics of these clerics are reprehensible, but the question has to be asked, who is responsible for the appalling behavior by certain Catholic clerics? Is it really just the clerics themselves, or is it also the Vatican State who preside over a centuries-old, entrenched culture that stubbornly refuses to move forward, acknowledge human rights, and allow priests to marry?

The reason why I raise this question is because it seems to me that there is a powerful faction in the Vatican that is against relaxing mandatory celibacy and this faction seems to have survived the centuries. This can be seen in the many bishops who break their vows and 'cover up' for priests who have also not been faithful to their vows. Additionally, a significant number of bishops have spoken out against mandatory celibacy but the determination to maintain it remains resolute. One has to wonder what is really behind this, and to raise the question as to whether those who 'fall from grace,' and engage in sexual activities, are also the victims of something quite ungodly that is lurking in the walls of the Vatican State. Why is the determination to hoist 'celibacy' onto priests adhered to despite continuous calls for reform? Why is the sexuality of priests denied, and why are their subsequent sexual activities covered up?

The 'celibate show' appears to be a theatrical circus, a façade that covers up the true humanity of its priests. These priests are human beings like the rest of us. They have a natural sex drive like everyone else. They also have faults and failings like everyone else and are, excepting their career choice, no different from anyone else. Perhaps the desire among those in the Vatican to create, at the First Council of the Lateran (1123) and, later, at the Council of Trent (1563), the myth that priests were superior beings has now been passed down through generations and has gained such a hold on the hierarchy that they feel it simply cannot be abandoned? The New Testament knew of no elite priestly caste that was better than the rest of humanity. The writer of the First Letter of St. Peter was quite clear that every Christian belonged to a royal priesthood—not just a few celibate men if, indeed, there were any celibate men at the time (1 Pet 2:9).

The Vatican has, since the First Council of the Lateran, created a system in which priests are forced to deny their own sexuality, in order to sustain, and continue, an elite misogynist 'celibate' cult which has nothing to do with the teachings of Jesus or the practices of the early church. As has already been noted, this celibate cult was born at the time of the Gregorian reforms and the slightly later First Council of the Lateran when priests were forced to abandon their wives and families and leave them destitute. The Vatican has never apologized retrospectively for this appalling treatment of women, and it is well time it did so. Perhaps the reason why it has not done so is because this celibate cult has been reaffirmed by later councils like the Council of Trent and Vatican I. Presumably, they still think it is okay that priests were forced to abandon their wives and families in the twelfth century?

Regardless of the myth that the Vatican itself has created, mandatory celibacy has been a complete and total failure because it has driven normal human sexuality underground, as priests have been forced to deny their own natural sexuality. The desire to have sex is a normal and natural urge.

While it may be true that some people have a much lower libido than others, the fact remains that the majority of men have no desire to be celibate. This also applies, from the evidence we have seen, to a significant proportion of Catholic priests who are, in reality, not celibate.

It can also be argued that driving sexuality underground can create a perverse subculture where suppressed sexuality comes out in distorted ways.[1] Indeed, some have argued that it causes a cycle of promiscuity. This is due to the fact that the 'straying' priest may be reluctant to remain in a sexual relationship with one woman (or man for that matter) for very long, in case it is noticed, so he quickly ends any sexual relationship to start yet another fling. He then ends that fling prematurely and so on…

Who is truly responsible for this? Surely the real responsibility for these kinds of behaviors should be laid at the foot of a corrupt hierarchy in the Vatican who insist on mandating celibacy to keep power and control in the hands of the elite 'celibate' sect? Mandatory celibacy (the forcing of candidates for the priesthood to deny their natural sexuality) is an abuse of human rights *and it appears to indoctrinate and create a significant number of abusers*. The system also betrays other good men with a truly holy vision who accept the system to pursue a love of God, only to find that the system then betrays them. How do men who join this priesthood currently fare? Both Sipe and Murnane have demonstrated that some men are completely corrupted by the system while others try to work within it and remain celibate (perhaps occasionally failing), while still others, like my co-author, finally decide they cannot entertain the system, and its hypocrisy, and eventually leave the priesthood altogether.

In modern times, due to a greater understanding of the psychology of human sexuality, there have been repeated calls on the Church hierarchy to lift the requirement that all Latin priests are celibate, but all these calls have fallen on to deaf ears. That is why I have suggested that a desire to be different and exclusive, a kind of power lust, has gained a grip on the men behind Vatican walls. For example, at the time of Vatican II, there was a widespread feeling among both the laity and many clergy that celibacy should become voluntary for priests, but the council still ploughed ahead with the decree, *Presbyterorum Ordinis*. This decree did not resolve the debate, and the immediate aftermath saw large numbers of priests leave their ministry. Then, in 1971, the Synod of Bishops again reaffirmed clerical celibacy. Vocations to the priesthood have declined ever since and one could say that this is a direct message from the Holy Spirit that mandatory celibacy is not God's Will; however, the hierarchy have ignored over fifty years of decline and

---

1. For further discussion of this issue, see Blackstock, "Gay Mafia."

have continued to ask 'the faithful' to pray for more men to embrace the priesthood as celibates!

Similarly, during the years before the recent Synod on Synodality, there were again calls for the Vatican to relax the celibacy law. Some of these calls came from bishops themselves, such as two very senior bishops in Belgium in 2010, Bishop Ramón Alfredo de la Cruz Baldera of San Francisco, Bishop Felix Gmur of Basel, and, later, in 2018, the entire Belgian Catholic Bishop Conference, who voted in favor of married priests. All these calls for an end to mandatory, or 'forced,' celibacy fell on deaf ears, as did the voices of the priests and laity who also questioned this rule at the synod itself. The Synod report stated, "Different opinions have been expressed about priestly celibacy. Its value is appreciated by all as richly prophetic and a profound witness to Christ; some ask, however, whether its appropriateness, theologically, for priestly ministry should necessarily translate into a disciplinary obligation in the Latin Church, above all in ecclesial and cultural contexts that make it more difficult. This discussion is not new but requires further consideration."[2]

One wonders how repeated sex scandals are a 'profound witness' to Christ. The majority of ordinary people in the West regard them with disgust as a turn-off from the Church. Isn't the Christian faith meant to attract people rather than drive them away? Isn't that what the early church did? Once again, the issue of mandatory celibacy has been avoided, and one has to ask the question as to why the pope bothered to call a synod at all if both the voices of the laity and of priests were not going to be heeded. The synod has also refused to restore the female diaconate. It has ignored the voices of many lay people, particularly in the West, and made no changes whatsoever. It may as well not have taken place.

In regard to priestly celibacy it should be obvious to any normal person that if celibacy was voluntary, it would gain more credibility and become more respected in the secular world, as there would be fewer scandals. There are a very small number of men with low libidos who can, and do, actually manage celibacy, and would actually choose it as a way of life if it were not mandatory. They are shining examples of a holy life. However, sadly, when this small group of men are thrown into a group of reluctant celibates their exemplary examples of a different kind of holy life are eclipsed by all those who fail.

While the Catholic hierarchy refuse to acknowledge that mandatory celibacy is not only cruel and inhuman but also a failure, there has been some movement from the Vatican in acknowledging that many children of

---

2. Cernuzio, "Synod Report," para. 21.

priests exist and this is largely due to the efforts of Vincent Doyle, a son of a Catholic priest.

Doyle had a relationship with his father, Fr. John J. Doyle, until his father died, but Doyle did not realize that he was Fr. John's biological son until many years later. Fr. John was his godfather and Doyle called him JJ. Sixteen years after Fr. John's death, Doyle realized that his godfather was his biological father. He was very moved, but not entirely surprised, stating in a TV interview with ABC News, "It was the antidote to the worst day of my life, that I had lost him – because I got him back…. There was a huge kindness about him. He was a father in everything but the word."[3]

Doyle then went on to found Coping International, an organization for the children of priests, which he set up in 2014. Since then, in excess of fifty thousand people have approached the organization. This gives an idea of the number of liaisons between priests and women that have resulted in pregnancy. As a result of Doyle's efforts, the Catholic Church has since acknowledged more publicly the need to help the children of priests and it improved its canonical guidelines concerning this matter in 2019. Prior to this, the Church already had secret guidelines in place. These had been composed by Pope Benedict XVI and Cardinal Claudio Hummes in *Congregazione per il Clero a proposito dei chierici con prole* (2009).[4] The existence of this document was little known, but, due to the efforts of Vincent Doyle, the existence of the children of priests was highlighted by the media and the guidelines were improved. These now state that any priest under the age of forty years who fathers a child can obtain a dispensation from the clerical state without waiting to reach that age.[5]

Nonetheless, these guidelines also insist that the loss of the clerical state is imposed on priests who have fathered children, claiming that paternal responsibility creates permanent obligations which, in the Latin Church, do not provide for the exercise of priestly ministry. Some implied exemptions are made to the rules: for example, if arrangements have been made by both parents of a newborn baby to have the child adopted, or in the case of a priest who has been reported for a past indiscretion from years' ago without any further breaches of misconduct and the child has since grown up. Yet, overall, the Vatican continues to view marriage as generally incompatible with priesthood.

Really? One wonders how the Orthodox Church has survived for almost two thousand years with married priests with families when marriage

3. Millar and Reed, "'Hidden Children' of the Catholic Church."
4. See Horrowitz and Povoledo, "Vatican's Secret Rules."
5. Congregatio Pro Clericis, "Vatican Guidelines."

is so 'incompatible' with the priesthood. And what about the married priests in the Eastern rite of the Catholic Church? Clearly, the Vatican must have some other agenda in banning married priests from the Latin part of its church. One has to wonder whether this is perhaps because there may be hidden documents that married people would find unpalatable in their walls. Who knows why these men persist on a path which is undermining not only the credibility of priests, but their own credibility to boot.

Moreover, there have been a significant number of contradictory changes from the late Pope Francis. Prior to becoming pope, Jorge Mario Bergoglio (then Archbishop of Buenos Aires, later Pope Francis) stated that mandatory celibacy was a matter of discipline, not of faith, and it could therefore be changed. He further explained that he was in favor of maintaining celibacy for the moment because there were ten centuries with positive experience of the rule. However, later, in 2014, as Pope Francis, he proposed a possible mechanism for change through national bishops' conferences that could seek and find a consensus for reform and take their suggestions to Rome. Still later, in 2018, Pope Francis claimed that he wanted the subject discussed, beginning with remote areas like Amazonia where there was a shortage of priests. The subject was indeed discussed and, in November 2019, the Amazonas Synod voted by 128 to 41 votes in favor of married priests. Sadly, following the synod, Pope Francis rejected the proposal in his post-synodal apostolic exhortation, *Querida Amazonia*.

It seems that no matter how many clergy, or laity, cry out for an end to mandatory celibacy, the Vatican, for reasons known only to itself, will simply not have it. This denial also makes it clear that, despite all its exhortations to the faithful, to revere the Blessed Sacrament, the Vatican values enforced celibacy more than ensuring the eucharist is available to the people. The shortage of vocations in the West is certainly due to mandatory celibacy and it is making it increasingly difficult for lay people to receive communion. In Northumbria where I live, many priests preside over four of five parishes, and some of those parishes no longer have a Sunday Mass. Other parishes have closed down altogether. The Church is dying on its feet in the West, but mandatory celibacy remains.

Since the Amazonas Synod there have been further calls for an end to mandatory celibacy when, in 2023, 75 percent of German Catholic bishops supported married priests at Synodal Path. Later, in January 2024, the Maltese Archbishop, Charles Scicluna, called for married priests in the Catholic church, and, in February 2024, the Belgian Bishops developed a document requesting optional celibacy. As has already been noted, all such calls to end mandatory celibacy have been ignored by the powers that be at the Synod on Synodality.

Returning to Vincent Doyle, he has managed to have a significant effect on the Catholic Bishops in Ireland. These bishops have now stated that a priest who leaves ministry after fathering a child must be financially supported by their diocese as they transition to the lay state with a view of fulfilling their parental role. Doyle has welcomed the move and stated that it will have worldwide significance for the Church because other bishop's conferences in other countries will follow suit. Doyle maintains that priests having children is inevitable and the remedy is married priests.[6]

The children of Catholic priests are often referred to as the' children of the ordained' and many have testified that being the offspring of a Catholic priest has been a very traumatic experience. Vincent Doyle has stated that, in his case, he was very fortunate to have known and had a loving relationship with his father, albeit believing that his father was his godfather. However, even he will have experienced some trauma, for he grew up not knowing who his real father was, when his father was right beside him the whole time. The trauma of other children of priests has been much worse because they were not so lucky. In many cases they have failed to have their emotional, legal, and financial needs met.

Some children of priests were very young when they learned of their father's identity, but were sworn to secrecy. Often, in these cases, the priest has been making secret payments to the mother of the child but wishes to remain in ministry and therefore cannot acknowledge the child. In other cases, the priest has been making payments to the mother and has had a relationship with the child, but the child has been told that his/her father is a priest and sworn to secrecy. So, the child has been ordered never to refer to their father as a father in public; outside the home he must be an 'uncle.' One woman in this position, Chiara Villar, stated that she had always loved her dad as a child but had never understood why he couldn't be her proper dad. All she had ever wanted as a child was for him to take her out in public and tell people that he was so proud of his daughter.

There have been other children of priests who have been adopted, perhaps because their father was a priest and their mother was a nun. Sometimes these nuns became pregnant because they felt bullied and coerced into sex and had therefore been abused. In the 1990s, leaders of several religious orders issued a series of confidential reports to the Vatican about the sexual abuse of nuns living in Africa. One report described an incident in Malawi where the local bishop dismissed leaders of a women's congregation after they complained that local priests had impregnated twenty-nine

---

6. Qtd. in McDonald, "Priest Who Leaves Ministry," para. 7.

sisters in 1988. The sister who wrote the report stated that she was aware of similar incidences in other countries including the US, Ireland, and Italy.[7]

Some priests and nuns had consensual sex but went on to have the child, who was the product of their union, adopted. One Brendan Watkins, who was adopted and grew up in Melbourne, was curious to find his biological parents. However, when he asked for his original birth certificate, he found that it only bore his biological mother's name and his father's name was missing. Eventually he located his biological mother who was a nun, but she refused to tell him who his father was. It turned out that the priest concerned had sworn her to secrecy. Later, when the priest died, she confirmed that he was the son of Fr. Vincent Shiel who had been thirty years older than her and whom she had revered as a kind of older role model. Watkins rightly stated that the fact that Shiel had sworn her to secrecy was a form of spiritual abuse.[8]

There has never been any study regarding the number of children who were fathered by priests and nuns. However, in 2022, Dr Doris Reisinger, a former nun who had herself been abused (although not impregnated) by a priest and is now a senior academic at Goethe University in Frankfurt, published a landmark report on the issue in the US.[9] She claimed that mothers were put under pressure by priests to have abortions or go into hiding and further stated, "I actually think we can assume that this is still going on because none of the contributing factors has been erased, the clerical power of priests, mandatory celibacy that often works as a perfect excuse and cover for reproductive abuse — all of that is still fully in place. And no major research has [looked] into reproductive abuse. So, there is still lots to be done."[10]

The failure of the Catholic hierarchy to allow priests of the Latin rite to marry has created psychological pain and hurt all round, as well as messy and dysfunctional families. Everyone has suffered. Priests have suffered because the system has contributed to their growing predatory behavior or, in the case of more caring priests, because the system will not allow them to have a normal sexual relationship with a partner and thereby exercise the natural human right to reproduce. Women have suffered, either because they have been abused, or because they have had the misfortune of loving someone with whom they can never have a public relationship unless he sacrifices the job he loves and his livelihood. Children have suffered because

7. Winfield and Muhumuza, "After Decades of Silence."
8. Watkins, "For 30 Years."
9. Reisinger, "Reproductive Abuse."
10. Qtd. in Smith, "Hidden Children," para. 30.

they have, either, not known their father, or they have never had a proper relationship with him.

One wonders what all this suffering has to do with Christianity. The question has to be raised as to why convert priests of other denominations are allowed to bring their wives and children over with them and to continue to minister in the Catholic church when cradle Catholic priests have celibacy hoisted on to them? There is also the question as to why the Catholic priests of the Eastern rite are allowed to marry and have children while those of the Latin rite are not? How is it that these men are allowed to have a normal sexuality which is denied to those in the Latin rite? If a married priesthood works in the Eastern rite Catholic Churches, then surely there is no reason why it cannot work in the West? It would be valuable to carry out research into the number of sexual scandals in both traditions, but that is for another study.

Part 2

The Sins of Mandatory Celibacy

*A Personal Experience
by Paul Murphy-Sanderson*

Introduction

When Debra approached me, asking if I would be willing to contribute to this book, *The Sins of Mandatory Celibacy*, I immediately agreed. The timing couldn't have been better, as I had only recently begun writing down my memories of being sexually abused by a Roman Catholic priest. Initially, these notes were intended to be private. However, the prospect of sharing my experience with others and potentially aiding someone else in their journey of recovery made me believe that something positive could come out of the decades of suffering I had endured. As I embark on this journey, I want to emphasize that healing is attainable, and I hope that my story can instill hope and positivity in those who walk a similar path. I believe that by sharing our stories, we can create a future filled with hope and optimism.

I can, without a doubt, say that this will be the most challenging piece of writing I have ever undertaken. For many years, I have borne the burden of abuse in silence. Even during the investigation, the trial, and up to the present day I have remained anonymous, known only as 'the victim.' However, in telling my story, I am not only exposing myself to potential judgment, but, more importantly, I am embarking on a healing journey. In sharing my experiences, I hope to offload some of the destructive memories that I have been carrying for decades and thereby move further away from being 'the anonymous victim' to becoming 'Paul the survivor.'

I want to emphasize that the information I will be sharing is based on my own experiences and observations, and while it may shed some light on the issue of abuse in the clergy, it's important to remember that my story is just one piece of a much larger puzzle. Sadly, it is a puzzle made up of countless human pieces. Some have found their place, but many are still lost and broken. The beautiful, completed image, of which all these human lives are a part, will only be made whole when the Roman Catholic Church acknowledges the role it has played in crushing the human image, the image of God Himself.

Blessed are you, when men shall revile you, and persecute you, and shall say all manner of evil against you falsely, for my sake. Rejoice, and be exceedingly glad: for great is your reward in heaven: for so persecuted they the prophets which were before you (Matt 5:10–12)

Early Childhood and Religious Vocation

Attending a Roman Catholic primary school in the 1970s was a formative experience to say the least. In many ways, it instilled in us a strong sense of spiritual discipline and community, or you could simply say, that it brainwashed us. The school day began and ended with prayers, thereby fostering a daily connection with our faith. We expressed gratitude for our meals at lunchtime by saying 'Grace' and observed important religious occasions such as Christmas and Easter. Additionally, we devoted time to saying the rosary daily in May and honored the dead in November. Our school also celebrated Major Feast Days, such as St. Patrick's Day (the school's patron saint) and, at the beginning and end of each term, there was a Mass celebrated by the parish priest for the entire school. On top of all of this, we were also expected to attend Sunday Mass in the parish church each week. Then, during Monday morning assembly, the headmistress would ask those who had not attended the Sunday Mass to stand up and be disgraced as she spoke to them directly about sin and laziness—the two things that separate us from God. Luckily for me, my dad took my brother and I to church most Sundays, and only occasionally was I made to feel the shame of being a sinner.

As if this wasn't enough to impact a child for life, at seven years old, we were shown by the teacher and the parish priest how to make our First Confession in church. On the chosen day, the entire class was escorted to the church, and then, one by one, was made to go into the 'confessional box' and close the door. In front of us was a grill, behind which, in a separate cubicle, sat the parish priest. We were told to kneel down and say clearly, "Bless me, Father, for I have sinned, this is my first confession…," after which we told our sins—the things that we had done wrong and which had offended God. Next, we had to express our remorse, saying how sorry we were to have offended God, after which, the parish priest on behalf of God would forgive us. Whilst for all of us this was our First Confession, I think for many it was also their last. In all honesty, it was terrifying, and for someone like me, who was a worrier and always seeking reassurance, it simply added fuel to the fire of my apprehensions.

A few weeks after we had all been absolved of our sins, we made our First Holy Communion at St. Patrick's Church in Heysham. It was May 10, 1975, a very significant day in our school year. The girls wore white dresses, resembling little brides, whilst the boys wore their school uniforms. It was the day we were to receive Jesus for the first time in the form of bread and wine, in fact, at that time only the priest received the wine. Even though I didn't fully understand the theological significance of receiving Christ's body and blood, I do remember feeling that something very special was happening, and, to mark the occasion, my grandparents gave me a statue of the Sacred Heart of Jesus, and my parents gave me a wooden crucifix for my bedroom wall, both of which I still have.

For most of the children in my class, making their First Holy Communion was just another boring church service to be endured, but for me, it was the day when Jesus, who had previously been just a statue in the classroom, became my actual friend. I began to feel close to Him. I started to pray on my own, reciting at home the prayers we had learned by heart in school, such as the Our Father, Hail Mary, and the Glory Be. I said them every night before I went to sleep, and if ever I forgot, I would feel the terrible weight of my Catholic guilt bearing down upon me. Then, one day in class, the parish priest announced that he was recruiting for new altar boys, and I volunteered immediately.

I cherished my time as an altar boy. I loved carrying the candles, ringing the bells, and assisting the priest at communion. What I loved the most was kneeling on the altar steps; from there I could see the tabernacle (the brass box, where the body and blood of Christ, was kept safe). There was something about it that drew me in, and even at seven years old, I sensed that a real person, Jesus, was present there. I never mentioned this to anyone; it remained my secret, but from then on, I always felt at home in the church. It became my safe place, my home from home.

I served as an altar boy for almost four years, until I left St. Patrick's Primary School to attend Our Lady's High School, Lancaster, in September 1979. On the whole, the years that I spent at this school were mostly uneventful. I could have been a better student, but I wasn't particularly interested in most of the subjects. The only one I really excelled in was Religious Studies. I had been top of the class in primary school and continued to do well in secondary school; it just came naturally to me.

Nevertheless, there were two events in my first couple of years at high school that had a huge impact on me. The first was an announcement from the headmaster that St. Peter's Cathedral in Lancaster were auditioning for a new boys' choir. I was keen to attend the auditions and encouraged my brother to come along, too, and, surprisingly, we were both accepted. It was an excellent opportunity on many levels. We learned about posture, breathing, projecting one's voice, and how to read music. Personally, it helped me to feel that I belonged to something; so often as a child I felt unconnected and on the outside of things—like a spectator watching the world going on around me, but never quite feeling a part of it. I used to look forward to our weekly choir practices, but, for me, nothing could beat singing at the High Mass every Sunday and on important feast days—often with the bishop present. I loved processing into the cathedral wearing my red cassock and starched white ruff; it was better for me than any football strip. The sound of the choir and the congregation singing in harmony, as one voice, used to lift my soul; it created within me a feeling of unity and a sense of intimacy and closeness with God. You could say that singing in the choir helped me to connect both the physical and spiritual realities, which became as real to me as each other.

I have many happy memories of my time as a cathedral chorister.

Occasionally, we would be invited to sing in the Metropolitan Cathedral of Liverpool, in front of the archbishop and we also participated in several radio broadcasts across the UK. In 1980, our choir had the opportunity to perform at a major international choir festival in Rome, and, in contrast, on one rainy day in April 1981, we made a recording of our usual repertoire, capturing the essence of the Church's different times and seasons, and, to our delight it was released as a vinyl record. My years in the choir really helped to broaden my understanding of, and love for, the liturgy.

The second significant event occurred during a history class. The teacher was handing out sheets of paper on which was a detailed ground plan of a medieval monastery. I don't really have the words for what happened next, suffice it to say, that as soon as my copy landed on the desk, I instantly knew that one day I would live in a monastery. I cannot explain it any other way, other than to add that it came as a complete and utter shock at the same time as being as real, and tangible, as the chair that I was sitting on. I didn't even know if monasteries still existed, or if wanting to be a monk was the same thing as desiring to be a gladiator or a medieval knight; both were very appealing to a twelve-year-old boy—but with extremely limited opportunities in the modern world.

Nevertheless, I couldn't get the idea out of my head; it was well and truly lodged there. I remember travelling home on the bus with my hood up, and when asked by my friends what I was doing, I said that I was going to be a monk. As soon as I arrived home that evening, I told my mum of my monastic plans for the future and, to say that she wasn't impressed, would be a huge understatement. Taking the hint, I kept my thoughts on the matter to myself for the next few years. Yet, from that point onwards, I began to attend Mass most evenings after school, and whenever I had any pocket money, I would buy small C.T.S. (Catholic Truth Society) booklets about the Church, Prayer and Catholic teaching.

Also, around this time, my paternal grandparents were on holiday in Devon, and whilst there, they visited Buckfast Abbey, a Benedictine monastery of some renown. On their return they gave me a guidebook to the Abbey as a gift, even though they knew nothing of my budding monastic vocation. I loved this booklet and spent many hours thumbing through it. But, as much as I loved looking at the photographs of Buckfast Abbey, there was one particular picture that stood out for me. It was a tiny black and white drawing of some Trappist Monks from the Abbey of Soligny in France. They were on a train, which I believe was transporting kaolin, a soft white clay essential for manufacturing porcelain, china, and paper. Whatever it was about, this picture deepened the desire within me to become a monk.

In the summer of 1983, my parents decided to move to Lytham St. Anne's, Lancashire, the town they both originally hailed from, with the result that I had to change schools one year before my final exams, which was not an ideal time, and so, in the September, I became a pupil at St. Bede's R.C. High School in Lytham. With this being the fourth school I had attended, you would think I would be used to fitting in, but I found it incredibly difficult and didn't make any friends during my year there. I continued to attend Mass whenever I could at our new parish church, St. Alban's (the church where I had been baptized as a baby), and in no time, I was serving the Sunday Mass and drawing religious cartoons for the weekly parish newsletter.

One Sunday, early in 1984, the parish priest, read out a letter from the bishop about vocations to the priesthood, and it felt as though he had written it especially for me. Once Mass was over, I couldn't wait to get home and tell my parents that I felt God was calling me to be a priest. Initially, they were a lot less enthusiastic than I was, and it took me the entire Sunday afternoon to convince them that I was serious and that it wasn't just a passing fad.

Thankfully, by early evening they were onboard, and, within a couple of weeks, I was being interviewed by my parish priest and the Vocations Director for the Diocese of Lancaster. Happily, the meeting went well, and soon my parents and I were on our way to visit St. Joseph's College, Upholland, to have a look around and meet the headmaster. St. Joseph's was the only junior seminary left in England, and it educated boys from eleven to eighteen years of age who believed that they might have a 'call' to the priesthood. As the college came into view I was struck by the imposing gothic edifice; it was huge and very impressive. Once inside, I remember thinking that the long corridors lined with oil paintings, the huge dormitories, and old-fashioned classrooms, wouldn't have looked out of place in a period drama. But, in spite of its solemn appearance, I longed to go there, and all that stood in my way was an interview with the bishop set for May 30, 1984.

I remember feeling incredibly nervous as we pulled up in front of 'The Willows' Presbytery in Kirkham on that critical day. There were to be two interviews: the first with the Diocesan Doctors, and the second with the Diocesan Vocations Board, which consisted of two Bishops, two Monsignors, the Vocations Director, and three priests, including the Headmaster of Upholland.

The two doctors were both elderly gentlemen who had already studied my medical record and wanted to ask a few further questions. One concentrated on the physical, measuring my height, blood pressure, hearing and eyesight, whilst the other was more concerned with why I felt called to the priesthood and if I was more attracted to girls or boys. I was horrified and embarrassed by such a question; I didn't even know what he meant as it was clear to me that boys liked girls, and I was no different; I had never heard of homosexuality at that time.

Following my meeting with the doctors, I entered a large, very old-fashioned room. On one side sat two bishops with three priests on either side. Facing such a formidable panel at the age of sixteen was an incredibly daunting experience, and, even more so, when I had to answer their questions. I was asked about my prayer life and my involvement in the local parish and school, and about my home life, hobbies, interests, and, finally, my motivation for wanting to enter the seminary and train for the priesthood. The first few questions were easy to answer, but the last one was much harder. I attempted to explain how I believed that God was calling me, though finding the precise words was really hard. Nevertheless, I must have said something right, for, later that evening, my parents received a phone call telling them that I had been accepted as a Junior Seminarian and would begin my studies at Upholland College in the coming September.

I was over the moon and so excited; I couldn't wait to tell the headmaster and my form teacher at St. Bede's. However, my news quickly spread among the student body, and, as is often the case when teenagers don't understand something, several of the students saw an opportunity to make me the butt of their jokes. I remember some boys pulling me down to the floor while a group of girls tried to kiss me. They knew that priests weren't allowed to marry and used it as an excuse to embarrass me. On another occasion, some boys kept saying swear words and asking me to repeat them; when I refused, they would mock me and call me names. At lunchtime, I used to go and sit in the school chapel to avoid everyone, but often the bullies would wait outside and, as I left, they would call me 'Father' and make jokes about my not being allowed to have sex. This was really the first time that I became aware of 'celibacy' as something connected to priesthood, although it was not a word I had ever heard mentioned in school. I knew that priests didn't marry, but I had never given it any thought; it was just how things were, and I was happy with it. Due to such experiences the end of term couldn't come quickly enough, and, in June 1984, I left St. Bede's without so much as a backward glance. My schooldays were over, and I couldn't wait to begin my new journey from seminary to priesthood.

Upholland College—Junior Seminary

My arrival at Upholland College will be forever etched in my memory. The buildup had been exciting: buying the college uniform, acquiring a large antique blue trunk for my clothes, a new fountain pen, a hot water bottle, and a pair of new shoes. I couldn't wait for Saturday, September 15 to arrive. Yet, as my dad drove my mum and I up the college driveway and I glimpsed the enormous sandstone building looming over the extensive grounds with its twin lakes, my excitement was replaced with a wave of anxiety and apprehension. The thought of being a priest, a figure of such reverence and responsibility, seemed too grand for someone like me. Who was I to think I could be a priest? These doubts and fears swirled in my mind, but it was too late to back out now.

At the colossal front door, we were greeted by a member of staff and some students. After being introduced, they kindly assisted in carrying my luggage upstairs to my new room, with my parents following behind. I soon discovered that the students were from the year I was about to join, and their warm demeanor and friendly chitchat put me at ease. They told me how fortunate I was to be starting in 'Poetry,' which was the college's name for the 'lower' Sixth Form, and how lucky we were to be allocated our own rooms, as the 'lower school' still had to sleep in large dormitories, and study in the 'Prep Hall' outside formal classes.

Just to expand on this a little. Ever since the sixteenth century, when Cardinal William Allen had founded a college for the training of English clergy at Douai, in France, the course of studies had lasted for twelve years: five years in the humanities, including Low and High Figures, Grammar, Syntax, Poetry, and Rhetoric, followed by two years of philosophy, and four years of theology. However, in the early 1970s, the Bishops of England and Wales made an important decision to reorganize priestly training in the North of England. This led to a new era, in which all the junior seminarians, from low Figures to Rhetoric, pursued their studies at Upholland College, and all of the senior seminarians studied their Theology and Philosophy at Ushaw College, Co. Durham.

The Sixth Form rooms were situated over two floors, with a priest member of staff having his living quarters at the end of each corridor, in order to watch over the students. My room was a decent size. The floor was covered with extremely old and very brittle Lino, and there were two large sash windows overlooking a large quadrangle framed by a pair of timeworn, paper-thin, and uneven curtains. The furniture was functional and consisted of a large Edwardian bureau with a hinged writing flap, a mahogany wardrobe, an old captain's chair, a sink with large brass taps, and a very high nineteenth-century black-framed former hospital bed. I felt like Nicholas Nickleby arriving at 'Dotheboys Hall,' and the look on my mother's face told me that she was thinking the same. Years later, she told me that, on seeing my room, she just wanted to turn around and take me home, and, with hindsight, maybe she should have done.

My first few weeks at Upholland were tough; I could have no visits from home, but I could receive letters, which were handed out in the refectory at lunchtime. After what seemed like an eternity (but, in reality, was only a few days), a letter arrived from home. I couldn't wait to get back to my room and read it. But, as soon as I had closed the door, sat on my bed, and read the first line, I burst into tears. I suppose, all the pain and loneliness of leaving home and having to settle into a totally new way of life with new people had taken its toll. After all, I was only sixteen. Writing this forty years later, I wonder at how young and inexperienced I was. In many ways, I had had a very sheltered childhood, and, because of my faith and early attachment to the Church, I probably hadn't matured as quickly as some other boys had. I wasn't alone, though, as most boys in junior seminary had similar childhoods. In fact, all but three of my new classmates had been at Upholland since they were eleven or twelve years old and knew little else.

Each day began and ended with 'prayer,' in the college chapel, and there was also a daily Mass, the time of which fluctuated. Meals also began and ended with prayer, and the food was plain and predictable. In my very first letter home, I wrote, "It is Sunday night, and at 6.20 p.m., I shall attend church for evening prayer. At 4.45 p.m., I had my tea: two slices of bread and butter and a cup of milk. For dinner, I had two roast potatoes, three slices of meat, gravy, and a glass of water. I had one bread roll with butter, a glass of milk, and some cornflakes for breakfast, but our table had no bowls, so we did without."

In many ways, Upholland was a place of equality and inclusivity, and, as with most boarding schools, the regime was intended to be character-building so as to produce holy priests, or good, upstanding, lay members of the Roman Catholic Church, and, in many ways, it achieved this. The student body consisted of two-thirds Church students, sponsored by their bishop, and one-third lay students, whose parents paid the college fees. Regardless of which group you belonged to, all were treated equally. We were all there to discover God's call for our lives and were encouraged to fervently respond to it.

It would also be true to say that Upholland was a place of contrasts. During the evenings of the Christmas term, I would attend rehearsals for the annual performance of a Gilbert and Sullivan operetta. Having previously received my education in mixed schools, I couldn't help but be surprised to see some of the younger boys dressed as women, as well as a priest or two. It was all new to me and contrasted greatly with the solemn portraits of past headmasters, bishops, and benefactors, who solemnly watched over us as we studied, prayed, and played. I learnt lot about the seriousness of becoming a priest, but, also, that it was ok to have fun. In a strange way, the priests who lived and worked alongside us embodied this contrast; some were great fun and inspirational, whilst others were austere and to be avoided.

Our weekdays were filled with small, intimate, classes, each accommodating no more than six students. This ensured a close-knit learning environment, where the student-teacher ratio was excellent. Occasionally, our lessons would take place in the private rooms of the priests, and, sometimes, we would study while munching homemade biscuits and drinking coffee. Both Tuesday and Thursday afternoons were dedicated to sports; we had a variety of options, including football, cricket, and even canoeing on the larger of the two lakes. We were also fortunate to have a full-sized nine-hole golf course, and, within the first few weeks, I joined the golf club and spent most of my sports afternoons playing a round or two with some classmates. Our sports activities also often spilled over into Saturday afternoons, and it was not uncommon for one of the priests, Fr. Michael Higginbottom, our physics teacher, to join us.

The college had a total of thirteen teaching staff with ten of them being priests. Additionally, the Procurator of the college was a priest, and there was also a bishop and a composer of Church music, Fr. Ernest Sands, living in the college. The only female presence in the building was represented by the French and Art teachers, College Matron, and Domestic Staff, who were responsible for cooking, cleaning, and doing our laundry. There were very strict rules regarding interactions with others. Speaking to the domestic staff was discouraged unless it was for a specific request about washing or food. Members of the Sixth Form were further prohibited from speaking to those in the 'lower school,' and there were severe consequences for breaking this rule. The aim was to prevent the formation of 'particular friendships,' as they were often referred to, especially between older boys and younger ones. There was an ever-present fear of anything sexual taking place. But, ironically, it wasn't the upper school that was a threat to the lower school, but some of the priests themselves.

In the Sixth Form, we were fortunate to have sinks in our rooms, but the communal showers were in a large room in the basement. On either side of the door were two wooden cubicles housing large cast iron baths, none of which had plugs, so toilet paper was used to block the drain. Along one wall, there was a bench for depositing clothes, and, on the other side, there were about twenty shower heads, each around two feet apart. There were no partitions, so all the boys had to shower together, regardless of age. An eighteen-year-old student wasn't permitted to talk to a fifteen-year-old, but he was allowed to shower with him.

Furthermore, as if this wasn't embarrassing enough, a priest would often walk around, checking everything, and it was almost always Fr. Higginbottom, particularly on sports afternoons. Everyone was wary of him as he had the reputation of being a strict disciplinarian and was undoubtedly the most unpopular priest on the staff. I only had one proper run-in with him. I had taken a canoe out on the lake without 'his' permission, but very soon it began to fill with water, causing it to become unstable and capsize. I was left with no choice but to swim back to the landing stage where I was met by Fr. Higginbottom, with a sly grin on his face. My punishment was to spend the next Wednesday afternoon, which was normally free time, cleaning every single drain around the college of the dead leaves, and whatever else was lying in them, needless to say there were a great many.

Often, Higginbottom would sneak about at night with another member of staff, who was contactable via a walkie-talkie. Their sole aim was to catch someone, anyone, out of their room after lights out. It was as if he spent all his spare time looking for minor misdemeanors that he could punish tenfold. There was always lots of gossip about Fr. Higginbottom, from hitting boys with a length of rubber Bunsen burner tubing to giving out electric shocks in Chemistry classes. As a rule, he tended to pick on those boys who were gentle and quiet, the ones who didn't particularly enjoy football or cricket, the ones he could bully and, unfortunately, sexually abuse, without any fear of repercussion, or so he thought.

Sadly, he wasn't the only one. Not long after arriving at Upholland I encountered another priest with a dubious reputation. He approached me in the corridor, hugged me tightly, whilst claiming to be my grandfather's half-cousin. So as soon as I got the chance, I asked my grandad, and he confirmed it. He went on to tell me how this priest-cousin used to visit him at his 'cash-and-carry' in Preston to get some free sweets to give to the children in his parish. This family connection appeared to give him an excuse to hug me at any opportunity. He would often grab me and pull me into his pot belly, which felt like molestation disguised as a friendly cuddle. I recall his peculiar smell, the stubble of his chin against my cheek, and, occasionally, feeling something hard pressing against me. It was clear that hugging teenage boys turned him on.

I clearly wasn't the only one he 'hugged,' as, amongst the student body, he was not-so-affectionately known as 'Grasper.' It's strange how some of life's experiences remain as physical memory. Writing about it now, many years later, I can still feel the same repulsion and shame that I felt at the time, and it isn't pleasant.

Each evening, after dinner and night prayer, it was usual for students to gather in one of the priest's rooms to unwind, watch television, or play board games. It created a kind of homely atmosphere, but, like anything, it could also be misused, as two of my classmates and I discovered. Fr. Ernest Sands, who was known to us as Ernie, was a well-known composer of Church music and had written several popular hymns. He often used to 'try out' his compositions on the students during choir practice in church. I remember him once saying to a struggling student, "If God has given you a lousy voice, then make sure that He gets to hear it." These kinds of humorous remarks, delivered with his trademark wit, never failed to amuse us. He was always the entertainer and loved being in the spotlight. *The Canterbury Dictionary of Hymnology* describes him as a "bucolic, witty and charismatic priest and composer." It goes on to say that "Ernie Sands sprang to fame and ultimately (in the USA) notoriety as the composer of 'Sing of the Lord's goodness,' described by one critic as a 'rip-off from Dave Brubeck's 'Take Five.'"

In fact, "Sing of the Lord's goodness" was chosen for the enthronement in 1991 of the Archbishop of Canterbury, George Carey. Before his ordination to the priesthood in 1973 for the diocese of Shrewsbury, Ernie Sands had attended school at St. Bede's College in Manchester, followed by seminary studies at the English College, Lisbon, and the Venerable English College, Rome. He also studied for a doctorate at the Graduate Theological Union (G.T.U.), Berkeley, California, but never finished his dissertation.

Instead, he devoted his energy to writing several books on music and ministry.

Ernie, who wasn't officially part of the staff, often travelled to America and spent extended periods away from the college. One time, when he returned from the United States, I clearly remember him cruising up the long college driveway in a white M.G. sports car with the top down. Clad in a stylish white clerical shirt and suit, he resembled a trendy Pope in a sleek little Pope Mobile. Ernie exuded an extraordinary level of self-confidence, and his bold and unconventional nature made him stand out.

As seventeen-year-old boys, we found his rebellious spirit captivating, so when the thirty-seven-year-old Ernie invited two friends and myself to his room after supper, we eagerly accepted. His sitting room was adorned with a grand marble fireplace, substantial mahogany bookcases, an impressive oak desk, and several inviting chairs where we relaxed. Although the details of our conversations have faded over the last forty years, I distinctly recall his earnest efforts to earn our trust and be 'one of the lads.' He achieved this by regaling us with risqué jokes, treating us to expensive brandy, and offering us enormous Churchill cigars. In our youthful naivety, we felt like the chosen few, unaware that his actions were a form of grooming. Looking back, it was inappropriate, and he cautioned us to keep our visits confidential. Despite this, we frequented his room for drinks, cigars, and daring conversations, until an unwitting action on the part of my friend and I greatly upset him.

Among the students he was affectionately referred to as "Porky Sands," although the reason behind this nickname still remains a mystery. One day, my friend and I stumbled across an empty packet of pork scratching's, and we decided that it would be amusing to cut out the word "Pork" and affix it to the nameplate on his door, as a lighthearted prank. Unfortunately, Ernie didn't see the funny side and demanded to know who was responsible. It soon became evident that we had unintentionally hit a sensitive spot. Suddenly, the jovial, up-for-a-laughErnie didn't like it when the joke was on him.

On top of our normal schedule of prayer, study, and rest, we would occasionally receive visits from local parish clergy who would talk to us about the life we were aspiring to. They would share insights into the busy daily timetable of a parish priest, including weddings, funerals, and baptisms. They would always stress the importance of prayer by warning us that as soon as a priest stops praying and spending time with God, his vocation will begin to suffer, which, in turn, will lead to struggles with loneliness and the possibility of engaging in 'unhealthy behaviors.'

I recall one occasion when I nipped to the toilet at the half-time break. No sooner was I standing at the urinal when in walked the visiting priest, exclaiming, "*So this is where the big knobs hang out is it*," followed by a hearty laugh. As if that wasn't disconcerting enough, once he had finished relieving himself, he tapped on the side of the urinal with his knuckles in order to show that he was so well-endowed that he couldn't help but hit the sides of the urinal whilst shaking off the drops. This might sound like a joke, but it shocked and confused me; how could this priest, who just minutes before had spoken so fervently about prayer and living a holy life, joke with me in such a sexual way? The hypocrisy was clear, and any respect I had for him vanished.

A Sexual Abuse trial and a Suicide

In 1998, a decade after he had left Upholland, Fr. Michael Higginbottom was appointed parish priest of St. Augustine's R.C. Church in Darlington. He earned a reputation among his parishioners for being respectable and hard-working. So, it came as asurprise to them when, in 2004, he was suspended from his parish. Fr. Higginbottom stated that he could not discuss the details of his suspension for "legal reasons," and his absence caused great anger and disappointment among his parishioners. Even Euro-MP, Stephen Hughes, criticized the Church for its "farcical" handling of the case, saying that "all of the parishioners feel that Fr. Michael has not seen justice."[1] A spokesperson for the diocese of Hexham and Newcastle responded, expressing that "the distress felt by parishioners and friends of Father Michael was also felt by the bishop," and while not intending to be unhelpful, he was unable to make any further comments.[2]

    Almost ten years of speculation went by before the true nature of the suspension became clear. After decades of silence, a victim of Higginbottom opened up to a friend about the sexual abuse he had endured as a boy of thirteen at Upholland College in the late 1970s. Understandably, his friend encouraged him to report everything to the police, which he courageously did. He told them that Higginbottom would whip him with a cane or a strap if he were late for an 'appointment,' telling him that he could make this as straightforward or as hard as he liked. He would then be ordered to undress himself before being molested by this 'so-called' man of God, who on many occasions would commit buggery on him, causing him excruciating pain. At other times, amidst tears, he would be forced to perform oral sex on this priest who would tell him that it was good for him, that the devil was inside him and that he, Higginbottom, was the only one who could save him.

---

1. Qtd. in "No Charges, but Priest Still Told to Stay Away from Parish," para. 6.
2. Qtd. in "No Charges, but Priest Still Told to Stay Away from Parish," para. 19.

As a result of this testimony, in 2015, Higginbottom was arrested. When he heard the allegations, he denied them, describing them as "total lies" and saying he did not even remember the boy.[3] Higginbottom admitted to working at the college from 1974 to 1987 and, whilst not being a qualified teacher (few of the priest staff were), had enjoyed his time as a physics master, football coach, and form teacher. He often allowed the boys to make coffee and watch television in his room, adding that it was common practice, but he was never attracted to any of them.

Nevertheless, the case went to trial and Fr. Michael Higginbottom was found guilty on April 12, 2017, of four counts of indecent assault and four counts of buggery. Seven of these were specimen counts, implying that the offences happened on numerous occasions. The following day, at Liverpool Crown Court, he was sentenced to seventeen years' imprisonment for offences the Judge called a "significant and wholesale breach of trust."[4] In summing up, the Judge also spoke of how Higginbottom had targeted the victim and systematically abused him in a calculated manner for his own sexual gratification. Furthermore, the assaults had destroyed his pupil's childhood as well as the religious faith which he had held so dear. He went on to say that Higginbottom's legacy "will only ever be that of a priest who abused a young boy."[5]

Consequently, it came as a huge shock when, in November 2018, the Court of Appeal, Criminal Division, overturned Higginbottom's convictions on the basis that details of fraud by misrepresentation relating to the complainant were not made available to the jury during the original trial. They decided that a retrial should take place and that evidence of the fraud be placed before a jury to assist them in assessing the complainant's credibility.

A re-trial could quite easily have caused Higginbottom's original conviction to have been overruled had not a second complainant come forward to say that he, too, had been abused by Higginbottom in the mid-1980s. He had seen a news report about the trial in 2017, which brought back memories of what he had endured at the hands of Fr. Michael Higginbottom. As a result, during a two-week re-trial at Burnley Crown Court, the jurors heard that Higginbottom "regularly, systematically and horrifically" abused the boys, and "they were both threatened with violence and struck with a strap or a belt."[6]

---

3. Qtd. in "Father Higginbottom," para. 22.
4. Qtd. in Crawford, "Father Michael Higginbotton."
5. Crawford, "Father Michael Higginbotton."
6. PA Reporter, "Priest Who Abused Schoolboys," para. 2.

The seventy-six-year-old Higginbottom was found guilty of "five counts of buggery and seven of indecent assault" and was sentenced to eighteen years in prison, with half of the sentence to be served behind bars and half on license. The Judge told Higginbottom that he abused his position of trust and specifically targeted the boys. He used threats or violence disguised as normal school punishment, leaving the boys with feelings of shame and guilt, and believing that no one would believe them if they complained. The Judge emphasized that the victims were psychologically impacted and still lived with the pain decades later. When Higginbottom passed away on June 5, 2022, after serving only a couple of years of his sentence, most people's thoughts and sympathies were with the victims and their families, highlighting that the passage of time does not protect abusers.

Following the closure of Upholland in 1987, Ernie Sands was in demand as a workshop leader and speaker, and for several years, he was General Secretary of the Department for Christian Life and Worship of the Bishop's Conference of England and Wales. In 1993, along with musical composer, Paul Inwood, he coauthored a guide for producers of religious TV broadcasts, the fruit of several training courses that they had offered across the UK in the late 1980s and '90s. Then, in later years, he withdrew from active ministry and the public eye, dividing his time between a remote cottage in Wales and a friend's apartment in Tenerife on the Canary Islands, which seemed very much out of character. All the same, he was back in the public eye in 2015 when Lancashire Police arrested him on suspicion of historical child sexual abuse involving five boys aged between eleven and fifteen. The allegations related to his time serving as a Catholic priest in the late 1970s and '80s. One of the offences was said to have occurred at Upholland College, while the others occurred at different locations.

The year after, on April 11, Sands was supposed to report to Lancashire Police. However, he never showed up, which raised suspicion. Following a request from Lancashire Police, an officer from Dyfed Powys Police in Wales visited Sands' home in the remote village of Hirnant. Upon reaching the property, the officer noticed that the shed door was open and, upon closer inspection, found Sands' lifeless body inside. After searching the address, a note dated April 10 was discovered on the bed in the main bedroom. The note explained Sands' intention to take his own life and was signed 'Ernie.' In the concluding remarks at the subsequent inquest, the coroner stated, "There is no evidence from the police that anyone else was involved in the events on April 11th of this year, nor is there any evidence to suggest a disturbance at the scene. So, I can conclude with some certainty that Mr. Sands acted deliberately and alone."[7] A verdict of suicide was recorded.

---

7. Qtd. in Mears, "Priest's Suicide," para. 19.

Castlerigg Manor, Keswick

My own time at Upholland came to an end in the summer of 1986. I had experienced and learnt a lot, both good and bad, made some wonderful friends and been accepted to begin studying theology and philosophy at the senior seminary, Ushaw College, Co. Durham, the following October. I was so excited to be progressing along the road to priesthood, and the icing on the cake was that I would be doing so alongside nine of my Upholland classmates, who had also been accepted to study at Ushaw College. The summer break couldn't go quick enough, so I was glad to be distracted by a four-day retreat at Castlerigg Manor, Keswick in the English Lake District. It was a unique opportunity to meet all of the other Lancaster students who were studying in various seminaries, such as Oscott College in Birmingham, Valladolid in Spain, the Venerable English College in Rome and, of course, Ushaw College, Durham. Castlerigg Manor began life as a private mansion but was subsequently purchased by the Diocese of Lancaster and run as a Catholic Youth Centre for school groups. It had lovely grounds, a private chapel and even a bar; it would be an enjoyable few days of prayer, reflection and making new friends, or so I thought.

On the first evening, after dinner and evening prayers, everyone headed to the bar for a relaxing drink at the end of our first day together. The bar was the perfect place in which to socialize and make new friends, friends who would one day be colleagues. I remember, as the evening progressed, chatting with Stephen Shield, a somewhat overweight twenty-six-year-old student from the English College in Rome. I was highly impressed by him, as it was common knowledge that only the best students were chosen to study in Rome. I recall a story he shared with me concerning the previous year's Christmas Pantomime, *Robin Hood*, which was a slight deviation from the usual nativity storyline.

Following the performance, an article appeared in *The Universe*, an English Catholic newspaper, with the headline "Boys will be girls."[1] He explained to me how the leading 'lady,' Maid Marion, had received the 'Miss Universe 1985' award from the Rector for her (his) magnificent performance. This unexpected twist in the story reminded me of seeing Higginbottom and several boys dressed as women in *H.M.S. Pinafore* at Upholland, an image that continued to make me feel uncomfortable.

As the evening drew to a close, everyone began to leave until only Stephen Shield, and I were left. I wanted to go to bed, but he kept talking, and without being rude, I couldn't find a suitable opportunity to go. Eventually, out of shear desperation and tiredness, I attempted to stand up and leave, at which point he jumped up and wrapped me in a tight embrace. Initially, I thought it was just a friendly hug, until he started trying to kiss me, that is. I can still 'feel' his whiskers brushing against my neck and cheek whenever I think about it.

I was shocked to my core, and after a struggle, I managed to escape his grip and rush back to my room, but I could hear him following me. I started to panic as I approached the door to my room, and no sooner had I begun to close it than he forced his way in and shut the door behind him. I was terrified and felt extremely threatened as he began to tell me how much he liked me, and how wonderful I was. Initially, he was full of flattering comments, which made me very uneasy. I was also conscious that he was standing with his back to the door, blocking my exit, and also that sleeping in the room next door was the 'Vocations Director,' whose job it was to guide us on our journey of discernment towards priesthood. The longer he was in my room, the more suggestive he got. He began to talk about what was in my trousers, telling me what he thought it looked like and how much he would love to see it.

I was sick with panic and fear. I just wanted him to leave, but he wouldn't, and I was also terrified of someone hearing him and coming into the room to see what was going on. I wasn't a streetwise eighteen-year-old who would have told him where to go; I was introverted and scared of getting into trouble. I don't know how long he continued to ask me to show him my penis, but it was a considerable amount of time. Once he realized that he wasn't getting anywhere he changed tack and asked if I would just sit next to him on the bed. As this seemed like the lesser of two evils, I

---

1. In *The Venerable* (the Annual Magazine of the English College, Rome), Kenny writes, "Leading panto 'lady' Maid Marion (Simon Peat) receives the 'Miss Universe 1985' award from the Rector after the 'Universe' prints a story about the panto headlined 'Boys will be Girls'. Ad libs come pouring in on this the last night, alternative props as well as alternative lines." Kenny, "Saturday 28th December," 72.

agreed. Yet, no sooner was I sitting beside him than he started again with the appeals. I didn't know what to do; he had his hand on my leg and was rubbing it up and down whilst saying, "Just undo your zip," or "Unfasten your trouser button" and I'll do the rest. And so, unable to see a way out, and to my immense shame, I gave in to his request.

I undid my trousers, but it wasn't enough for him, he wanted more. By now, I felt utterly powerless and so he succeeded in getting me to pull down my trousers and underpants. I don't have the words to describe how appalled I felt then, and how angry it makes me now. It was made infinitely worse, in that being a teenage boy, and for reasons beyond my control, I became aroused. I was frightened and confused; I was heterosexual and had never felt any sexual attraction to men, so why was this happening? How could I be so terrified, opposed to his wishes, yet be aroused? Stephen Shield, on the other hand, was ecstatic and just sat there staring at my penis. To this day, as unbelievable as it may sound, I cannot recall if he touched me or did anything else, I expect that I was so numb with embarrassment, shock and humiliation that my memory has blocked it out. I don't recall him leaving the room, but I know he did at some point.

When I awoke the next day, I couldn't believe what had happened; I just wanted to escape and go home. I was in a daze and believed that everyone else would know what had happened; maybe it was normal behavior in the senior seminary. With great trepidation, I entered the dining room for breakfast and was surprised to find everyone chatting and eating like normal. Even Stephen Shield sat there 'like butter wouldn't melt in his mouth.' He didn't seem to be the slightest bit concerned, embarrassed, or ashamed, at what had happened, so I just sat down and tried to forget and focus on the day ahead.

Thankfully, one of my classmates from Upholland was also at Castlerigg with me. Once you have lived alongside someone for a couple of years, you begin to know them well enough to spot any subtleties in their behavior, and John perceived that something had happened to me. So, after breakfast, I told him in detail all that had happened the previous evening. Initially, he was horrified and disturbed, as like me, he had never encountered anything like this before. But unlike me, his horror turned to anger, and he told me he had a plan, a plan to confront Stephen Shield, and ensure it never happened again.

So that evening, after a few drinks in the bar for courage, John and I positioned ourselves in the large entrance hall, from where we could see the main staircase. Shortly after, Stephen Shield came out of the bar and went up the stairs to his room. We continued to wait a little while, allowing him to fall asleep, before creeping silently up the stairs towards his room. With a nod, John grabbed the handle, and we entered the dark room. Shield was in bed, but as soon as he saw us, he sat bolt upright in shock. John then took charge and in his anger shouted, "If you effing do that again, I'll smash your effing face in, after which we both turned on our heels and quickly left the room.

High on adrenalin, we made for the bar, bought another drink, and returned to the foyer to discuss the evening's events. Sometime later, as we were sitting in the dark, the fire door at the top of the stairs creaked open, and Stephen Shield stood there, carrying his bag. He quickly descended the stairs, crept across the hallway and slipped out of the large front door, quietly closing it behind him, before scurrying off into the night.

The following morning, at breakfast, the Vocations Director went from table to table, asking if anyone had seen Stephen Shield, who appeared to be missing. Of course, no one had, and John and I just kept silent. In fact, I kept quiet for almost two decades, but I never forgot what Stephen Shield had done and the memory of him leering at me and wanting to touch me has had a hugely negative impact on my life, particularly on my spiritual life, which was, and still is, central to everything that I stand for.

Ushaw College 1986

In October of 1986, I arrived at Ushaw College, and, in spite of the traumatic experience at Castlerigg Manor, I was just as committed to my religious life. However, the summer had left me feeling vulnerable, lacking in confidence, and confused. I knew that what had happened was wrong, but I was afraid that no one else would believe me, especially since Stephen Shield was a student at the prestigious English College, Rome. Furthermore, I was terrified of being thrown out because I truly believed that God was calling me to the priesthood, and I couldn't imagine living any other life. I was always obedient, considerate, and kind, and I trusted and respected those in authority. Causing trouble simply wasn't in my nature and I think this made me an easy target for some of the more predatory homosexual students at Ushaw. It would be true to say that many of the men who were abused in the seminary were similar to me in personality and outlook, that is to say, quiet, and unlikely to cause a scene.

Even though I had never visited Ushaw previously, it felt like home to me, as I was the thirty-sixth member of my family to study for the priesthood at Ushaw. Knowing that so many of my relatives had studied there before me gave me a strong sense of belonging and I wasn't prepared to let Stephen Shield spoil that, no matter what he did. I used to enjoy having my meals underneath the watchful gaze of some of my relatives' portraits hanging on the refectory walls. I've always been passionate about history, especially the history of the English Roman Catholic Church during penal times. So, I was thrilled to find out that our first course in the seminary would be "The History of the Church in the Twentieth Century," followed by "The Theology of the Church." After that, we would be studying both the New and Old Testaments, Philosophy, and the year would draw to a close with Epistemology (the theory of knowledge or the relation of the mind to reality). It was going to be a very full academic year, but one I was greatly looking forward to.

In many ways, life at Ushaw was similar to life at Upholland. Our schedule included daily Mass, morning, evening, and night prayers, as well as lectures and private study. I suppose that the main difference was the increased independence we were given at Ushaw. We had free afternoons and could visit the local pub in the evenings or relax in the college bar when it was open. On most Saturday afternoons we would explore Durham and maybe visit the beautiful twelfth-century cathedral or do some shopping for small luxuries, like decent coffee or biscuits.

Another significant difference between Ushaw and Upholland was the diverse student body, made up of men of varying ages and professional backgrounds. Many were in their twenties or thirties and came from professions such as office workers, police officers, teachers, solicitors, and shop assistants. Additionally, many of them had already attended various universities or colleges before starting life at the seminary and so were used to academic life. Unfortunately, for those of us attending Ushaw straight from Upholland, our lack of worldly experience made us more susceptible to grooming and abuse by some of the more predatory members of the student body.

I imagine that the majority of people would expect a Roman Catholic seminary to be a place of exemplary behavior and safety. Where good men strive to outdo each other, not in wealth or academic prowess, but in compassion and kindness. Men of true faith and deep prayer, ready to go out into the world, and teach the good news of the Gospel of Jesus Christ. And while the majority of students were, I believe, genuinely seeking God, there were some for whom seeking God had become no more than a cover for sexual predation and often they were the ones who, externally at least, appeared to be the most holy and devout, but of course it was all show.

The problem with the seminary system at the time was that it allowed these sorts of behaviors to exist unchallenged, and it wasn't only the students who were inclined to such double standards. Several of the staff were also prone to gathering groups of 'admirers' around themselves, thereby creating a very unhealthy atmosphere of in-crowds and favoritism. While it is generally limiting to categorize people by their sexuality, it is fair to say that there was a noticeably 'gay subculture' in existence at Ushaw, and an extremely unhealthy one at that.

Such subgroups, within any community, would be classed as being divisive and unjust in their effects, and, when it comes to the priesthood, they represent the total opposite to the openness and transparency that is expected of followers of Christ. For example, it was common for some students to give each other female names, and it wasn't unknown for seminarians to frequent Newcastle's gay nightclubs at the weekends. In fact, the very year before I commenced my studies at Ushaw, several students had traveled to Newcastle in one of the college minibuses and parked it right outside a gay nightclub before going in to enjoy their evening. Much to their regret, the minibus was spotted, and all but one of them was expelled. On another occasion, two students, who had overindulged in the college bar, became quite amorous in the refectory over dinner. As soon as the meal was ended the two of them went off to a room and commenced having sex with no intention whatsoever of keeping it quiet. In fact, things got so loud that a neighbor started to play his music at full volume, in order to drown out the noise. Unfortunately, it ended up having the opposite effect of drawing a larger crowd.

It may come as a surprise then to learn that officially the Roman Catholic Church is strictly opposed to ordaining gay men to the priesthood, citing the belief that homosexual acts are sinful in the eyes of God. However, studies by such respected figures as A.W. Richard Sipe[1] and Fr. Donald Cozzens,[2] estimate that not only is there a significant percentage of homosexual men within the Roman Catholic priesthood, but that they probably outnumber those who are heterosexual. Yet, in spite of such evidence, the Church continues to issue documents outlining the various restrictions on ordaining men with, as they would put it, "deep-seated homosexual tendencies."[3]

As recently as 2018, Pope Francis expressed a clear stance on the issue of homosexuality in the church in a book-length interview titled *The Strength of a Vocation*. He stated that individuals with ingrained homosexual tendencies should not be accepted into the ministry or consecrated life. He urged homosexual priests and men and women religious to live celibacy with integrity and to be impeccably responsible, emphasizing that it's better for them to leave the ministry or consecrated life rather than to live a double life. Therefore, the real challenge lies in the failure of seminaries to adequately prepare students for managing celibacy while dealing with sexual feelings.

In actual fact, and somewhat surprisingly, I don't ever recall receiving any formal education on sexuality and celibacy throughout the six years that I spent in seminary. Of course, there was the occasional mention of Church documents on celibacy, such as Pope St. Paul VI's *Sacerdotalis Coelibatus* [Encyclical Letter on the Celibacy of Priests], or Pope St. John Paul II's *Pastores dabo vobis* [Post-Synodal Apostolic Exhortation on the Formation of Priests in the Circumstances of the Present Day]. The primary focus

---

1. Sipe, *Celibacy in Crisis*, 51.
2. Cozzens, *Changing Face of the Priesthood*, 21.
3. Congregation for Catholic Education, *Instruction,* para. 2.

of Seminary education was on academics, pastoral work, and spirituality, with very little emphasis on personal growth. Needless to say, we did have regular one-to-one sessions with the Spiritual Director, but they too had been educated and formed within the same system and so were relatively inexperienced when it came to questions of sexuality.

Naturally, not all occurrences of sexual abuse in the Catholic Church can be directly attributed to inadequate seminary training. Yet, there are several factors associated with seminary formation that could, in some way, contribute to the vulnerability of seminarians and priests to perpetrating sexual abuse.

I think it would be true to say that the seminary environment does have a strong tendency to foster repression and secrecy around the whole area of sexuality and thereby creates unrealistic expectations for celibacy. There is, on the whole, a total lack of open discussion around the area of sexual desires and impulses, and so those seminarians who are striving to live a celibate life are left to suppress their natural urges without adequate support. This, in turn, can often lead to unhealthy coping mechanisms, such as pornography, masturbation, inappropriate relationships, both inside and outside the seminary, and the list goes on. Furthermore, the structure of seminaries, which suppresses normal sexual development, can contribute to psychosexual immaturity among seminarians. This immaturity can sometimes manifest itself in inappropriate and abusive behavior, especially when the student is faced with sexual temptations or challenges in their future ministry outside of the seminary.

On top of that, the seminary system intentionally isolates seminarians from the real world, thereby limiting their interactions with women and other social and cultural influences. Such an absence of healthy socialization can hinder the development of appropriate boundaries and interpersonal skills, both of which are essential qualities for anyone working in a pastoral, people-centered environment. The result of this is that seminarians and priests are often more susceptible to engaging in abusive behavior. What's more, seminary training does not adequately prepare future priests to address issues related to human sexuality and sexual abuse in the parish. The focus on academics, pastoral work, and spirituality neglects the practical skills and knowledge necessary to navigate complex sexual dynamics and provide appropriate support and guidance to parishioners and victims of abuse. Heartbreakingly, this often results in the Church downplaying sexual abuse by using euphemisms like 'inappropriate conduct' or 'boundary violations,' thereby focusing on the vulnerability of the adult rather than the actions of the abusive and psychosexually immature cleric.

At this point, it is important to emphasize that not all priests who undergo seminary training engage in sexual abuse. Sexual abuse is a complex issue influenced by various individual, societal, and institutional factors. However, I do believe that the seminary environment and formation process does contribute to the vulnerability of some priests to engage in abusive behavior. Fortunately, efforts have been made in recent years to enhance seminary training and address these issues. It would seem that seminarians are now encouraged to develop a deep understanding of their own sexuality, including their desires, attractions, and emotions. Such self-awareness will help them to navigate their celibate life and therefore make informed choices. Hopefully, they are also guided towards accepting their sexuality as an integral part of their identity. This will involve them embracing their sexual desires and attractions without any shame or guilt while, at the same time, recognizing their call to celibacy and finding ways to express their sexuality in a chaste and appropriate manner. The focus must always be on understanding healthy boundaries, developing self-control, and channeling sexual energy towards their vocation and service to others. In essence, the goal is to help seminarians integrate their sexuality into their whole person, thereby fostering a healthy and balanced approach to celibate living. If the system had focused more on relationships and friendships, self-knowledge, integrity, and celibate chastity in the past, then it could have been more successful at producing fully grounded, sexually mature men for the priesthood. This, in turn, would have hopefully resulted in less grooming and abuse taking place both inside and outside of the seminary system.

For example, I can recall, on more than one occasion, standing outside the refectory waiting to go in for supper, when suddenly I would feel a hand rubbing and squeezing my bottom. Unfortunately, we didn't queue in a formal line at mealtimes, it was more of a large crowd, so it was relatively easy for someone to inappropriately touch you without being seen, and it wasn't uncommon. On another occasion, I remember ordering a drink at the college bar when a deacon in his final few months of college and who was standing beside me began stroking the back of my hand whilst at the same time offering to pay for my drink. I was shaken. Not only was it unwelcome, it was also very visible and anyone could have seen him doing it. I quickly paid for my own drink and left the bar as soon as possible.

These sorts of things were pretty standard; on some bar nights, if it hadn't been for the large crucifix and a photo of the pope on the wall, you could have been mistaken for thinking that you were in a gay bar. It was that obvious! I remember walking around the college grounds one afternoon when I happened to look up at the 'East Wing,' an accommodation block built in the 1960s. To my utter astonishment, right before my eyes, were two students standing completely naked in front of one of the windows. Furthermore, it was abundantly clear what was going on, as they made no attempt to hide it. In fact, I later discovered that it was common knowledge that the two of them were in a sexual relationship, but nothing was ever said or done about it. Only one of them eventually made it to ordination and he is still in ministry to this day.

As my first year at Ushaw came to a close I began, possibly for the first time, to question my vocation. I had real concerns about what had happened to me at Castlerigg Manor and about the secretive and abusive nature of seminary life. Being shut away from the society that I would one day serve, didn't sit comfortably with me at all. It just didn't seem to make sense. How would I be able to understand the day-to-day joys and difficulties of ordinary men and women, if my preparation required me to live in a comfortable little clerical bubble, a sort of camp gentlemen's club, where belonging meant everything, and being outside was kind of second rate? I needed time to think, and so I decided to wait until after the summer break before making any major decisions about my future.

Having said that, it was customary, as part of our seminary training, to spend one month of our summer break experiencing parish life. But, one month was nowhere near enough to have any real impact, and living alongside clergy meant that it wasn't any different to being in seminary. I was assigned to The English Martyrs Church in Preston, where Canon Taylor, an experienced and somewhat traditional Parish Priest, would be there to guide me. He had trained in Rome, prior to the Second Vatican Council, and expected me, a nineteen-year-old, to wear a clerical collar when visiting parishioners. While I understood the reasoning behind it (that it would help people identify me as a church representative), I felt uncomfortable with the effect it had on how others treated me, even in public. Preston was traditionally a very Catholic town, and the clergy commanded great respect. I couldn't shake off the feeling that I was being inauthentic. I felt unworthy! There I was, walking through the streets of Preston dressed like a priest, knowing that Stephen Shield had abused me, and furthermore, I had also been touched and caressed by several students at Ushaw. Of course, I now know that none of it was my fault, but back then I didn't have such clarity. I wondered if I was to blame, was there something about me which attracted such unwanted behavior, had I in some way solicited it? All of this caused me mental torment and distress, and I didn't enjoy my time in Preston at all.

With the end of the summer break, I half-heartedly decided to return to Ushaw for my second year. Initially it was great to be back with my friends and to catch up on all of the holiday gossip over a pint in the local pub. But, once the novelty of being back had worn off, I knew deep down that I couldn't remain; my soul felt damaged, burdened by the weight of expectations and the pressure to conform to an image that now seemed corrupt to me. As a result, I contacted my Bishop and asked if I could have some 'time out.' At first, he wanted me to take one year off seminary, but I felt it wasn't long enough. So, he agreed that as long as I kept him informed of where I was and what I was doing, my 'time out' could be open-ended. Relieved, I decided to leave on December 19, 1987, just before Christmas.

Years out and more abuse

After leaving Ushaw, I somewhat naively believed that I would easily reintegrate into my previous life at home with my parents and be able to leave the trauma of abuse behind me. How wrong could I have been? As the reality proved to be much more complex. The four years that I spent, from the age of sixteen to twenty, in an all-male, misogynistic and mainly homosexual environment, had a permanent impact on me. Instead of experiencing the usual confusion and self-discovery of adolescence, I was living in an environment of strict rules and conformity, which stunted the journey towards independence that should have characterized that period in my life. I began to develop negative beliefs about myself, which in turn led to a lack of self-confidence. Relating to others, especially my family and friends, was hard, and I had difficulty expressing my emotions and sharing how I really felt. Resentment began to consume me, and within one month of returning home, I left again.

Through a contact, I had managed to get in touch with a religious sister who worked for a charity called the DePaul Trust, UK. Upon hearing my story and the challenges I was facing, she generously offered me a room in a hostel for people experiencing homelessness in Heaton, Newcastle. Despite my internal struggle, I decided to accept the offer, as it was a chance for me to start anew while still remaining close to the familiar surroundings of Newcastle, Durham, and my friends at Ushaw. I may have moved out of Ushaw, but in no way had I moved on.

I arrived in Newcastle in early January 1988, hoping to settle into my new home. However, I found it challenging and felt very isolated. During the day I would wander around Newcastle, and in the evenings I would sit in my room, reflecting on my life, writing my thoughts in a journal, and listening to the radio. Over time, I started to harbor further negative beliefs about myself, stemming from the shame and guilt that I was carrying. Some evenings, when my internal struggles became intolerable, I'd buy the largest bottle of wine I could afford, drink the lot, and then wander into the city center, visiting various pubs and clubs until I had forgotten my pain. Miraculously, I always managed to make it back home but seldom remembered how.

On one particularly memorable day, I received a letter from a friend at Ushaw, inviting me to spend the weekend there, and I leapt at the opportunity. I arrived on a Friday evening in late January, and it felt comforting to be back on familiar ground with people I knew. I had only been away a month, but it felt much longer. Everyone was thrilled to see me and some even treated me to a pint in the college bar, but I couldn't shake the feeling that I no longer belonged. Apart from our shared memories, I soon became aware that I no longer had much in common with anyone and that realization left me feeling empty and sad. I did try to make the most of the visit, enjoying the chance to catch up and reminisce, but the pain and trauma were never far away.

On Sunday, as lunch was drawing to an end, a former classmate approached the table and invited me to his room for a coffee after lunch. I was somewhat surprised, as he wasn't someone that I was particularly close to, or even considered a friend. So, in my uncertainty, I decided to ignore the invitation and returned to my own room. Nevertheless, he was determined, and after about half an hour there was a knock on my door and in he walked, expressing his disappointment that I hadn't accepted the invite. Feeling under pressure I apologized and agreed to join him in a few minutes. Arriving at his door I gave a quick knock and he immediately shouted for me to enter. But, as soon as I was inside he locked the door behind me with a key, and despite it only being mid-afternoon the curtains were drawn and only a desk lamp illuminated the room.

It all seemed very odd, and as I nervously sat down he began making the coffee. I didn't know him very well, as there had been thirty-three students in my year and he wasn't generally someone I associated with. All I knew was that he was from Gibraltar and his family were good friends with his bishop. He began by making small talk, asking me how I was managing since leaving college and appearing genuinely concerned. At Ushaw, the college provided everything we needed and so he wanted to know if I was ok for money. I told him that I was, but he didn't seem convinced. He then pointed to an envelope on a shelf, which he said contained a cheque for twenty-five pounds, which was mine if I would allow him to perform oral sex on me. I was stunned and made it clear that under no circumstances was that going to happen. I could see that he was taken aback and beginning to become agitated, so I tried to change the subject, but to no avail. He offered me more money and again I refused. This went on for some time, until eventually he sat down beside me on his small, two-seater settee and offered me one hundred and twenty-five pounds. By now he was highly agitated and covered in sweat. I believed that at any moment he was going to get violent and punch me as his fists were clenched and he was shaking. In frustration he aggressively said, "Just lie on the bed, close your eyes and pretend I am a woman. I have had loads of lads in this room and there has never been a problem." Thankfully, at that very moment, there was a knock on the door. As he couldn't really ignore it, he reluctantly went over and unlocked it. A classmate stepped into the room and appeared to instantly know what was going on. Much to my surprise, he said that he wanted to see me and asked if I would come immediately with him. I didn't need asking twice; I was out of the room in a shot.

Once in the corridor, the other student, who could see that I was traumatized, asked if I would like to have afternoon tea with him in the refectory, to which I agreed. Just before going in, I decided to nip to the toilet, and no sooner was I standing at the urinal than in walked the Gibraltarian student. He stood in the doorway, tall, overweight and intimidating, declaring "You've got it out now, so why don't you just turn around and let me see?" I refused, and then he said, "What would you do if I came over right now and grabbed you?" I answered, "I don't know," as I quickly fastened my trousers. Then, he moved towards me and made a grab for my waist, and even though he was large and heavy, I managed to spin around and push him so hard that he fell backwards into one of the toilet cubicles. I didn't wait to see if he was ok; I just ran out and went straight to the refectory where, thankfully, some of my Upholland classmates were sitting together at a table, so I joined them. Instantly, they knew that something was wrong. I was shaking and all of the color had drained from my face. As soon as I began to tell them what had happened, they told me I wasn't the first; others had suffered the same. All were younger than him, and in fact two of them were part of our Upholland group. So, as soon as tea was over, I tracked them down and told them of my experience, and as I was leaving the following day, they agreed that the two of them would report him to the College President, which they did, and he was dismissed from Ushaw.

Five years later, I was in conversation with a priest when suddenly he asked, "Guess who I bumped into in Rome this summer?" Needless to say, I didn't have a clue, and so it came as a complete shock when he said the name of this Gibraltarian student. Apparently, after having been thrown out of Ushaw with a reference stating that the college would not recommend him for ordination, his bishop (totally ignoring it) enrolled him in a seminary in Rome, from where he was ordained a priest in 1992. Moreover, he is still working as a priest now, thirty-two years later, in Spain.

About thirty years later, I spoke of what had happened to me to the Safeguarding Coordinator of Lancaster Diocese and initially, at least, I believed that they were taking me seriously. At that time, the Diocese of Gibraltar was without a bishop, so the diocese was being administered by Bishop Ralph Heskett C.SS. R who had been appointed Apostolic Administrator of Gibraltar on July 10, 2014, the same day as he was installed Bishop of Hallam Diocese. He ceased being Administrator of Gibraltar in September 2016. I was told that the Safeguarding Coordinator passed on my statement to Bishop Heskett but, to this dayin 2025, I have had no response. I have asked the Safeguarding Coordinator for an update on more than one occasion, but I have yet to receive a proper answer, which makes me suspect that nothing has been done and nothing ever will be.

When I returned to my lodgings in Newcastle, I felt utterly lost and alone, filled with guilt and shame. I started to believe that something must be wrong with me, otherwise why had these things happened? Was I somehow causing them? I felt weak; why didn't I physically defend myself? Stephen Shield and the Gibraltarian were both effeminate and overweight, so how did I allow this to happen? I was punishing myself both mentally and physically, I felt tortured. For the next couple of months I drank myself into oblivion almost every day. It was the only way, so I thought, to forget what had happened. But the drink just caused me to sink deeper into my pain. I even began to self-harm, cutting my arms and hands as a further means of punishment. I didn't see anyone until one day my parents unexpectedly turned up and immediately saw that I was struggling. They suggested that I go back home to them, and I agreed.

To begin with, I managed to get a job with an Insurance Company, but I only lasted three months. I couldn't settle or focus and being tied to a desk all day doing paperwork and answering the telephone just wasn't me. I needed something with human contact and, luckily, I saw an advert for a job in a hotel in the Lake District; I applied and was accepted. I loved working there. It was a small hotel/pub in the picturesque village of Hawkshead and very soon I made friends and became part of the village community. Gradually, I began to put all the pain of abuse behind me and move on with my life, though, in reality, it was just being bottled up and stored away somewhere deep inside of me.

After a year or so of living and working in Hawkshead, I started attending a Roman Catholic mass each Saturday evening in a transept of the Anglican village church. It began at 6 p.m., the same time as my shift behind the bar, but I got permission to start at 6.30 p.m. on Saturdays. Word spread around the village that I had previously been studying for the priesthood and so my attending mass was no great surprise. I was lucky in that I never blamed God for what had happened to me, and in many ways, my faith was more vital than ever, a more mature faith perhaps? This weekly dose of religion started me thinking about priesthood again. The priest who said the mass, Fr. Bede, was a Benedictine monk stationed in the village of Coniston, a few miles away. I got on well with him and had many conversations with him about my vocation, though I never mentioned the abuse I had suffered. He encouraged me to get back in touch with the bishop. After all, I hadn't left, just taken time out, so I hesitantly wrote a letter and posted it a few days later.

English Martyrs Church, Preston

It wasn't long before I received a reply from the Vocations Director, and I was surprised to discover that he was my old headmaster from Upholland. He came to visit me just before Christmas 1991, and together we decided that instead of working in the pub until the following October (when I would hopefully return to Ushaw) I should work for six months at The English Martyrs Church in Preston with Canon Taylor—the same church where I had spent my summer parish placement back in 1987. So, in January 1992 I left village life in Hawkshead for good and returned to parish life in Preston. I was happy to see Canon Taylor when he welcomed me at the door and ushered me in, but my joy quickly turned to dread and dismay when there, in the hallway, stood Stephen Shield, wearing a clerical shirt and smiling at me. Seeing him made me feel physically sick and the thought of having to live in the same house as him was almost unbearable. Were it not for my desire to become a priest, I would have turned on the spot and left immediately, but I felt trapped. Stephen Shield was not only now a priest, but he was also the parish curate. Therefore, it would be much easier for the Church to get rid of me than him, so I gritted my teeth and went to my room. As the weeks passed, I found that I could avoid him most of the time apart from daily mass and mealtimes. Alongside Canon Taylor, Stephen Shield, and myself, two more priests, and another student lived in the house. Stephen Shield and the student were great pals and spent a lot of time together, so I was left to myself as the priests were all busy with their own business, which suited me fine, and as time went on I began to settle down and feel more at home.

Every twenty years, the town of Preston celebrates its Guild Day, which began in 1179 with King Henry II granting Preston its first royal charter and establishing the right to have a Merchant Guild. All the local churches take part in the parade, after which there are many costumes and props to be stored away. Behind the High Altar of the English Martyrs Church was a room containing an enormous wooden chest full of objects from previous Preston Guild's. Canon Taylor wanted it cleaned out and so he asked myself and Stephen Shield to clean it, and surprisingly it went okay. He was pretty chatty and polite and made no mention of Castlerigg Manor or what took place there. We just got on with the job, which turned out to be quite interesting to me as a lover of anything historical, for this vast chest was full of old costumes and religious props dating back at least sixty years.

To this day, I still have trouble understanding why I never told anyone what happened at Castlerigg or mentioned it at the time. The only thing I remember is the fear of not being believed and it backfiring on me. I had full faith in my vocation, my calling from God, but I was also fully aware that its outcome depended mainly on the opinions of those in charge of my formation. Abusers also know this and that is how they get away with it. I firmly believed in the Gospel and what Jesus taught about forgiveness, but I also acknowledged my limitations. I couldn't forgive Stephen Shield and the student from Gibraltar, and this only added to my guilt and despair. All I could pray was, "Lord, I can't do this! You'll have to take over," and in a way, this simple act of surrender, allowed me to find some relief and move forward, one day at a time.

Not long after Easter, in mid-April, Canon Taylor went away for a break leaving Stephen Shield in charge. The house was Victorian and had a grand dining room with a large mahogany table that would comfortably seat over a dozen people. So, Shield decided to make use of it and host an evening for some of his friends. I helped to set the table and decorate the room whilst the German cook prepared the meal. Only the finest silver cutlery and candlesticks, the best crystal glasses, and decanters, as well as place cards and linen napkins were to be used, and by the time we had finished the room rivalled any stately home. He also insisted that we wear formal dress, so reluctantly I wore a jacket and tie. I remember being one of the last to enter the dining room, as I didn't know any of his clergy friends, and discovered, to my horror, that he had seated me right beside himself. I felt so uncomfortable being made to sit there, but with a dozen priests around the table I didn't have the courage to cause a scene. I felt awkward and shy and only really spoke if someone asked me a question. Thankfully, there was another student who I knew there, but he was sat on the other side of the table and not directly opposite me.

As soon as the main course was over and everyone was chatting, I felt Stephen Shield's left hand on my lower back and then on the outside of my trousers, trying to slip under my bottom. I was seized with panic but somehow managed to keep eating. This went on for some time, with him rubbing my bottom through my trousers. Until, that is, he pushed his hand down inside and I felt his fingers in the cleft between my buttocks. In those days I was very slim, and my clothes were loose, which made it easier for him. He pushed down as far as he could and kept his hand there. I didn't know what to do, I felt paralyzed; why couldn't I push him off, stand up or leave? It is easy to think like this with hindsight, but he had power over me at the time, and I couldn't stop him. I was certain that the other priests around the table knew what was happening, but no one said or did anything. And as the conversations continued, his hand, which was reasonably well covered by my jacket, slid around to the front of my trousers until he could feel my penis, at which point he just kept it there. I was in a trance, frozen with fear and in a perverse way I felt as though I had to help hide his arm or I too would get into trouble for allowing this to happen. My world was upside down; I was numb with panic. Stephen Shield, however, was acting like nothing was wrong. He was chatting away and laughing with his friends, as though he were two different people, one hidden and one on show. In the end someone suggested putting some music on, which meant that Stephen Shield had to remove his hand and leave the table in order to go and get a CD.

He returned wearing a cassock and biretta, a rather funny square hat with three ridges and a tassel on top, usually worn by clergy of a certain traditional persuasion. The music he chose to put on was an ABBA, which went down surprisingly well with the other priests and before long, about half a dozen of them, including Stephen Shield in a cassock, were dancing around the room in their clerical attire. As if that wasn't bizarre enough, they were doing so in a very 'camp' way, like a group of drag queens skipping about with innuendo's flowing as freely as the drink. Stephen Shield wouldn't leave me alone and was constantly trying to get my attention. It was obvious that he wanted more than just an enforced fondle. But thankfully I managed never to be alone and so all his attempts came to nothing. Nevertheless, I found myself in a state of utter confusion and disbelief. The feminine pronouns were flying about, and it all felt very wrong.

Somewhat ironically, in an article about the relevance of modern forms of worship, entitled "The Traditional Latin Rite in the Church Today," Stephen Shield wrote, "How can we call swinging in the aisles, the waving of hands in the air, participation? Such behavior may satisfy the ego for a moment but nothing of it speaks of eternity, it restricts souls to the present."[1]

Yet, there they all were, dressed in traditional clerical dress, swinging and waving their hands in the air, full of their own egos, showing no respect for the tradition that Stephen Shield supposedly held in such high regard. They were all living a lie, a life of double standards. I just wanted to become

---

1. Shield, "Traditional Latin Rite," 7.

invisible, but instead I remained at the table, silent and self-effacing, hoping to be left alone. In the end I could take no more and so I made my excuses and left. I knew that no one would be bothered, and in many ways I had felt like an intruder at a private party. I couldn't wait to get back to my room and lock the door.

That night I was restless, my mind kept on replaying the evening's events, from the inappropriate touching to effeminate dancing priests. But, when morning arrived, I pretended that everything was fine, putting on a brave face, whilst inside I was lost in a maze of pain and confusion. I was twenty-four years old; how could this have happened again? Why had I allowed it to happen? I was consumed by anxiety, guilt and shame.

At breakfast, I recall making a huge effort to be extra considerate and helpful, focusing all my attention on others to keep my mind off the pain I was really feeling. Later in the morning I decided to go to Mass and was utterly shocked to see Stephen Shield standing there in his vestments, looking like 'butter wouldn't melt,' and holding the sacrament with hands that just a few hours earlier had touched my penis. I recall an elderly lady sitting next to me and expressing her admiration for Stephen Shield, saying how much she enjoyed his Masses, as he was "reverent and kind, such a lovely priest." I am reminded of another quote from his article on "The Traditional Latin Rite in the Church of Today": "Liturgy is about the worship of Almighty God and the sanctification of the world, it has nothing to do with our being entertained by a priest masquerading as an out of place, second-rate comedian. Obedience to the Church is our security and our only defense. Once we take the law into our own hands, once we step outside her domain, we can't be taken seriously because we have disobeyed the truths we have been given."[2]

Stephen Shield penned this article while he was curate at The English Martyrs Church, Preston—the very same place where he took the law into his own hands on several occasions. You could say he was a sexual abuser masquerading as a priest. I didn't go up for communion that day because I could not take him seriously, and I didn't want anything that he could give me, even if it was Jesus Christ.

As soon as I returned to the house, one of the students who had been present at the previous evening's meal approached me to ask how I was. It was evident from his tone and body language that he was referring to the previous evening and all that I had endured at the hands of Stephen Shield. I was taken aback, not because he knew, as I suspected most of them were aware, but because he cared enough to ask me. I muttered that I was ok, but,

---

2. Shield, "Traditional Latin Rite," 7.

in reality, I knew that everything had changed and that nothing would ever be the same again.

That being said, I did my best to carry on with my daily round of Mass, visiting the sick, talking to school groups and avoiding Stephen Shield as much as I could. It was easier this time because he was even more distant than usual, which suited me fine. Outside I was my usual conscientious self, but inside, I was riddled with confusion and feelings of isolation. I couldn't think straight, and I was full of guilt and shame. So, it was a huge relief when my time at The English Martyrs church came to an end. I couldn't wait to return to my parents' house for the summer break and be looked after. I very much needed to be loved as I felt totally unlovable and good for nothing. There was only one cloud on the horizon and that was that I had to return to The English Martyrs for the ordination of one of the students, which thankfully meant staying only for one night.

The ordination and the reception in the parish hall went well and it was a very joyous occasion for the newly ordained priest, his family, friends, and the parish. Everyone had a great time, and I enjoyed myself, as the pain and the fear subsided a little. At about ten o'clock in the evening, I decided to return to the parish house, as I wanted to wind down a little before bed. The house was empty, so I went into the main sitting room and put the television on. A short while later I heard someone coming in the front door, and after a few moments, who should walk into the sitting room but Stephen Shield. I felt very uncomfortable and didn't know what to say to him. He made his way over to the corner of the room where there was a drinks cabinet and to my surprise, he asked me if I would join him in a whisky. To begin with I refused, which seemed to annoy him, so when he asked me a second time, I reluctantly agreed. After handing it to me he perched himself on the arm of the chair next to where I was sitting. Feeling very unsure, I took a sip of the drink, and it seemed to be incredibly strong. At the time, I put it down to having a whisky on top of the four or five pints of beer that I had already consumed, but, with hindsight, and considering the effect that it had on me, I suspect that he may have added something to it. After all he poured it with his back to me, so I couldn't see what he was doing. Either way, the rest of the evening is broken up into fractured memories.

I do, however, clearly recall him sitting on the arm of the chair with his hand on my upper thigh, saying, "Oh, you are so funny." He did this several times. The next memory that I have is of him walking beside me as we ascended the stairs, his arm around my waist. But instead of going to my usual room, he took me down a long corridor which led to a room at the rear of the house, which had once been the servant's quarters. Once there he somehow managed to undress me, and we both ended up on the bed.

To this day, and, as I write this now, I cannot explain how any of it happened. There was just no way that I would have gone with him by choice. Nonetheless, what happened next is very clear to me, even though part of the memory appears as though I was watching it from the door. Everything seemed to have a red hue around it, and I can physically remember him performing oral sex on me. It was as if I couldn't function, move or stop him. I have spent decades reviewing it in my mind, and I still have no answers. Remembering trauma as though one is watching it take place is not uncommon and is due to disassociation, which is one of the many defense mechanisms the brain uses to cope with the trauma of sexual abuse. Often it is described as an 'out-of-body' experience where one feels detached from reality and that is precisely how I felt.

When I awoke the following morning, the bedroom door was firmly closed, and a cup of coffee was on the bedside table. I was lying completely naked, with no sheet over me and my clothes were on the floor. Aching all over, especially in my shoulders and ribs, I tried to stand up but could hardly walk to get my clothes. Worse than any physical pain, however, was the spiritual pain I experienced; it was as if my soul had been ripped out and replaced with his evil. It sounds as horrific to me now as it felt then. There was nothing left; I was an empty shell. Slowly, I began to get dressed, but it took me so long that I missed the newly ordained priest's first Mass in the church. I did, however, manage to walk around to the local convent, where the sisters were preparing Sunday lunch for us all. I gingerly took my seat at the table and tried to act as normal as I could. Then, to my absolute horror, Stephen Shield arrived and took the seat directly opposite me. It was a narrow table and so for the next few hours I sat facing the man who a few hours earlier had sexually abused me. I felt physically sick; every single mouthful of food was an effort to chew and swallow. I didn't know how I was going to make it through. Yet all the while, he sat there leering at me and chatting away as if it was just another Sunday lunch, and everything was good in the world.

As soon as the meal was over, I quickly said my goodbyes, and went back to the church to meet my parents. Years later, my mother told me that she knew something was wrong as soon as she saw me. She asked if I was alright, but I couldn't bring myself to tell her the truth, so I just said, "I'm tired." On the way home, we stopped off to visit my great aunt, who lived en route. I still remember walking into her house and seeing a picture of the Sacred Heart of Jesus with a small, red, electric light attached in the hallway. It upset me to see it, and I had to look away. On one level, I knew it wasn't God's fault, but the phrase "Alter Christus" (another Christ) kept repeating in my mind, signifying that by his ordination, Stephen Shield acted as "another Christ." In that moment I felt deeply betrayed. I had tried my best to answer God's call, and then this happened. No words can fully capture the physical, psychological, and spiritual pain that I felt that day and continued to experience for decades to come.

The Roman Catholic Church desires compliant and easily influenced men and the seminary system is designed to mold them accordingly. The term 'seminary' originates from the Latin word 'seminarium,' meaning 'seed bed.' In a seminary, students are metaphorically like seeds, nurtured to grow and flourish in their ministry. The Church seeks men who will unquestioningly follow its directives and overlook any problems or issues, individuals who can be shaped into unwavering supporters of the Institution and, at the time, that was me. On the other hand, the Church has always been wary of independent thinkers who might challenge its beliefs and practices or expose its numerous inadequacies. So, after already spending four years in the seminary system from the age of sixteen to twenty, where I was taught to remain silent and 'roll with the punches,' I kept my experiences to myself, and, in October 1992, at the age of twenty-four, I returned to Ushaw College, Durham, hoping that things had changed.

Ushaw College 1992

Returning for my second year in 1992, I was relieved to discover that my original class, or those who had completed the six-year course, had been ordained priests the previous summer. This meant I had a fresh start in a place where very few people knew me. It's hard to believe now, but at the time, I was completely unaware that I was repressing all of my traumatic memories. This was not a conscious decision, I hasten to add, but an involuntary response known as dissociative amnesia. I must have been doing it quite effectively, for the Director of Studies, in April 1995, wrote: "Paul first came to Ushaw in 1986 and stayed for a year. He was rather immature at that time, a fact that is reflected in his academic performance. He returned in 1992, much more mature and indeed an impressive young man. Again, the maturity is reflected in his academic performance (not to mention other areas which do not concern this particular reference)."

However, I didn't feel like an impressive young man at the time. I harbored feelings of humiliation, remorse, anger, and terror. I was full of self-doubt and worthlessness, especially in my relationships with others, my relationship with God, and my true self as a child of God. If you asked my classmates if they were aware of any of this, they would almost definitely say, 'Not at all.' Nevertheless, I was ashamed and refused to share my true self with anyone, always presenting a cheerful and balanced exterior. I still felt genuinely called to a deep and abiding relationship with God, but the shame simultaneously pulled me away. I felt as though I had offended Him due to the deep wound in my soul. This internal conflict was extremely difficult to bear, and it severely distorted my spiritual life, as well as making genuine relationships with others almost impossible. Maintaining secrecy and hiding shame consumed a lot of my energy. Abuse is profoundly isolating, and it creates a powerful and unbearable sense of being cut off from those around you. College, on the other hand, is an intensely social place, but I always felt separate from others, as if I was watching life through a window, and this made me even more vulnerable to the devious.

One such student, whom I had previously met in Preston, and was due to be ordained a deacon at the end of the year, picked up on my vulnerability, and tried to take advantage of me. At our first meeting, he came across as 'one of the lads,' and I certainly would never have thought of him as anything other than heterosexual. At college, I had only spoken to him in passing until, one Friday evening, as the bar was about to close, he invited me up to his room for a whisky. I decided to go, as we had been having a good chat, and it seemed a shame to stop. Everything was fine; we enjoyed the drink and put the world to rights. A few weeks later, the same thing happened again, and it became a regular occurrence until one evening, just as I was leaving, he handed me a book, a St. Luke's Daily Missal, which he said I could keep. He told me that someone had given it to him as a present, but he already had one so he thought I might like it. It wasn't a cheap book, it was brand new and would come in handy, so I thanked him and took it to my room. A few days later, I was chatting to a student from his year and told him his classmate had given me the book. He immediately looked concerned and advised me not to go to his room again, and when I pushed him to explain, he said that this student was well-known as a predatory homosexual. He would invite younger students to his room for a drink, buy them presents, and then, after some time, when he had their trust, he would ply them with drink and then sexually abuse them. The following morning, he would go to their room and lay all of the guilt on them, telling them that they were disgusting, and putting all of the blame for what had happened onto them. Some students had even left the seminary after such an encounter. Needless to say, I never stepped foot in his room again and avoided him whenever possible.

Shortly after this, at the end of the academic year, the diaconate ordinations took place in the college chapel. The local bishop came to perform the ceremony, which was followed by sherry in the bar and a celebratory meal in the refectory. Whilst sipping my sherry, I overheard one of his classmates say to him, "You will have to change your ways now that you have just promised celibacy," to which he replied, "No, I won't. I had my fingers crossed," implying that he didn't take his vows seriously. The following Christmas, this same student along with two others were officially told to leave Ushaw. The college was refusing to recommend them for ordination to the priesthood the following summer. Despite this, however, all three were ordained to the priesthood by their local Bishops, with their sordid reputations intact and two of them are still working as priests to this day.

Over the course of the summer break, and to cover living expenses, students from Lancaster Diocese received £325, which came to £25 per week. I decided to use my allowance to book a return flight to Rome where I had secured a position at the Venerable English College's Villa Palazzola. During the summer months, the villa became a hub for parish groups whilst the seminarians were away on holiday. Located just outside Rome, in the hills of the Castelli region, south of the city, the villa overlooks Lake Albano and offers views of the Pope's summer residence, Castel Gandolfo. It has an extremely rich history, initially serving as a Roman Villa and later becoming an abbey for Cistercian monks in the thirteenth century, followed by Carthusian monks, and then Franciscan friars in the fifteenth century.

I had a wonderful time there, along with another student from Ushaw, a schoolteacher from Hartlepool, and three young women, two of whom were nieces of Fr. Anthony who managed the place. While none of us received payment for our work, we were provided with board and lodging, as well as sixty lire every Friday evening to enjoy a pizza together. Our main tasks involved setting tables for the visitors' meals and washing up afterwards. We also had ample free time for sightseeing and relaxation, including taking advantage of the villa's swimming pool, often frequented by some of the Swiss Guard from Castel Gandolfo. Interestingly, they mentioned that Pope St. John Paul II would not permit them to use his private pool, which seemed a bit mean.

Once a week, we used to take the Villa's minibus to Rome and, whilst Fr. Anthony attended to some errands, the six of us had the opportunity to explore the city and see the sights. On one notable trip, as we drove up Via di Monserrato (the road where the Venerable English College is located) Fr. Anthony honked the horn in order to attract the attention of a priest walking along with a group of tourists. To my shock the priest turned out to be Stephen Shield. He recognized Fr. Anthony straightaway and rushed over for a chat. Unfortunately for me, I was sitting immediately behind the driver's seat and so couldn't avoid being seen. Then suddenly he addressed me by name, asking how I was. His voice went through me and instantly took me back to the room where he abused me; it was as if it was happening again, and I was left feeling physically ill. I must have looked visibly shaken, because Rachel, who was seated beside me, noticed my distress, and asked how I was. As a result, I confided in her about the sexually abusive encounters I had had with Stephen Shield in the past and she was incredibly supportive. In fact, she has continued to be a pillar of strength and support to me over the past thirty years, and she has been there through some of the best, and also the most challenging times of my life.

All in all, I had an amazing time working at Palazzola, surrounded by the stunning Italian landscape and the great company, and as luck would have it, the six of us ended up on the same flight home. After passing through security and finding our way to the departure lounge, I was horrified to see Stephen Shield, smugly sitting there, waiting for the same flight. Thankfully, we didn't have too long to wait before our flight was called, and once we were on the plane, I felt a bit more at ease. As a group, we all sat together, I was next to a fellow student from Ushaw while Rachel and the others were in the row in front. I felt safe, until that is, Stephen Shield appeared beside me, looking anxious, and asking about my onward journey from Manchester Airport. I told him that my dad was picking me up, at which point he returned to his seat. Rachel could tell that I was uneasy and later confided that he was definitely putting undue pressure on me. After this, the rest of the flight was fairly uneventful, but still, I was greatly relieved once we were off the plane and heading towards the arrivals lounge. Stephen Shield, on the other hand, had other ideas. As I stood waiting for my dad to arrive, he approached me once again, asking about my journey home. He told me to call my dad and tell him not to come, as he could drive me home. But, despite his insistence, there was no way that I was getting in his car. Finally, the tension finally melted when I saw my dad's car pulling up. I had never been so relieved to get out of an airport, and thankfully, to this day, I have never met Stephen Shield again

I spent the rest of my summer break on a parish placement at St. Mary's Church in Barrow in Furness with Canon Frank Cookson, a remarkable priest.

Our connection was uncanny: he had studied for the priesthood at Ushaw College, just like me, and was ordained to the priesthood at The English Martyrs Church in Preston on July 19, 1953. Our shared experiences and interests made our time together enjoyable, and we decided to visit Furness Abbey one day. The Abbey, founded in 1123 by the Savigniac Order and later transferred to the Cistercian Order in 1147, until Henry VIII had it suppressed in 1537, was a fascinating place to explore. Its history reminded me of the previously mentioned drawing of Cistercian (Trappist) monks on a train in the book that my grandparents had bought at Buckfast Abbey. This memory, in the midst of the pain of abuse, was a source of solace. It rekindled my passion, reminding me of my initial interest in monasteries when I first encountered them in a history class in school, and before long, it was time for me to return to Ushaw for my third year.

As was customary on the first night after the summer break, everyone went to the local pub for a few pints and a catch-up. We were all eager to share stories of the exciting places we had been to and everything we had seen and done. It was great to be back amongst friends. On returning to college the conversations continued over coffee until about midnight when we broke up and returned to our own rooms. Turning on the light, I was startled to find a fellow student lying on my bed, with the duvet thrown back and his trousers pulled down, exposing himself to me. I had no idea how long he had been waiting for my return, but what he had in mind was very clear. I didn't know him all that well as he was not in my year or even one of my friends. All I knew was that he was in his late thirties and had previously had a career as a British soldier. In spite of my fear, I managed to gather my wits and as he attempted to stand up and approach me, I grabbed him by the shoulders and pushed him out through the open door, quickly closing and locking it behind him.

I felt disgusted and disturbed but also violated, shocked, confused, and angry. It was as if all the trauma of being inappropriately touched at Upholland, sexually humiliated at Castlerigg, locked in a room and offered money for sex at Ushaw, seriously sexually assaulted at The English Martyrs Church, then groomed again at Ushaw, was all welling up inside of me. I collapsed in tears on the floor of my room; how could I go on? Why did this keep happening? I felt like the only one. No one else ever said or hinted that it had happened to them. I felt dirty and unclean, and my room seemed contaminated. I didn't sleep in my bed for quite some time as each time I lay on it all I could see was the image of this student lying there exposing himself. Instead, I slept on the floor, which was pretty uncomfortable but preferable to my bed.

Due to my experiences, I found it very difficult to express myself openly and honestly in the seminary environment. I was very guarded and unable to share my experiences of sexual abuse with anyone. The burden of guilt weighed heavily upon me as I struggled to find the courage to speak out. I had a deep-seated fear that my words would fall on deaf ears and be met with disbelief and blame. Living in a close-knit community meant that I had to rely extensively on those in authority for guidance and support, which I believe created a sense of dependency in me, thereby making it a challenge to speak out against abuse for fear of rejection. A sense of hopelessness encompassed me, and I was convinced that seeking help was futile, as there was no one who could free me from the constant anguish and turmoil that I was feeling.

Yet, in spite of the significant damage and deep wounds to my soul, my unwavering faith in Jesus Christ and his teachings continued to sustain me through these challenging times. The fervent desire to be ordained a priest and to serve the Church was not merely a passing whim but a deeply rooted longing within me. As I look back now, I can appreciate that it was my faith in God's calling that led me to endure and rationalize the inappropriate behavior I encountered. But, at the time, I attributed everything that had happened to my own flaws and weaknesses, whilst at the same time failing to recognize the underlying harmful dynamics and structures within the seminary system. When confronted with the decision to abandon the seminary and the Church entirely, or to reaffirm my commitment to my journey with Christ, I always chose the latter. Steadfastly refusing to give in to despair and instead redoubling my efforts to center myself on my spiritual life and my relationship with God, acknowledging that this was where the deepest wounds lay, and where my true strength resided. Finally, it was within this renewed dedication that I discovered the glimmer of hope that enabled me to move forward and be open to promptings of the Holy Spirit.

Ever since my 'mystical experience' in a history class at the age of twelve, I'd had a deep sense that one day I would live in a monastery. The image of the Cistercian monks on the train often came to my mind, as if the Holy Spirit was prompting me to explore further. One Saturday afternoon in early October 1993, I was browsing the University Bookshop in Durham when I came across *The Cistercian Alternative* by Dom André Louf. The 'blurb' on the cover described the book as "the first comprehensive look at and guide to Cistercian spirituality today," and it ended with, "this is an excellent and straightforward guide." It was just what I needed, so I bought it and read it cover to cover in a few days. It spoke to me like no other book had, as if it had been written for me. I had never felt at home in the world, and my experience of seminary life hadn't exactly filled me with longing at the thought of working alongside people like Stephen Shield, especially as he was a priest of Lancaster Diocese and we would therefore be colleagues. In fact, the very thought left me cold.

There was one particular phrase that stood out for me, "we leave the world."[1] It spoke of the significant sacrifice made by the monks as they gave up all former connections, including families and friends, and, instead, were drawn to another place—not by its outward appearance, but by its spiritual ethos. As I have already stressed, I never really felt like I belonged in the world, and I think that sexual abuse only added to my sense of disconnectedness and alienation. Often, I would speak with a friend about the strong pull that I was feeling towards monastic life. Until one day I received a large envelope in the post. It contained several brochures and pamphlets about Mount St. Bernard Abbey, a Cistercian Monastery in Leicestershire. Straight away I knew that my friend was responsible and when I later questioned him about it, he told me that he had also arranged for me to stay at the

---

1. Louf, *Cistercian Alternative*, 45.

monastery guesthouse over the Christmas holiday. He also offered to drive me there, saying that he would stay with some friends nearby, which would allow me to fully immerse myself in monastic life for the weekend. What better way could there be test a monastic calling?

Over the course of that weekend, I threw myself in the rhythm of monastery life, participating in the seven church services that took place from 3:30 a.m. to 7:30 p.m. These times of prayer provided a structured and contemplative framework, which allowed me to engage in a deeper way with my own spiritual journey. Whilst there, I also had the opportunity to have several in-depth conversations with the Novice Master, who offered me invaluable guidance and support. These interactions helped me gain clarity and perspective on my journey and I found myself wondering if this contemplative environment held the potential for a new direction and a deeper sense of purpose in my life.

In the spring of 1994, I made a second visit to the monastery and, once again, I immersed myself in the daily rhythm of its life. This time, not only did I participate in the church services, but also, I worked alongside the novice monks in cleaning the church, tending to the flower beds, and assisting with the washing up. Despite the mundane nature of these activities, they fostered a profound sense of solidarity and purpose amongst us. In the quiet moments between tasks, I valued the opportunity to engage in heartfelt conversations with some of the more senior monks—listening to their personal stories and the deeply spiritual journeys that had led them to embrace such a rigorous monastic existence. As my departure date loomed, it seemed as though the very walls of the monastery were beckoning me to remain, and so I took 'the plunge,' and I arranged to return for one whole month during the following summer break from Ushaw.

The final term of the year couldn't go quickly enough. Thankfully, the prospect of spending one whole month in the monastery helped to distract me from the constant juggling act that was going on in my mind. It was like having three little voices whispering in my ear: stay at Ushaw, join the monastery, or leave altogether. But what else would I do, though? The Church was all I knew, and I couldn't imagine any other life.

Finally, the time came for me to immerse myself in the contemplative life once again. I ate, worked, and prayed alongside them for the whole of August in an attempt to seriously discern if my future lay within their community. This unique experience also allowed the monks to view me and see if I was a suitable candidate. It was a two-way street. Each week I would have a formal meeting with the Novice Master. I remember my surprise when I first visited his room and saw the phrase 'Keep death daily before your eyes' scrolling across his computer screen. This powerful quote from the Rule of

St. Benedict made a huge impression on me. It felt as though I was being shown how to focus on what's really important in life and to shift my attention from material things to spiritual ones.

Instead of hiding my pain of sexual abuse, I realized the importance of being honest and embracing the truth. I learnt that the biggest obstacle I faced was my lack of understanding and the belief that death and trauma only affected others. In fearing these things, we tend to avoid thinking about them, or preparing for them, which distracts us from living a truly spiritually fulfilling life. The reality is that death and trauma touch everyone, regardless of their age, and once we acknowledge this we can begin to live authentically, to be true to ourselves, and appreciate the same qualities in others. This realization of the importance of being authentic and true led me to approach the Abbot and ask permission to enter the monastery. I didn't receive an instant answer, but, instead, a few days later, and after consultation with the community, he said yes! However, I couldn't enter straight away, as there were a number of details that needed to be addressed at Ushaw first, such as telling them of my decision.

So, upon my return, with no time to waste, I arranged to meet with the President of the College to tell him of my intention of joining the monastery. Much to my surprise, instead of disappointment or attempts to dissuade me, he confessed to feeling envious, as the idea of joining a monastery had crossed his own mind several times. I was taken aback by his unexpected response, which in turn brought about a whirlwind of relief and validation within me. With the weight of having to tell him off my shoulders, the next step was to inform the Bishop of Lancaster and begin preparing myself for monastic life.

I decided to notify the bishop by letter, and his swift reply conveyed his disappointment whilst at the same time assuring me of his full support. His words provided a sense of solace and encouragement, despite the underlying tinge of being let down. The relief that washed over me at the thought of never having to work alongside Stephen Shield, or anyone like him, was immense. In that moment, I truly believed that I would never have to encounter him, or anyone like him, again.

A few weeks into the Christmas term, an announcement from the President appeared on the student notice board. It was informing everyone that the third-year students were being considered for the "Rite of Admission to Candidacy," which is an essential step for each seminarian on his journey toward the priesthood. It is an opportunity for a seminarian to publicly express his intention to receive the Sacrament of Holy Orders as a deacon and, later, as a priest. The process involves a close scrutiny of the candidate, which includes a thorough examination of the seminarian's readiness for the priesthood, and the blessing of the candidate in church. The student body plays a crucial role by providing their own observations and insights. Therefore, the notices stressed that if anyone knew of a reason why a particular student shouldn't be admitted, they were conscience-bound to let it be known.

Thus, I found myself in a state of moral obligation, as the student who had exposed himself to me in my room was now on track for Candidacy. I knew that I had to speak up, but at the same time I was plagued by the fear of not being taken seriously, or worse, having my experience dismissed entirely.

Nevertheless, driven by an unwavering sense of duty, I mustered up the courage to approach the President. As I spoke of what had happened, he listened attentively. Once I had finished, he expressed his gratitude for bringing the matter to his attention. However, he stressed that action couldn't be taken solely on my testimony, and he suggested that if I could find one or two other students who had had similar experiences to come forward it would greatly aid him in addressing the issue.

I left the room feeling utterly deflated, my mind swirling with conflicting emotions. How could I, a victim, be expected to take on the role of an investigator and seek out other victims? It was very unfair of him, and I couldn't help but question whether it was truly my responsibility. Furthermore, not once was I given the opportunity to express my feelings or seek support, and this lack of empathy only reinforced my disillusionment with the process of reporting abuse. It became apparent that the Church's priorities lay in protecting its reputation and making it arduous for victims to come forward. The request from the President to find other victims clearly demonstrated that my testimony alone wasn't enough. And, whilst he was quick to say that he believed me, he left me in no doubt that, unless other victims came forward, his hands were tied. But what if there were no other victims?

I decided, under the circumstances, to reach out to a few close friends for help, and if nothing came of it, I would let it go with a clear conscience, satisfied that I had done my part. However, it wasn't to be the case, as the very first person I spoke to knew of someone who had been victimized, but the situation required careful handling. The student in question was just eighteen years old, and this former British soldier had been bombarding him with letters demanding sex for some time. He was a quiet, good-looking lad, the type that homosexual predators often preyed upon in the seminary, and the contents of the letters were repulsive and disturbing. As a result, my friend and I encouraged him to report the incident to the President and thankfully he did so, and the abuser was dismissed from the seminary. In spite of his ordeal, this young student continued through the seminary and was eventually ordained a priest. However, the impact of the earlier experience was still clearly evident and, after approximately a year as a priest, he made the difficult decision to leave the Church.

Mount St. Bernard Abbey

My heart was heavy when the time to bid farewell to Ushaw and the Lancaster Diocese finally arrived on Easter Sunday, 1995. It wasn't just a goodbye to the physical places, but also to the priesthood, as there was no assurance of ordination in the monastery. The role of monastic priests is solely to serve the community, and it is the decision of the Abbot as to who should be ordained.

Nonetheless, on April 29, 1995, which happened to be the Feast Day of St. Catherine of Siena, my parents accompanied me to Mount St. Bernard Abbey. On the way we made a stop for lunch, during which I devoured an enormous steak, fully aware that it would be my last taste of meat; the monks followed a strict vegetarian diet. As we approached the entrance gates of the Abbey the radio played "Back for Good" by the British boyband, 'Take That,' a song whose bittersweet lyrics resonated deeply with me. The melody served as a poignant soundtrack to my inner turmoil, symbolizing the need to let go of the past, and embrace a new beginning.

This was in stark contrast however to my parents, who found it very difficult to let me go. Monastic life was completely alien to them and not something they had ever considered for their son. After all, I would get no holidays and would only be allowed home if a close family member was ill or had died. Of course, they could visit me in the monastery, but I could only meet them in the guesthouse or for a walk in the grounds; there was no leaving the property. I recall the novice master showing me to my room, furnished with a wooden bed, some bookshelves, a desk, a chair, wooden shutters on the window, and a plain wooden floor. All of the furniture was made in the monastery carpenters' shop and what struck me most was that when I sat on the bed there was no 'give' in it; it was as hard as a brick. I later discovered that the mattress was homemade and filled with tightly packed barley straw, which I was informed was a lot softer than wheat straw, but it certainly didn't feel so.

After bidding my parents farewell, I returned to my room and collapsed on the bed in a wave of sorrow. My tears were not for myself, for this was my chosen path, but for my parents and friends who had to bear the pain of my departure. I felt a profound sense of solitude in the presence of God. From my earliest days, I always believed that God required my unwavering devotion, and that He yearned for me to surrender everything to Him. Until that moment, I had always held back a significant part of myself, but now I was confident that I had given it all. I had cut myself off from the world through what was essentially a movement of love for God. I pondered if this was the essence of monastic life and, in that moment, I was convinced that it was.

Throughout the initial years of my monastic journey, I dedicated myself to laying a strong and constructive groundwork. It was a time when I consciously set aside the painful memories of my past abuse and instead fully embraced and integrated into the daily rhythm and way of life within the community. I adjusted to the unhurried pace of monastic life within its serene and unadorned surroundings. My daily routine encompassed prayer, contemplative reading, and physical work. I found this engagement in monastic activities to be deeply fulfilling and affirming—allowing me to realize my purpose and nurture my vocation. It became an all-encompassing experience and exactly what I needed at that point in my life. I endeavored to remain open to the formative influence that the natural rhythm of this life brings, recognizing that many profound truths gradually permeate one's spirit through the act of living, often without conscious awareness. Most of my monastic day was spent in silence, in order to create a space, an emptiness in the depths of one's being where God can be heard without any other noise.

After spending two and a half years in the novitiate, I took a significant step in my journey. I made my temporary vows; a commitment lasting for three years. These vows consisted of three solemn promises: 'Conversion of Life,' which meant giving oneself entirely to the monastic way of life and which also included poverty and chastity. 'Obedience,' which was primarily obedience to the Abbot, but also to each other and 'Stability,' whereby a monk vows to remain with his community in the monastery until death.

As part of my preparation to make these vows I explored, in some depth, the theology and practice of celibacy. Regardless of spending six years in seminary, celibacy, as I have already stated, had never been a topic of study or conversation. It was simply assumed that individuals would somehow come to terms with it themselves in a mature and balanced manner, as if by psychological osmosis. The idea that this could occur in an all-male community of sexually repressed men, many of whom were homosexual and only understood celibacy as abstaining from marriage, with no consideration for sexual abstinence, is astonishing. Moreover, we were largely isolated from the outside world, making it even more challenging; yet the seminary staff and the bishops expected it.

The reality, however, was very different. From my own experience, many of the seminarians who eventually 'committed' themselves to celibacy were psychologically underdeveloped. Thanks to the seminary system, their psychological and spiritual growth had been stunted, and their level of maturity was often much lower than their age. For example, consider the Ushaw student mentioned earlier, who crossed his fingers as he made his promise of celibacy. Such behavior is similar to that of a child attempting to avoid making a genuine commitment. He had no intention of openly binding himself to celibacy because it would require him to change his behavior and he wasn't mature enough. Men like him, who claim to be celibate while engaging in sexual activity, contribute to a culture of deception within the priesthood in several significant ways. Firstly, the celibacy requirement can lead to priests engaging in sexual activity while publicly claiming to be celibate and thereby fostering a culture of secrecy and dishonesty. Secondly, non-celibate priests may be reluctant to expose others engaged in similar behavior due to their own guilt, leading to a tolerance for misconduct within the priesthood. And thirdly, priests and bishops engaging in sexual activity while pretending to be celibate compromise others in the system and perpetuate a culture of secrecy and dishonesty.

The psychological impact of this is that celibacy can leave priest's feeling unfulfilled, which in turn often leads to compensatory behaviors such as overeating, alcohol abuse, excessive travel and secret relationships, all of which further contribute to a culture of dishonesty. It is essential to understand that the very system that they live under often prevents many priests from realizing their full natural and spiritual potential. Like any transformative change in life, celibacy necessitates a series of choices and crises with both gains and losses. For celibacy to truly benefit the priest, he must fully embrace its spirit, with all its implications, even if it means embracing spiritual solitude.

Unfortunately, many priests are enticed by the system, with its power and career compensations, often at the cost of their spiritual journey. A.W. Richard Sipe writes, "At any one time, 2% of vowed celibate clergy can be said to have achieved celibacy – that is, they have successfully negotiated each step of celibate development at the more or less appropriate stage and are characterologically so firmly established that their state is, for all intents and purposes, irreversible."[1] These remarkable individuals, and I have met some, demonstrate a deep sense of inner freedom and harmony, which unites their unique qualities and their unwavering commitment to serving others. Their tireless efforts and remarkable accomplishments testify to their deep spirituality and connection to a higher purpose.

It is essential to understand that celibacy is not about suppressing emotions or sexual desires but rather about channeling them in a different direction. According to St. Paul, celibacy is intended to free individuals for love of the Lord Jesus, and such freedom is closely linked to the practice of prayer, and to be honest, this concept resonated more with me during my time in the monastery than in the seminary. St. Paul further suggests that embracing celibacy enables individuals to "wait on the Lord without distraction" (1 Cor 7:35), which, again, can be interpreted as engaging in uninterrupted prayer. Ultimately, this kind of prayer becomes the most compelling evidence of celibacy as it blossoms into a profound love for God.

Like all forms of self-denial, celibacy is a practice that requires careful consideration. The act of renunciation can leave a wound that may continue to chafe for a long time, maybe a lifetime. Celibacy is not just about abstaining from physical pleasure; it is about creating an emotional space that does not diminish one's capacity for affection. In fact, it should enhance this capacity, directing it towards the service of God, His Church, and, particularly for monks, their fellow brothers. This state of being is only ever achieved gradually and prayer always plays a central role.

Having witnessed the transformative power of prayer, I determined, as a monk, to embrace it with all my being. Whenever I met with temptation, I would pray to remain at peace, depending solely on the power of God to help me through. Sometimes, things would get so bad that the only way out was to cry to God for help, repeating the words from St. Matthew's Gospel, "Lord save us, we are sinking" (Matt 8:25), which was always sufficient. In time, I discovered that prayer doesn't require many words; it is simply a movement of the heart. Monks strive to be continually in the Lord's presence. They cling to Him and fill the silence by calling on His name. It is through this constant prayerful communion that the faith, which joins them to Him, begins to grow stronger and more profound. In time, the solitude of celibacy becomes a communion of love through prayer, and, in this way, a fullness will enter the monk's heart, which will be both human and divine. None of the personal richness that flows from love in the human being will be lost, or lie fallow, for the monk because of his celibacy.

---

1. Sipe, *Sex, Priests and Power*, 67.

It will all be taken up and used to the full, and, through his deep bond of love with Jesus Christ, he will be open to the fullness of divine life, and united more closely with His God.

Moreover, the beauty of this journey is that it extends beyond the solitude of a monk's cell. It is a journey that unfolds within the Church, where any growth in authentic love also strengthens the bonds of union between Christ and His Church. Love, nurtured through prayer, has the potential to bear fruit in the life of the Church as a whole. Whether it's priests actively serving in the world, or a religious community living out a shared vocation, the love that springs from prayer can also touch the lives of all those they encounter in the course of daily life. This philosophy emphasizes the collective responsibility and unity that prayer fosters within the Church, making it a powerful force for positive change and spiritual growth.

Many have written about the connection between the priesthood and celibacy in Christ-centered terms. Numerous authors have delved into the subject, highlighting celibacy as a clear demonstration of unwavering and exclusive devotion to God and His sacred mission. It is portrayed as an emblem of perfect love for God and humanity without any reservation, purely driven by an ardent longing for the Kingdom of heaven. Lovely words!

However, when we examine practical realities, celibacy presents itself as a daily struggle for most, and a less frequent struggle for others. Having experienced this firsthand, I decided to make a conscious effort to reaffirm my vows each day, ensuring they remained at the forefront of my mind. For me, this practice was incredibly worthwhile. Approaching vows such as celibacy with genuine sincerity involves making a sincere commitment to personal growth and embracing the unique opportunities for spiritual development that such commitments offer. It is important to prioritize honesty and build a strong foundation of prayer for support. It's also essential to recognize that this journey may come with challenges and complexities, but, with patience and perseverance, one can overcome them and continue to grow.

During my three years in temporary vows, my connection to the community grew stronger as I embraced the monastic lifestyle. This period also marked the beginning of my pursuit of a Bachelor of Divinity Degree from St. Patrick's Pontifical University in Maynooth, County Kildare, Ireland. I dedicated time to delving into the profound Cistercian heritage, immersing myself in the teachings of early Cistercian figures like St. Bernard of Clairvaux, Stephen of Sawley, and Baldwin of Forde. Through my studies, I discovered the significance of humility and honesty in fostering self-awareness. I realized that monks and nuns are not escaping from life, but rather, embracing their own truth and humanity. The monastic way is about diving into life, not shying away from it.

During the initial years of my monastic life, everything felt relatively easy. I had no major vocational crises and everything appeared to be going well. That is, until one day in the summer of 2000 when the Abbot summoned all the monks to the Chapter House (meeting room) to make an important announcement. He told us that Fr. James Deadman, a sixty-nine-year-old monk of the community, had been accused of sexually assaulting five women. This was the first time that I heard of him, as he had left the monastery in 1993, two years before I joined, to undertake therapy. One of the women later said that she had informed the Abbot at the time that the abuse was taking place, but nothing was done about it. I believe this to be true; otherwise, why did the Abbey send him off for therapy seven years before his case went to court? It says a lot about where the priorities of the community, and the Institutional Church, lie. In fact, it is striking that there are a large number of treatment centers for priests who abuse throughout the world, but, as far as I know, there are no centers for their victims.

Still, in November 2000, James Deadman was found guilty of sexually assaulting four women. He was cleared of seven counts of indecent assault in relation to a fifth women. During the trial, the jury heard that James Deadman molested the women at Mount St Bernard Abbey in Leicestershire between the years 1983 and 1993, where he lived as a monk. It appears that he groped and sexually abused vulnerable women who were 'brainwashed' into believing it was spiritual therapy during counselling sessions. One of the women told *The Irish Sunday People* newspaper that he stroked her breasts while praying with her, touched her with his 'healing hands,' kissed her on the lips after each counselling session and hugged her so tightly she could feel he was sexually aroused under his habit.[2] James Deadman denied all nineteen charges of indecent assault against the five women, claiming that nothing sexual had ever happened and, if it did, then it was purely accidental or unintentional.

I was genuinely shocked to my core by the revelation of sexual abuse committed by a monk. It was particularly disturbing to learn that some of the abuse took place in a confessional box in the church, a place that is meant to be sacred and safe. As I attempted to process what had taken place, I couldn't help but admire the bravery of the women who came forward to speak their truth. In total contrast, I was taken aback by the response of some senior monks during a community meeting following the guilty verdict. Instead of prioritizing support for the survivors, they appeared to

2. Cook, "My Ordeal," para. 7–10.

be more concerned about potential legal repercussions and the possibility of being sued by the women. The Abbot and his Council decided that it wouldn't be beneficial to reach out to individuals outside the community who were affected (the victims), as it could potentially cause more harm than good.

In response, I couldn't help but wonder who would experience more harm - the community or the victims? As a victim myself, I believed that receiving compassion and support from the Church would have been immensely helpful to these women. To me, it was a no-brainer that the viewpoint of the victims should always be taken into account, but I was definitely in the minority. Witnessing this lack of empathy and accountability deeply troubled me. It seemed to contradict the values of compassion and justice that are at the core of Christian religious teachings. And, as I reflected on the situation, I found it difficult to reconcile the actions of the community with the teachings and example of Jesus Christ. It was an intensely upsetting experience that led me to question the integrity and values of the institution that I had previously trusted.

As a result, I began to notice a change within myself. I came to realize that, for years, I had been concealing a significant part of my truth—the impact of sexual abuse that I had experienced. As a 'Junior Monk,' I regularly engaged in discussions with the Junior Master, who tracked my progress and addressed any concerns that I had. In one of these sessions, whilst we were talking about the James Deadman affair, I mustered the courage to share with him my experience of sexual abuse, and, even though I didn't reveal all the details at the time, it was still a pivotal moment for me. It was the first time that I had spoken to anyone about what Stephen Shield had done to me, and, though I didn't want anything to be done about it at that time, it was still a huge release for me. Shortly after, on April 28, 2001, I made my Solemn Profession, affirming my lifelong commitment to the Cistercian community of Mount St. Bernard Abbey. This moment marked my wholehearted dedication to the monastic way of life that would endure until my last breath, or so I believed at the time.

Following my Solemn Profession, I continued to study for my degree, and then on March 19, 2004, I was ordained to the Diaconate and six months later, to the Priesthood. Shortly afterwards, the Abbot appointed me as Junior Master and in preparation I was enrolled in a course of studies for those involved in monastic formation (Novice Masters and Junior Masters), which was to take place in Rome, with the final few weeks being spent in Assisi—the home of St. Francis. This was a wonderful opportunity for me, and I learned and experienced so much. It just so happened that my time in Rome coincided with the death of Pope St. John Paul II on April 2, 2005.

I was actually standing in St. Peter's Square at the time. Shortly after, I then had the opportunity to pay my last respects in St. Peter's Basilica, attend the opening Mass of the Conclave, the Requiem Mass, as well as witness the newly elected Pope, Benedict XVI, address the crowd in St. Peter's Square. All of this, as a newly ordained Roman Catholic priest, was a once-in-a-lifetime experience. I even had the opportunity to celebrate Mass in the Chapel of St. Elizabeth of Hungary in the crypt of St. Peter's Basilica. Following this, a religious sister who worked in one of the Vatican Congregations, offered to give me a tour of the inside of the Vatican and, needless to say, I leapt at the chance.

As I reflect on this now, I am fully aware that anyone reading this may wonder why someone who had been sexually abused by seminarians, and two priests would excitedly visit the headquarters of the very institution to which his abusers belonged. All I can say is, at the time, I was in complete denial without even realizing it. I had well and truly buried the memories of abuse and was focused on being a devout follower of Christ. The Church was my whole life, and I didn't want to confront the fear and anger associated with those memories. I was afraid to acknowledge what had happened, terrified it might bring further pain, and even more suffering. It is important to emphasize that none of this was intentional. I was just too deeply engrained in denial and confusion to address any of it at that stage in my life. For whatever reason, the timing wasn't right, and I wasn't prepared to face it.

Upon returning home from Rome in late June 2005, I felt revitalized and ready to immerse myself, once again, into the daily round of prayer, reading, and manual work, as well as take on my new role within the community as Junior Master. This involved being there for three junior members of the community: assuming the roles of advisor, spiritual mentor, educator, and confidante—all of which proved to be quite a challenge for me. Teaching, in particular, presented a formidable trial, as I lacked prior experience, and the three juniors came from diverse backgrounds. One had previously served as a Cambridge Don and theologian (now a Bishop in Norway), another held a degree in estate management, and the third had worked on a construction site before joining the monastery. Tailoring the classes to suit their individual needs and knowledge levels proved to be my most formidable task, and I am sure it must have tried their patience too.

In the autumn of 2005, I found myself, once again, in Assisi for the General Chapter of the Cistercian Order. This was a significant event, gathering all the Cistercian Abbots and Abbesses from around the world, along with a delegate from each region. I was elected as the delegate for the Region of the Isles, which included all the monasteries in England, Scotland, Wales, Northern Ireland, the Republic of Ireland, and Norway. In the course of this meeting, I was appointed to the role of 'Regional Secretary for Formation,' a job, which, amongst other things, involved organizing various courses of studies, as well as two week-long residential sessions each year for all the junior monks and nuns in the region—about twenty in total. I found this new responsibility to be quite daunting, and I often felt out of my depth. But I had taken a vow of obedience and tried my best to accept this role as God's will, even though I often felt like the "useless servant" in the Gospel of Luke (17:10).

For decades, I have been plagued by a deep sense of inadequacy, which I believe stems from the trauma of sexual abuse. The inability to shield myself from harm has led me to internalize feelings of inferiority, which, in turn, has led to the misguided belief that only perfection would ensure my safety. Even today, I still grapple with a sense of incompleteness and imperfection, convinced that the only way to shield myself is by aspiring to perfection. In my roles as 'Junior Master' and 'Regional Secretary for Formation,' I found myself acutely aware of my own imperfections and constantly haunted by the fear that others would perceive me as worthless. In my world, it often felt as though there existed only two states of being: perfection or worthlessness, and I keenly recognized that I did not measure up to the former.

Following my return from the General Chapter, the Abbot approached me with a request to represent him at a conference, as he had prior commitments. The conference was being held at Hyning Hall, a convent in Lancaster Diocese, and was intended for all the Abbots and Abbesses of the region. The meeting was entitled: "Savouring Our Experience of God: A Contemplative Approach to Spiritual Direction." Eager to expand my knowledge, I gladly accepted the invitation to attend.

I arrived feeling nervous, as I was the only non-superior present, aside from a few sisters from Hyning Hall, and I was also the youngest by at least a decade. The sessions were led by an American Sister of Mercy, who promised to delve into some thought-provoking topics. These included, cultivating a contemplative mindset, sharing our personal experiences of God, honing effective listening skills, and gaining a deeper understanding of the interconnectedness between spiritual direction and counselling. One of her teaching methods involved role-playing real-life scenarios to demonstrate her method of spiritual direction. She would select a volunteer who was comfortable discussing a personal problem and conduct a spiritual direction session in front of the entire group. I was deeply moved by one particular session, which involved a very senior Abbot of the region. He was incredibly open and honest as he shared his struggles during his many years as a monk and his sincerity made a lasting impact on me. So, one evening, when she approached me to ask if I had anything that I would be willing to discuss with her in front of the group, her compassionate and understanding approach prompted me to disclose to her that I was a victim of clerical abuse. Initially she seemed shocked, and suggested that we both take time to consider it, and that she would check with me again in the morning to see if I was still comfortable with discussing it publicly.

The following day, with the promise that I could stop at any time, I agreed to proceed with the session. Gradually, over an hour and a half, I shared the sexual abuse that I had suffered at the hands of Stephen Shield, leaving nothing out, in front of all the Abbots and Abbesses of the Region of the Isles—my superiors. It is one thing disclosing abuse in privacy to a counsellor, but it is something else reliving one's experience of clergy abuse in front of a group of priests and nuns. I remember at one point feeling a wave of panic coming over me. I began to wonder: "How they would react?" "Would they believe me?" "Would they blame me?" "Would they think less of me or treat me differently?" "Would everyone in the region end up knowing?" "Would Stephen Shield find out?" "Will he seek revenge against me or a loved one?" "What will happen to the information and who will be told?"

All of these questions raced around my head as I continued to speak. I also began to worry about the consequences of my disclosure. Would I be asked to leave the monastery? And once my experiences were public, would I lose all control over what would happen next? I needn't have worried, as several of the group were in tears, and the pain of what they were hearing was written all over their faces. The room was filled with a collective anger, so thick that it was tangible; you could feel it in the air and, more importantly, it wasn't directed at me.

Over two decades have now gone by since I first opened up about the trauma of clergy sexual abuse and still I often reflect on what prompted me to share such a deeply personal and agonizing part of my past. At times, it feels almost absurd that I disclosed it, especially in the presence of others, and I've often questioned whether I should have done so. Yet, if I hadn't broken the silence back then, I might never have found the courage to speak out about it at all. In a peculiar way it had become precious to me, my secret. Not only had my body been violated, but also the deepest part of my being, my soul, had been defiled. But, at least on a subconscious level, I could keep 'my secret' intact. Yet, as the Third Book of Ecclesiastes tells us: "For everything there is a season, and a time for every matter under heaven" (Eccl 3:1) and I do believe that the session at Hyning Hall was the right time. By the end I felt like the widow in the Gospel who had given everything she had, and thankfully, the group, much like Jesus, recognized the extraordinary value of this painful gift (Mark 12:41–44).

In the days that followed, I felt supported and more importantly believed, especially by the women on the course who showed me such kindness and love, providing some respite from the awful isolation and pain that I had been carrying for years. Yet, like a bandage on a deep wound, it could only soothe temporarily, the true healing had to begin from within and once I was back in the monastery, the pain that I thought I had left behind resurfaced, overwhelming me. Speaking out about my abuse was akin to releasing a force beyond my control, much like letting a genie out of a bottle. My decades-old secret, once securely locked away, was now free, and I struggled to regain my equilibrium.

Having received nothing but kindness and understanding from the superiors at Hyning Hall, I made the difficult decision to seek further assistance from my own Abbot and despite the sensitive nature of our discussion, he wasted no time in recommending a counsellor to me and offered to arrange an appointment. His supportive response was a great source of comfort and reassurance at the time, and it gave me both the courage and confidence to begin what would become a very long path to healing.

Reporting Abuse to Lancaster Diocese

Going to my first counselling session in September 2006 was an overwhelming experience. I can still recall the intense anxiety and physical trembling as I parked the car park in front of the house. With hindsight, I now believe that I should have asked for a different counsellor, as the one recommended by the Abbot was a catholic priest. I would have felt much more at ease speaking with a woman in a completely neutral environment, but this didn't seem to be an option, so I just put up with the situation for fear of 'rocking the boat.' At least I was given an opportunity to speak out. The silence, fear and intimidation had to be broken again, just as it had been at Hyning Hall. The world hadn't ended, and I took this as a beacon of hope that it was essential to keep speaking. Every time I voiced my pain and trauma, it became more real to me, emphasizing that it was necessary, and that I wasn't exaggerating or 'making a mountain out of a molehill.' Gradually, the counselling sessions led to a significant change in my focus. They allowed me to see my experience from different perspectives and to bring up more emotions. This shift eventually brought about a turning point in my journey, but it didn't happen overnight.

Initially, I was very matter of fact, almost as if I was recounting somebody else's story. I suppose I still harbored a deep fear of confronting the intense and painful emotions that I had hidden for so long. Employing a lighthearted and jokey tone at times allowed me to keep my true feelings at bay while conveying a sense that everything was under control, but, in reality, it wasn't. In fact, it took me several months of weekly sessions before I allowed myself to show any real emotions, and even then I still felt somewhat disconnected from my own words. There were moments of powerful and conflicting emotions as I grappled with feelings of vulnerability and uncertainty despite knowing that sharing my experiences was the right thing to do. It wasn't uncommon for me to stop on my way home feeling like I was falling apart or losing my grip on reality. The process of disclosure often left me confused and disoriented and a long way from the relief that I had hoped for.

My early recovery was a time of intense struggle, both internally and externally. I faced emotional turmoil, frustration, and overwhelming mental and physical exhaustion. Often, I felt like I was caught in a whirlwind, unable to keep up with the rapid pace of my journey. Even within the peaceful walls of the monastery, tranquility seemed elusive. After a counselling session, I would return to the abbey still wrestling with intense emotions of anger, fear, and resentment, all while having to pretend that I was 'fine' as I slipped back into the serene silence of the community who were completely unaware of my internal battles. My counsellor, some years later wrote: "I do remember he was severely traumatized by the experience of abuse and how the memories, which at the time prior to therapy and during his time, very severely impacted him. He reported feelings of severe distress and trauma, which were clearly visible in the sessions as he spoke of his experiences". This intense struggle forced me to deeply question and re-evaluate every aspect of my world as I sought to navigate my way through the tumultuous process of recovery.

The situation was further complicated by the fact that the monastery had been housing a priest who was awaiting trial for facilitating a known pedophile, and this wasn't the first time: the monastery had harbored several priests like him during my years as a monk. It was a distressing reality that dioceses often sought out abbeys to house priests facing charges of sexual abuse, simply because they didn't know what else to do with them. I found living alongside these troubled men increasingly difficult, especially being a victim of sexual abuse myself. I couldn't escape the feeling that they could sense my unease and the absence of clear instructions for handling such difficult and delicate situations only added to the complexity of the issue. They were always allocated a room alongside the monks without any opportunity for the community to express their thoughts or concerns.

It sickened me that amongst the community there was a general feeling of pity for the priest, but very little talk or concern was ever shown for his victim. He had been accused and charged with facilitating the rape of a twelve-year-old girl between May and November of 2005.[1] At his trial in May 2007, the jury heard that he had met a twenty-one-year-old man living in a hostel for the homeless in Dublin and initiated a sexual relationship with him. He knew the man was later convicted of raping an eight-year-old girl and jailed for twelve years, during which time he visited him and

---

1. For further information on the case, see "Disgraced Priest Is Released from Prison."

wrote to him. The priest admitted having a homosexual relationship with the man but denied knowing that he was repeatedly raping and sexually abusing the twelve-year-old girl. He said he was so besotted with the man that he was blind to what was happening. The priest gave the man £20,000 to lavish treats, clothes, and holidays, on the child. On Friday May 25, 2007, the jury found him guilty of one count of facilitating the abuse, and he was remanded in custody until June 14, when he would be sentenced along with the man, who pleaded guilty to raping the girl before the trial. When the day came, he was sentenced to five years' imprisonment for aiding and abetting the rape of a twelve-year-old girl.

Living alongside this man while trying to work through my memories of being abused was incredibly challenging. It felt like a constant struggle as I grappled with my emotions and tried to navigate my monastic responsibilities. I found it extremely distressing to be in the same vicinity as this priest, especially when I observed him forming relationships with the junior monks under my care. The situation became even more complicated when I noticed him taking one of the juniors to the farmyard after supper to have private conversations in the barns. Confronting them about their interactions only led to further conflict and I faced anger and displeasure from them both, which added to the strain that I was already under. Discussing these complex dynamics with my counsellor was pivotal in influencing my decision-making process. He stressed the importance of allowing survivors of abuse to be in control of their own recovery process, advising me not to take on too much too quickly, as it could lead me to feeling overwhelmed, stressed, and hopeless. Each step, he suggested, should only be taken when I felt ready. Trying to rush the process and skipping important steps would only lead to frustration.

The experience of living alongside this priest, who had already been accused of inappropriate behavior, significantly influenced my own decision to report Stephen Shield. However, it was not the only factor. The defining moment occurred during one Sunday Mass as the priest read the following from the Gospel of St. Luke: "Nothing is hidden which will not be revealed; and nothing concealed which will not be made known. Therefore, whatever you say in the darkness will be heard in the light, and whatever you speak confidentially in the innermost rooms will be proclaimed from the rooftops" (Luke 12:2–3).

These words struck a chord within me, resonating deeply with my inner turmoil and my strong sense of yearning for truth and justice. It was as if time had slowed down, creating a moment that felt as if I were having a personal conversation with Jesus. In that instant, everything became clear to me, and I knew that I could no longer keep quiet about the secret I had been carrying any longer. It was almost as if I could hear a gentle voice saying, "The truth will set you free," (John 8:32) and I longed to break free from the haunting memories that had been troubling me.

So, during my next counselling session,
I expressed my readiness to take things further and report the sexual abuse to the relevant authorities. So, with my counsellor's support, I reached out to the Child Protection Coordinator for the Diocese of Nottingham, and I was relieved to find him exceptionally supportive. His sincere willingness to assist me, including intervening with the Lancaster diocese on my behalf, was a ray of hope. His support, along with that of my counsellor, played a central role in my journey towards healing.

Subsequently, on April 26, 2007, he sent them my full disclosure about Stephen Shield, along with the following letter:

> Dear …, I met with Fr. Paul Murphy Sanderson [PMS] and his counsellor (who is a Priest of Nottingham Diocese) yesterday. Fr. [PMS] wishes me to forward his disclosure for your consideration. I outlined some of the possible processes which might unfold as a result of his disclosure. He is clear that he doesn't want the Police to be involved, but felt that Bishop Campbell should know of what happened to him and take appropriate action. He feels that there must be others who this happened to, given the nature of Stephen Shield at the time, and also the sort of behavior which he witnessed in seminaries. His fear is that his disclosure might become widely known in the diocese. He wants as few people as possible to know since his family are there and he knows many priests in the diocese. At present only the Abbot at Mount St. Bernard Abbey and his counsellor (and myself) know about this. Fr. [PMS] asked that he shouldn't be consulted directly about anything, but that, if possible, I should be the conduit between you and him.

As indicated in the letter, I was terrified at the thought of my disclosure becoming public knowledge. My primary goal was to ensure that the diocese was fully informed and that they would handle the matter internally with Stephen Shield, maintaining the utmost confidentiality. I was determined to avoid any unnecessary attention being drawn to the situation and I was deeply anxious about my family finding out, knowing how much it would distress them. The burden of shame and guilt, which I still harbored, was a heavy weight on my shoulders, increasing the importance of maintaining confidentiality. Therefore, I was taken aback when I received the following reply four days later from the Nottingham Child Protection Coordinator:

Dear Fr. [PMS], the Child Protection Co-ordinator for Lancaster Diocese, Fr. [A], has emailed me to say firstly that Bishop Campbell is taking your disclosure very seriously and is mindful of your concern that others may have been harmed by Stephen Shield. He has also asked if he could meet with you to discuss parts of your disclosure where there was some vagueness, particularly the 'out of body' experience. He has also told me the bishop would like him to meet your Abbot, though I don't know the reason for this. Do you have a view about either of these?"

I remember feeling frustrated, as I had never used the phrase an 'out of body' experience in my disclosure. What I actually wrote, when trying to describe my memory of being sexually abused by Stephen Shield, was: "The next image is one of two naked bodies intertwined on the bed, and the background is very red. However, when I see the image, I am not in it but looking at it from the door of the room, and this is, I believe, due to the trauma and the fact that I have dissociated myself from what happened."

It seemed totally unacceptable to me, that a priest, especially one serving as a Child Protection Coordinator, did not understand the concept of dissociation. Unfortunately, Lancaster Diocese had recently made a cost-cutting decision to replace their qualified Child Protection Coordinator with Fr. [A] who lacked the necessary qualifications and experience for the job. I never felt as though he really understood the seriousness of the situation. Had he known anything at all about the effects of sexual abuse, he would have understood that I was talking about dissociation, which is a widespread effect of abuse, where the trauma is so significant that the mind cannot cope with recalling it. Therefore, the person experiences themselves being abused as though they were watching it taking place from a distance. This does not mean it didn't happen, or the person was floating around the ceiling having an 'out of body experience.' It is something that happens in recalling the event, not that the person was not really there in the event itself. I felt as though I had to explain myself when what I really needed was respect and understanding to support me through the experience.

Following Fr. [A's] request to meet with me and because I felt that he didn't fully understand my disclosure, I agreed to the meeting in the hope that it would help clarify the situation. Fortunately, I was already scheduled to be in the Diocese of Lancaster, at Fernyhalgh, a local Shrine dedicated to the Blessed Virgin Mary, so I informed Fr. [A] about this, suggesting that we meet there. But, instead, he proposed that we meet at Forton Service Station, which was nearby, in order to avoid raising any suspicion from the local parish priest. Apparently, this was to protect my anonymity, but, in hindsight, I doubt whether the local priest would have even given our meeting a second thought. So, on the evening of Saturday May 5, 2007, at 7 p.m., I found myself seated at the Service Station café, anxiously awaiting my meeting with Fr. [A]. As the minutes ticked by, my nerves intensified, and I wondered if I would be able to maintain my composure. It seemed as though Fr. [A] was purposely keeping me waiting. I found his lack of punctuality to be very disrespectful, especially for such a crucial discussion, which you would have thought required extra compassion and respect for the victim.

Then suddenly, twenty minutes late, Fr. [A] nonchalantly strolled into the café, his casual demeanor sharply contrasting with my own apprehension. Drawing near to my table, with a huge grin on his face, he flippantly remarked, "You're a big lad; why didn't you fight him off?" I was totally stunned and didn't know how to respond. It was as if he thought the entire situation was some sort of joke. Such a comment was genuinely disrespectful and entirely out of order. Asking a victim of abuse, 'why they didn't just fight their abuser off,' is possibly the most insensitive and inappropriate thing one could ever say. It essentially implies that the victim not only brought the abuse upon themselves but also failed to take any action to prevent it. In his ignorance, he totally lacked any understanding of the dynamics of abuse and demonstrated an utter absence of compassion.

However, his unprofessionalism was not the only issue. His choice of location, a café in a service station, was entirely unsuitable for discussing such a serious matter. For example, halfway through our meeting, the café was invaded by half-drunk, thunderously loud, football fans. Such a public and noisy setting was a clear indication of his lack of understanding. What if I had wanted to express emotion, cry or shout with anger? It was as if he had no concept of my need for privacy and anonymity and this only added to my frustration and disappointment.

Nevertheless, and in spite of his insensitivity, the discussion continued with the focus turning to whether or not Stephen Shield had ever reached out to apologize to me. I immediately told him 'no,' and expressed doubt that such an apology would ever come to pass. In my view, abusers maintain their power through a potent mix of secrecy and fear. To apologize would mean breaking the secrecy and acknowledging their guilt, both to themselves and to a lesser extent, to the victim. This power dynamic left me feeling confused and uncertain about Fr. [A]'s interpretation of the situation. Did he believe that the absence of an apology was evidence of my delusion? Or did it only serve to deepen his understanding of Stephen Shield's callousness? I really couldn't tell.

At one point, Fr. [A] told me about a 'narrow escape' that he had experienced, when another student had propositioned him whilst in the seminary. Such unprofessionalism made light of my own trauma, and his 'narrow escape' was of no interest to me, but it did lead me into speaking of my regrettable experience with the student from Gibraltar, which seemed to interest Fr. [A]. Then, as soon as I had finished, he told me that he was now obliged to contact the Child Protection Coordinator for the Diocese of Hexham and Newcastle. At no point did he ask for my consent' and therefore he had no right to tell anyone, especially since I was not making a formal disclosure to him and I was an adult at the time of the abuse. I stressed that I did not want him to take any action and would not cooperate with the Diocese of Hexham and Newcastle if he did. As I have already stated, it is essential that victims of abuse have control over the pace and intensity of their own recovery. Every step should only be taken when they themselves are ready.

It seemed to me, that Fr. [A], having read the cover letter and my disclosure was clearly trying to use them against me. The cover letter explicitly stated the following about me: "His fear is that his disclosure might become widely known in the diocese. He wants as few people as possible to know since his family are there and he knows many priests in the diocese." Regardless of my clear decision not to involve the police, Fr. [A] persistently attempted to demonstrate how my fears could become a reality if I ever changed my mind. He vigorously stressed the high regard in which Stephen Shield was held in the diocese, being both Dean and a Canon of the Cathedral, and reminded me of the potential public exposure that any action against him would inevitably bring. It was clear to me that he was trying to manipulate the situation to his advantage, which only strengthened my resolve not to be intimidated or coerced in this way.

In addition, and while we were discussing the apparent high regard in which my abuser was held, I learned that in the past, the Diocese of Lancaster had consistently placed accused individuals on administrative leave. However, they had recently discovered that other dioceses had different protocols and so, in regard to Stephen Shield, they would be re-evaluating this practice. Yet again, it seemed that Fr. [A] was attempting to unduly influence me. I fully understood that any decision as to what would happen to Stephen Shield lay within their jurisdiction. Nevertheless, I got the distinct impression that he was uncertain as to what the next course of action would be.

I felt deeply unsettled after our discussion, which had come to a close with Fr. [A] asking me if I would be willing to meet Stephen Shield face to face in the presence of Bishop Campbell should he deny the allegations. This suggestion left me bewildered. What did they expect to achieve from such a confrontation? Did they want me to accuse him directly, for him only to deny it? It was evident to me that if Shields denied the allegations, there would be proper procedures that should be followed, none of which would involve a direct meeting between us. The question to meet and the implied pressure to agree troubled me deeply. It was my understanding that in such situations they should follow the established procedures, prioritize the victim's well-being, maintain the integrity of the investigation, and reassure everyone involved about the fairness and thoroughness of the process. So why couldn't they see that subjecting me to such pressure was both highly inappropriate and the very last thing that I needed?

A whirlwind of emotions consumed me as I made my way back to the monastery. The sense of betrayal, frustration, and disappointment that I felt towards the authorities of Lancaster Diocese was overwhelming. And, in spite of Fr. [A]'s repeated assurances that my allegations were being taken seriously, their incompetence was painfully evident. It seemed as though they were completely oblivious to the immense courage and emotional toll that it takes for a victim, particularly a priest victim, to come forward with allegations of sexual abuse. It is never a decision taken lightly, but one that involves profound soul-searching and painful questioning.

Over the course of the next few days, I found myself unable to let go of the encounter, replaying it in my mind and dwelling on the particular phrase, 'You're a big lad; why didn't you fight him off?' The seemingly indifferent tone in addressing such a serious issue felt like a direct attack on my emotional vulnerability, as if Fr. [A] was insinuating, 'We don't believe you' and, 'You must have somehow allowed this to happen.' Sadly, sharing my feelings had left me feeling exposed, and being met with a wall of doubt and suspicion, further deepened the emotional turmoil that I was already feeling.

Then, to add insult to injury, on May 18, 2007, Fr. [A] phoned my Abbot to ask if it would be okay for himself, and possibly one other member of the Lancaster Diocesan Child Protection Commission, to visit the Monastery. Apparently, he wished to meet with the Abbot to 'clarify a few issues contained in my initial disclosure.' To my surprise, the Abbot agreed to this, and a meeting was planned for Wednesday, May 23, at Mount Saint Bernard Abbey.

I must admit that the Abbot's decision left me feeling somewhat confused and slightly worried. I couldn't understand why the diocese needed to talk to the Abbot when I was the one who had made the disclosure, and as such, I was the only one who could provide accurate information about it. As I have already explained in some detail, I first met with Fr. [A] at his request, to clarify any queries he may have had in regard to my disclosure. Of course, I was under no obligation to meet with him, but I was eager to be as helpful as possible. So, in order to ease my anxiety, I approached the Abbot to see if he would call Fr. [A] back, as I wanted to find out exactly what it was that he was unclear about. It felt as if they were checking up on me, possibly trying to assess my character and personality and I was puzzled as to why they would seek information from someone else about matters that I was best qualified to answer.

The Abbot agreed and, during the phone call, Fr. [A] stated that he required my date of birth as a priority. Having been a seminarian for the Diocese of Lancaster for nearly six years, I found it hard to believe that my date of birth was not easily accessible to him. Also, if it was so important, why hadn't he asked me about it during our meeting at the service station? Fortunately for me, the Abbot stood his ground and refused to give Fr. [A] my date of birth, saying that he should have asked me directly. But still, Fr. [A] persisted, stressing that specific details in my initial disclosure needed further clarification. Once again, the Abbot made it clear that he couldn't comment on my disclosure as he hadn't read it, and he suggested that Fr. [A] contact the Child Protection Coordinator for the Diocese of Nottingham for any further clarification he required. It made absolutely no sense that Fr. [A] and his colleague were willing to undertake a six-hour journey just to find out my date of birth and discuss a few points from my disclosure.

Consequently, as soon as the Abbot explained to Fr. [A] that there was no reason for them to meet in person and that he was no longer willing to do so, Fr. [A] changed his tack and became quite threatening. He pointed out that the Abbot had been aware of the abuse since 2001 (when he was Junior Master), and had failed to report it, so there could well be serious consequences. He continued to stress that if Stephen Shield had harmed anyone else, then the Abbot would be answerable to the police. Such threatening behavior was not only unprofessional and inaccurate but also abusive. The conversation ended with Fr. [A] emphasizing to the Abbot that Stephen Shield's life and reputation were at stake, the fact that he never mentioned my damaged life said it all!

I was deeply upset when I learned what had been said during the phone call. It was evident that the threatening and unprofessional behavior of Fr. [A] needed to be urgently challenged. It was disheartening for me to witness Lancaster Diocese prioritizing their own reputation over my accusations of sexual abuse. So, after seeking advice from several safeguarding professionals, I decided to report Fr. [A] to the Director of the Catholic Office for the Protection of Children and Vulnerable Adults in England and Wales (COPCA), as well as to Bishop Campbell of Lancaster, and a member of the Chair of the Lancaster Diocesan Protection Commission. In the thorough report that I attached to the cover letter I provided explicit details of my interactions with Fr. [A], and emphasized the challenges and bravery required in disclosing sexual abuse. Coincidentally, no sooner had I sealed the envelope than I received an email from Fr. [A] informing me that the police had been notified, despite my explicitly telling him that I didn't want the police involved. I had stressed several times that I just wanted the Diocese to deal with the issue internally. He went on to say that his "first impressions [were] that they would be looking at sexual assault," and then mentioned that the "probability of getting a prosecution [was] doubtful without a thorough investigation," which seemed to imply that Stephen Shield would probably get away with it.

He continued to inform me that if I wished to speak to the police, they would be more than willing to visit me and explain in more detail what exactly would be involved. Whilst I appreciated this offer, as it reassured me that the police would take the matter seriously if I ever changed my mind, I was unhappy with Fr. [A]'s request that I email him back before Monday (it was Saturday evening), to let him know whether I wanted to meet with the police or not. I politely thanked him, but as soon as Monday morning arrived my only plan was to post my letters of complaint.

Surprisingly, Bishop Campbell was the first to reply. He began by thanking me for my letter and enclosure and abruptly ended with, "Obviously, you will understand that I cannot comment on your letter at the present moment but have been in touch with the Commission." Surprisingly, he added a postscript at the bottom of the page, mentioning that he had made his ordination retreat at Mount Saint Bernard fourteen years previously. His response left me puzzled, as if the casual mention of his retreat was intended to make up for his refusal to comment.

Two days later I received a response from the Director of COPCA:

Dear Fr. PMS,

I am concerned to hear of your experience in relation to informing the Diocese of Lancaster about your past abusive experiences.

I have spoken to Bishop Campbell of Lancaster about the appropriate way in which to take this matter forward and it is my advice that the incoming Chair of the Lancaster Diocesan Child Protection Commission, who is about to be formally appointed to the position, should take the lead in making enquiries into your situation, on the basis of receipt of your complaint.

This will of course run alongside actions to investigate the allegations of abuse you have made, which will be followed up in line with the National Child Protection Policy.

COPCA's view of the events which you describe may be requested in the course of the Lancaster CP Commission Chair's enquiries, and if so, we will be happy to provide them at the appropriate stage.

I regret that you feel that you have experienced less than adequate service at such a sensitive point for you.

While Bishop Campbell's response had left me feeling disappointed, COPCA's felt like an insult. The phrase 'I regret that you feel you have experienced less than adequate service,' sounded like 'it's not my fault you were born so sensitive,' and 'less than adequate service,' might be appropriate in a restaurant but not when speaking of sexual abuse. I felt disbelieved and disrespected. I had opened my heart and soul to people I thought would respect and support me—followers of Christ—but all I had received was mockery and incompetence.

Soon after I received another email from Fr [A] stating that because I hadn't met with the police, "they (would) simply log (my) complaint and refer the matter back to the diocese." He went on, "If that happens, the next stage would be for Bishop Campbell to have Stephen Shield in to address what is contained in the disclosure. I will keep you informed…"

He never kept me informed, as this was the last I ever heard from Lancaster Diocese. In fact, they remained silent and did not communicate with me again until March 2013, a gap of nearly six years. The lack of information about whether Bishop Campbell ever addressed Stephen Shield or took any action, combined with the knowledge that Shield still held the positions of Canon and Dean of the Cathedral for the intervening six years, implies that no significant measures were taken.

As I continued my counselling sessions, week after week, in the hope of a response from Lancaster Diocese, I couldn't help but notice the increasing whispers in the community about my Wednesday afternoons out. The diary in the Bursar's Office had made my frequent car use public knowledge, and this unwanted attention made me feel like I was violating an unspoken rule and thus further complicating an already challenging situation. Feeling misunderstood, I decided to share the reason for my weekly absences with the community. I decided to do this through a letter which the Abbot kindly agreed to read out at a community meeting in my absence. It would have been too traumatic to do it in person.

I longed for the community to understand and be compassionate, to comprehend the inner turmoil that I had been struggling with. Wednesdays were especially difficult. I would spend an hour sharing my feelings only to go back to the silent and reflective atmosphere of the monastery. The temptation to scream and let out all my bottled-up anguish was strong, but I forced myself to keep it in. This led me into a downward spiral of despair and intense self-blame. My hope in sharing my trauma with the community, was that I would find the acceptance and empathy I needed to heal.

However, once the meeting was over, there was a noticeable sense of disapproval amongst the community and, over the course of the next few days, I began to feel like I had somehow disappointed them all. I felt isolated and ignored; hardly anyone acknowledged me or offered comfort or support. These men were like family to me; I had lived alongside them for more than a dozen years. Yet, now that I had spoken out about being sexually abused by a priest, it felt like I had betrayed them. An American Bishop (James McHugh of the Diocese of Camden, New Jersey) called victims of clergy sexual abuse "Terrorists" and their desire to confront their abuse with the truth a "new kind of terrorism" in the Church, and in many ways, this is how I was made to feel.[2] One of the monks, to whom I was particularly close, and who had also studied in the junior seminary at Ushaw in the 1940s, approached me and said, "just get over it; when I was a student, it was common practice and acceptable for older students to play around with younger ones, for boys to fancy boys, and you are no different." I was stunned and snapped back, "it may have been acceptable to you, but it isn't to me," and from that day on he avoided me.

One of the most distressing memories I have from this time is of an intense interaction with a senior monk in the Abbey guesthouse. As the Assistant Guest Master, I had various responsibilities, from cleaning and polishing to welcoming guests and serving tea. One day, while walking through the communal sitting room, I heard my name being called. It was coming from a corner where a monk was sitting with half a dozen guests enjoying a cup of tea. As I approached, the monk began to admonish me in a loud voice, saying, "You should be ashamed of yourself. Instead of causing trouble, you should be fervently praying for that priest, praying that he finds his way to heaven, and also praying for his poor mother." His voice was so loud that everyone in the room heard it, and I felt as though everyone was judging me, even Jesus hanging on the wall. My only thought was to escape—I had to numb the pain and confusion that I was feeling and so, in that moment, I made a decision that would become both a crutch and a curse. I took a bottle of whisky from the kitchen storeroom. The burn of the alcohol seemed to match the fire in my soul, and for a moment, I felt like I could take on the whole Church. But very quickly the temporary relief gave way to a darkness in which I languished.

2. Keeler, "New Shepherd," para. 91.

From that day on, alcohol became both my confidante and my tormentor. It would reassure me that I was doing the right thing by speaking out, only to later turn on me with the damning words, "You should be ashamed of yourself." This phrase, like a relentless echo, began to chip away at my self-esteem. I sought refuge at the bottom of another bottle, often surprised that no one seemed to notice. But, then again, how could they? Most of them had already distanced themselves from me, and our relationships had become strained as a result of what they perceived was a betrayal of the priesthood, the community, and the Church.

I began to miss Vigils (the prayers at 3:30 a.m. every day) and stayed up after everyone else had gone to bed, wandering around the cloisters and gardens in constant torment. Was I mistaken? Should I just keep quiet? But, how could I? It was eating away at me; I felt like I was going mad. Why did no one seem to believe me? Why was I the one in the wrong? There was no escape from the pain which consumed me, that is until I found a scalpel in the monastery printing press. I began to cut the back of my left hand, gently at first and then harder until it bled. I was punishing my body; my abused body and the relief was instant.

The following day and to my embarrassment, the Abbot noticed my injured hand and inquired as to what had happened. Shamefully, I told him that I had accidentally put my hand in the bin without realizing that someone had dumped some broken glass in it. But, in spite of my earnestness, I couldn't tell what he was really thinking as he nodded solemnly and quietly left the kitchen. The shame that I felt further fueled my anger towards myself, the community, and the Church. I had gone from being a well-respected, competent, popular priest to a self-loathing shell. Thoughts of Stephen Shield, his voice, his stubble, the bed, and even the furniture consumed my thoughts day and night. I couldn't eat or sleep and continued drinking to numb the pain. Eventually, everything came to a head one evening in August. As soon as everyone was in bed, I ascended the spiral staircase of the church tower. Once at the top, I climbed onto a viewing platform, placed my hands on the parapet, and stared down the one-hundred-foot drop. I imagined what it would do to my body were I let myself fall and for almost an hour I remained there, contemplating the idea. My thoughts fluctuated between letting go and pulling back. It felt as if an imaginary rope was pulling me over and I was struggling against its pull. In the end, I managed to crawl to the door at the top of the stairs and will myself back down the stairs until I entered the cloister below. From there I managed to make it back to my room.

Over the next few months, I struggled with the terrifying realization that nobody was taking me seriously. Instead, I was nothing but a troublemaker, despite only ever speaking the truth. I began to have panic attacks along with palpitations, sweating, chest tightness, and an overwhelming fear of impending doom. As the stress of everything began to take its toll, the community began to notice physical signs of my declining mental health, which were reflected in my appearance. The monastery's infirmarian, responsible for caring for the sick, decided that I needed closer monitoring and suggested I move into one of the infirmary rooms. At that point, I was so emotionally exhausted that I didn't care where I slept. I was so desperate for any sort of relief that I readily agreed to the suggestion.

I was allocated a large room, on the ground floor, with a rather macabre view of the cemetery from the window. By this time, I was only eating a tiny amount of food once a day. It was a less obvious way of self-harming. I was still drinking alcohol, which I acquired by sneaking out of my room at night and taking it from the community storeroom.

On October 1st, I attended an appointment with the local GP. In his notes he wrote: "Paul is very angry and frustrated and has several cuts from a scalpel, on both his left and right arms. He is regularly seeing a counsellor and is due to see a Consultant Psychiatrist soon."

Three days later, I met with a Consultant Psychiatrist in Leicester and during the meeting he observed the following:

> There has been an increase in distress following the disclosure of sexual abuse, which was reported to the diocese in April 2007 without a satisfactory response. There have been instances of self-harm with a scalpel. The individual is currently residing in an enclosed Cistercian Monastery with thirty-two monks, and there is a growing tension in relationships within the monastery. During our interview, the individual appeared troubled and angry, with low mood, decreased appetite, and disrupted sleep patterns. There have been recent instances of self-injury, and the individual is exhibiting symptoms of depressive illness. It is essential for the individual to receive support in addressing the traumatic events from the past.

Whilst I was receiving support from my counsellor, I sadly wasn't getting it from anywhere else. It soon became evident to me that the Diocese of Lancaster was not taking my accusations seriously, and my community's response made it clear that many would have preferred me to have remained silent and continue to suppress the painful events of the past.

During my time in the infirmary, only one of the senior monks took the time to check up on me, while the three junior monks visited me regularly. However, the infirmarian had the most significant impact on my experience. He made sure I had a constant supply of beer and cigarettes, which I suspect was what made me so popular with the junior monks. The air in the cloisters became saturated with the scent of tobacco, reminiscent of a gentleman's club. Needless to say, this was not well-received by the monks, in spite of the fact that some of them indulged in secret smoking sessions in the garden.

While alone in the infirmary room, I felt an overwhelming sense of isolation. I was in desperate need of solace and understanding to help me cope with the aftermath of reporting the sexual abuse. Still, instead of finding the support I needed, I encountered a disheartening sense of blame from the community. It seemed that there was a belief that the abuse, seemingly permitted by God, must have some profound purpose and perhaps be ultimately beneficial. This deeply rooted conviction was intertwined with the idea that spiritual enlightenment and personal growth stem from the profound lessons learned during times of despair and tribulation. As a result, there was a tendency in monastic life to embrace life's hardships and the pain they brought as an act of accepting the apparent will of God. Trappist monks, the branch of the Cistercians to which I belonged, were known in the past for their practice of 'intentional humiliations.' This practice played a significant role in the monks' lives, often leading to the early deaths of some due to the lack of prudence in asceticism. At one point, the ascetic practices were so severe at the Abbey of La Trappe in France that the life expectancy of monks upon entering the abbey was a mere five years. The concept of not only enduring suffering but actively seeking it was still prevalent, although less so, among some of the senior monks in my community, which possibly explains their behavior towards me.

During my years as a monk, I came to understand that from every negative experience, a positive one can emerge if we choose to see it as an opportunity for growth. I also held a strong belief that God, in His infinite wisdom, can use suffering for good, turning it into a catalyst for our personal development. However, I did not see suffering itself as inherently good, nor did I believe that God directly caused it; instead, I saw it as a tool that God can use to bring about positive change. Recalling a phrase my grandmother often used to say, "God helps those who help themselves," I gradually realized that I needed a positive change in my life and so, after a lot of thought, I wrote a letter to the Abbot. I shared how difficult it had become living within an enclosed monastic community of men for whom sexual abuse, in fact sexual anything, was something to be avoided like the plague and I attempted to excuse them by blaming it on their unsatisfactory formation for a life of celibacy. I ended the letter by requesting a leave of absence. In summary, I wrote:

Dear Father, after careful thought and advice, I propose the following: I need some distance from the monastery but don't want to be too far away. I suggest having external accommodation while working in the monastery's farm and dairy as a way to provide financial support for my living expenses during this time. This will give me structure, freedom, and space to work through my difficulties. This plan will help me rediscover and reaffirm my vocation. I hope you can consider my proposal for my healing process and the reaffirmation of my commitment to my vocation. Thank you.

Somewhat surprisingly he agreed, and, within a week, I had moved out of the monastery and into a modest flat in Ibstock, a village a few miles from the Abbey. At first, the newfound freedom was exhilarating: having my own space and the liberty to eat whatever and whenever I pleased was a welcome change. However, this newfound independence only magnified my feelings of isolation, especially when I went to work on the monastery farm. I felt utterly marginalized, as if I were an unwelcome presence. The junior monks were explicitly instructed to avoid interaction with me, which created a profound sense of alienation. My days were spent in silence, whilst my evenings were spent in solitude, once again seeking solace in alcohol.

Sitting alone in the flat, my only companion was the bottle, but it brought no relief from the memories that tortured me. I was totally lost, adrift in a sea of uncertainty and confusion. In spite of doing what I believed to be the right thing in reporting the abuse, I was met by the Church with a deafening silence. No one reached out or offered me compassion as my world slowly crumbled. Overwhelmed by anger and pain, I discontinued my antidepressants and continued drinking in a futile attempt to numb my emotions. For ten months, I lived a life where alcohol was my coping mechanism. Yet despite this, I managed to function in my daily life. I continued to attend my weekly counselling sessions, seeking guidance and understanding as best I could. However, the bottom line was that the mishandling of my disclosure to Lancaster Diocese had a paralyzing effect on me, thereby thwarting my attempts to move forward along a path to healing.

To add insult to injury, in September 2008, I received the unwelcome news that the monastery was no longer prepared to provide me with financial support. This meant that, not only would I stop receiving payment for my work, but my rent would also go unpaid. This news was difficult to process, and I needed to consider my options carefully. There was no way I could return to monastic life, so I had a lot to think about and not much time to do it. In my resolve, I visited the Bishop of Nottingham to see if there were any potential job opportunities in one of his parishes. He greeted me with genuine warmth and wasted no time in offering me a position as a curate in a parish in Lincoln, thereby indicating his deep trust in my abilities. This unexpected show of faith rejuvenated my confidence, which had been waning for quite some time. I accepted the offer with a heart full of gratitude and, as I prepared to leave, he kindly escorted me to the door and stood on the street in order to bid me farewell.

I arrived at the parish the day before the parish priest, who also happened to be new to the job. Unfortunately, he seemed to have a knack for rubbing people up the wrong way and within the first couple of months, he had managed to alienate about half of the parish, causing the Sunday Mass attendance to drop drastically. My living conditions were also less than ideal. The accommodation consisted of a miserable, ground floor lean-to attached to an empty presbytery, which was used during the day by the local Catholic school as classrooms. As if that wasn't enough, I was twice woken in the middle of the night by gunshots, and the sound of breaking glass, while my bedroom window was shot at. And on top of this, the parish priest made it nearly impossible for me to receive my monthly wage and there was a period of six months where he simply refused to pay me. It felt like the whole world was conspiring against me and this was absolutely the last thing I needed. Also, my counselling sessions stopped when the monastery would no longer support me and so, for most of my time in Lincoln, I no longer had anyone to confide in.

One positive aspect of my time in the parish was that I took on a part-time chaplain role at HM Prison Moreton Hall, which had recently been converted into a women's prison. I would spend ten hours each week talking with the prisoners and then on Saturday afternoons, I would lead a Eucharistic service for those who wanted to attend, prior to which I would hear confessions. Throughout my years as a priest, I heard some incredibly honest, soul-searching, and moving accounts of people's lives, but none compared to the sincerity I heard from these women prisoners. Even though they lacked external freedom some of them had discovered a profound inner freedom. Reflecting on this, I came to realize that I had external freedom, but was constrained internally, a prisoner within myself. I was living in a perpetual past, while simultaneously shielding myself from what had already occurred. The memories of what Stephen Shield had done to me would never leave me, and I found it increasingly difficult to reconcile the sexual abuse with the positive aspects of the Church. The apparent incompetence of Lancaster Diocese seemed to be a deliberate strategy, a hope, or expectation, that I would lose interest or energy and give up. This experience felt like a cycle of re-traumatization, especially when I could never get an adequate response from those in authority.

After enduring two years in Lincoln, I reached my 'breaking point.' I had become so run down with stress and anxiety that in May 2009 I was diagnosed with glandular fever, which left me feeling incredibly poorly for six weeks, with aftereffects that lingered on for a good eighteen months. Feeling that I couldn't go on in the parish, I reached out to the Bishop of Nottingham once again, to share with him how challenging life in the parish had become for me and how immense the difficulties were that I was facing regarding the abuse. To my dismay, he showed no interest and seemed unwilling to even engage with my situation. His response left me feeling not only disappointed but also deeply hurt and abandoned. Following a brief and dismissive conversation, we reached an agreement for me to depart from the parish. This left me in a state of anguish, grappling with the uncertainty of once again having no source of income or a place to call home.

Luckily, I was fortunate to receive support from a close friend, which enabled me to move into a cottage in a small village named Newbold Coleorton in Leicestershire. I didn't have to pay rent, which was a relief, because I had no income. I spent my days walking in the countryside and contemplating my situation. The tranquil surroundings and the simplicity of everyday life in the cottage offered a renewed sense of freedom that I hadn't experienced in years. However, the downside was that my stay in the cottage was limited to just six months, which meant that in no time I had to begin the daunting task of finding a new place to move to.

Despite the obstacles I had encountered within the Church, I was determined not to let them deter me from my desire to return to the monastery. So, I persisted in my efforts to secure work within the Church once again. Therefore, I applied for a part-time role as a Naval Chaplain at HMS Nelson and the Dockyard in Portsmouth and I successfully secured the position. In addition, the local Bishop, who was also a friend of the monastery, entrusted me with a parish on Hayling Island. This arrangement allowed me to spend four days a week fully immersed in the parish community, whilst dedicating two days to the naval base and all that was required of me there. The prospect of commencing a new chapter in a parish, this time taking on sole responsibility, filled me with a sense of eager anticipation. And early in 2010, I excitedly moved into my new living quarters at the parish, ready to embrace the challenges and rewards that lay ahead.

During the first year everything went really well as I fully immersed myself in parish life on an island. I made some great memories, like buying a kayak and spending my days off rowing in the Solent. At the naval base, I officiated several weddings and, on Wednesday afternoons, I would carry out burials at sea for the cremated remains of sailors and navy veterans. One of the most memorable moments was conducting the very last baptisms to take place on HMS Ark Royal, just before she was decommissioned in 2011. The gravity of this moment, marking the end of an era, was not lost on me. It prompted me to consider the possibility of finally leaving the haunting memories of sexual abuse in the past and embracing a new, hopeful chapter in my life. However, if previous experience was anything to go by, I should have realized that the road ahead would be anything but straightforward.

Every couple of months, the clergy from the local Deanery, which was comprised of parishes within a specific area, would gather together to seek God's will for the mission of the local Church. This required that the participants be Christ-centered, prayerful, and open to the Holy Spirit's guidance. At one such meeting at the Sacred Heart church in Waterlooville, Portsmouth, it was brought to our attention that a woman who had been a pupil at the local convent school had made an accusation of sexual abuse against a former convent chaplain. To my horror and absolute disgust, one of the priests blurted out, "Typical! Another money-grabbing floozy comes out of the woodwork and jumps on the bandwagon," and they all laughed in agreement. Their dismissive attitude cut deep, and I tried in vain to get them to understand that this incident served as a stark reminder of the urgent need for awareness and action against sexual abuse. Unfortunately, my efforts were futile and driving home that evening I could not help but be overwhelmed by a mixture of anger and frustration. I struggled to shake off the feeling of being unable to escape the dismissive atmosphere that seemed to permeate every interaction I had with the Church. Having personally experienced its impact, I couldn't help but worry about the fate of this unfortunate woman. I can't say for sure what happened to her, but I truly hope she found the justice and comfort she deserved.

Following the deanery meeting, I was struck by a wave of pain, fear, and shame triggered by the actions of the clergy. Memories that had been mostly dormant since my departure from the monastery began to resurface, causing significant disruption and intrusion in my daily life. These distressing flashbacks were particularly marked when I was in church, becoming almost unbearable during the Sunday Eucharist. At the solemn moment of consecration, I would suddenly realize that Stephen Shield was saying the exact same words of consecration in Lancaster Cathedral. *The Catechism of the Catholic Church* tells us that "by this sacrament (the Eucharist) we unite ourselves to Christ, who makes us sharers in his body and blood to form a single body."[3] In other words, every Roman Catholic who receives the Body and Blood of Christ becomes a part of the Body of Christ in the world today. But I did not want to be joined to the same body as Stephen Shield or

---

3. *Catechism*, 1331.

anyone else who had abused me or others, and this caused me a tremendous amount of spiritual suffering. I longed more than anything to be connected to Christ, who was also a victim of abuse, but I couldn't stomach being connected to Stephen Shield and, according to the Church, I couldn't be a part of one without being a part of the other. So, once again, I turned to alcohol to ease my intense emotional pain.

Nonetheless, I endeavored to fulfill my parish duties and navigate through each day as best I could. I didn't know it at the time, but each drink was taking me to a darker place within myself until in January 2012 the situation took a distinct turn for the worse. My drinking escalated to such an extent that I resorted to feigning illness on numerous occasions and making frantic calls to arrange for another priest to conduct the Sunday mass. The downside to all of this was an all-pervading sense of failure, shame, and regret, which deepened the isolation and lack of support I felt. The sexual abuse and the failure of the Church to take me seriously had led me to a desolate and deeply distressing place, one where I was struggling to cope with the challenges of living.

It didn't take long before the area Dean noticed that something was wrong. Word had clearly got out and so he promptly came to see me to discuss the issue. I openly shared with him that I was a victim of sexual abuse and voiced my distress at the complete lack of response to my formal complaint to Lancaster diocese back in 2007. I told him of my urgent need for support, explaining how the prolonged silence was causing me immense emotional strain. As a result, he contacted one of the Vicar Generals of the diocese, who assured me of his support, and in an email wrote: "I just want to see how we can be of help. I know that the area Dean and the local clergy are supportive, and that the Diocesan Safeguarding Coordinator will give you whatever support she can. But I am wondering what else can be done to help you through this and into a better place. I know there are no easy solutions when the issues are big, but there is always a way forward if we are willing."

Finally, I felt like my voice was being heard and I genuinely believed that the diocese of Portsmouth was ready to provide me with the assistance I needed. The Vicar General had even gone as far as arranging to meet with me in person on May 4, which was just two days away. But then things took an unexpected turn for the worse the day before our scheduled meeting. Whilst entering the local Anglican Church, I slipped and fell on a moss-covered, makeshift disabled ramp and broke my ankle in three places. The damage was so bad that I quickly contacted the Dean to let him know what had happened. The following day and much to my surprise, some understanding parishioners offered me a room in their nursing home for a couple of weeks, to help me through the initial stages of recovery. So, I proposed meeting with the Vicar General there, but the Dean felt that it would be better to postpone the meeting until I was feeling better.

So, you can imagine my shock, when I received an unexpected phone call from the Abbot of the monastery informing me that under no circumstances was I to return to the parish and that the diocese was insisting on the immediate removal of all my personal belongings from the parish house. It was an alarming turn of events, especially considering that I had not received any official communication from the Bishop of Portsmouth or anyone else from the diocese. They had simply got the Abbot to do their dirty work, and so once again the Church had put its own interests ahead of showing support and compassion for a victim of abuse.

As you can imagine, losing both my job, and my home, in one phone call came as a devastating blow. The Church, an institution to which I had dedicated my life, had seemingly turned its back on me when I needed it most. The stress and worry about my uncertain future were overwhelming, and only when my parents kindly offered me a place to stay, did I feel a slight reprieve. The fact that not a single person from the Church reached out to check on me during this difficult time left me profoundly disappointed and hurt. It was a harsh realization that the institution I had dedicated my life to would not offer me the support and care that I had hoped for during such challenging times.

Contacting the Police

I spent the remaining two weeks of my stay in the nursing home feeling completely let down and betrayed. Throughout my forty-four years as a member of the Roman Catholic Church, I had actively and passionately participated, beginning with my baptism at just five weeks old. I had undertaken various significant roles, including fifteen years as a Cistercian monk, and several as a parish priest, demonstrating my adaptability and commitment to the Church. However, as soon as I spoke out about the sexual abuse I had suffered at the hands of another priest, I was met with a response that left me feeling completely dispensable and unappreciated, as if, in the eyes of the Church, I was nothing but a nuisance.

As I result, I couldn't wait to get back home to my parents' house. I hadn't actually spent much time there since leaving for Upholland College twenty-eight years earlier, in 1984. I must admit that it did feel strange being back home and also back in Lancaster Diocese after such a lengthy absence. I was also very limited in what I could do, as my left leg from the knee downward was confined to a plaster cast. On the plus side, however, this physical disruption left me with ample time for reflection. I spent days going over and over in my mind all that had happened since 2007, when I first disclosed having been sexually abused to Lancaster Diocese, and the shambolic way in which they had dealt, or rather, failed to deal with it. I recalled Fr. [A's] final email to me, in which he signed off, "I will keep you informed." Five years had now passed, and I had not heard one single word from them.

It was all so frustrating, as I had poured my heart and soul out to the Church in the hope of seeking validation for my pain and suffering. I yearned for a compassionate response and for decisive actions to be taken to ensure the safety of others. As a priest, my initial inclination was to seek some kind of justice from within the confines of the Church establishment. I was concerned about potential public scandal and, in my own way, was trying to safeguard the institution's reputation. My sole intention was not to cause trouble, but to merely alert the Church to a troubling situation involving a priest who had not only abused me but potentially others as well. Yet, my trust was met by a 'Church' shrouded in secrecy, deceit, and cover-ups, prioritizing its public image over the well-being of those it had wronged. The betrayal I experienced as a result of this profound disconnect was deeply disheartening, leaving emotional wounds that cut me deep. As a young man, Stephen Shield had crushed my soul. As a priest, the Church had broken my heart. I felt deeply betrayed and the wounds it left were profound and lifelong.

Realizing the need for a different approach to gain acknowledgment for the traumatic experience I had endured I determined, with some apprehension, to contact the police. This wasn't a decision I took lightly. I knew that, at the end of the day, it would be my word against his, and that there was a strong possibility that it may not even make it to trial. Plus, if it did get that far, there was no guarantee that a judge and jury would be sympathetic toward me. Furthermore, I had no desire to come face-to-face with Stephen Shield ever again. So, I spent a good deal of time weighing up the possible advantages against the stress and sacrifice involved and what I stood to lose. Also, I was acutely aware of the effect it would have on my family and friends, and I couldn't bear the thought of causing them any more pain. But, at the end of the day, and despite possible repercussions, it was evident to me that if I ever hoped to get any sort of justice and closure, involving the authorities seemed to be the only realistic course of action, particularly bearing in mind the Church's failure to address the matter.

Thus, only twelve days after returning to my parents, I found myself sitting in the living room, holding the phone and feeling incredibly nervous. I knew that making the call to the police meant that they would either pursue the matter or simply 'log it,' and, once I had disclosed the details, it would be out of my hands for good. I had come across an article mentioning that most survivors of sexual abuse choose not to report it to the police due to fear, humiliation, and shame. While I could understand their reasons, something deep within me insisted that if I didn't report it not only would Stephen Shield escape accountability, but the Church would also evade justice. Nothing would change. I felt passionately that victims of abuse needed to speak up about the deeply embedded hypocrisy within the Church if any meaningful change were ever to occur.

Happily, the phone call with the police officer surpassed all my expectations. I had mentally prepared for the worst, but the officer's calm and supportive manner brought me tremendous relief. She patiently listened to me without rushing or pressuring me. Her professionalism made me feel at ease during the entire conversation. Instead of discussing everything over the phone, arrangements were made for me to attend a formal interview at the police 'comfort suite.' These are dedicated rooms where victims of rape and serious sexual assault can talk in privacy and ease. Some are located in police stations, but the one I attended was a dedicated building designed to be a serene, private place where victims could feel relaxed and secure.

Three weeks later, on June 18, 2012, a police officer picked me up from home and drove me to Preston for the formal interview. Despite feeling very nervous, I was hopeful following my positive phone call experience. Upon arrival, I was greeted by a friendly female police officer who immediately put me at ease and offered to make me a coffee. I was then taken into a room set up for recording the interview on video. It was explained to me that if the case were to proceed to trial, I would have the option for the video to be played in court for the jury.

This meant that I wouldn't have to be physically present in the courtroom. Instead, I could be in a side room for my testimony and cross-examination via video call. This arrangement ensured that I would never have to come face to face with Stephen Shield, which was a great relief.

The interview lasted for a grueling one hour and twenty minutes. In the room were two female police officers: one led the interview and the other handled the recording. Basically, they covered four main areas: Who did this? What happened? Where did it happen? And when did it happen? Of course, it is not as simple as this and recounting the sexual abuse I endured at the hands of Stephen Shield was excruciating, but I held nothing back. Emotions ran high; I cried and felt fear and embarrassment, yet the police officers provided not just unwavering support, but also a deep sense of empathy and care, reassuring me each time.

Likening this experience to the one with Fr. [A] at Forton Service Station on the M6 motorway in 2007 is like comparing night and day. The police demonstrated unwavering support, respect and most importantly, impartiality, whilst Fr. [A] of Lancaster Diocese was the complete opposite, unsupportive, disrespectful, and blatantly biased. I found that this experience reinforced my strong belief that victims of clergy abuse should always seek assistance directly from the police, rather than the Church. I cannot emphasize enough the crucial role that the impartiality of the police plays in ensuring fairness and justice in the handling of such sensitive cases.

After my initial interview, I was assigned a 'dedicated officer' who had received advanced training in the handling of rape and serious sexual offences. This officer was my main point of contact throughout the investigation and his responsibilities included:

- Explaining each step of the investigation.

- Addressing any questions or concerns I may have.
- Facilitating access to essential support services.

Furthermore, he proved to be extremely diligent in keeping me up to date on the investigation's progress, providing regular updates at least every twenty-eight days and sometimes sooner if there were any significant developments.

One of the first jobs that I was required to do was to create a detailed list of potential witnesses, which in my case amounted to twenty-two names. Not surprisingly, given the nature of the allegations, only one of these individuals had actually witnessed any of the events. This specific witness happened to be one of the priests who had been seated across from me when Stephen Shield abused me at the dinner table. His simple inquiry the following morning, "How are you?" carried a significant weight given the circumstances. The rest of the names on the list included individuals whom I had confided in over the years, starting with my friend at Castlerigg Manor, and concluding with the Abbots and Abbesses at the "Contemplative Approach to Spiritual Direction" course at Hyning Hall. Within three days of receiving the list, the police had already made contact with my friend Rachel, whom I had first told when we worked in Rome and straightaway she responded with her initial disclosure statement, followed shortly after by all of the other witnesses.

Then, in October, a police officer came to my house to update me on the progress of the case. He told me that the investigation was moving forward, which was a positive sign, but cautioned that it would take time, due to the nature of such inquiries. He was very candid with me, stressing that getting a prosecution would be challenging. He didn't say this to discourage me but to help me understand the reality; I would need to be determined and persistent. It would be particularly challenging since the offences were not recent, making the evidence-gathering process trickier for the police compared with more recent cases. However, by reporting it to them, I had taken the first step in attempting to bring about a prosecution. Before he left, I was asked to sign some medical consent forms, which I did without hesitation. It was crucial for the police to collect as much evidence as possible to illustrate the impact of the abuse on my physical and mental well-being throughout the years.

After Christmas, in late December, I received an email informing me that the case file had been handed over to the Crown Prosecution Service (CPS) to determine how next to proceed with the investigation. The wait was extremely tough, and I was worried that the case would be dismissed. The situation became even more testing when a month later, on January

23, 2013, I received another email saying that the case file was still with the CPS. Their lawyer had promised to review the file the previous week, offering a glimmer of hope that the waiting period would soon come to an end. This excruciating period of waiting, filled with uncertainty, felt like it would never end, and it really took a toll on my mental well-being. The situation became so difficult that on March 21, my doctor referred me to the Community Mental Health Team and prescribed anti-depressants to help me cope. Thankfully, following this time of overwhelming frustration and worry, the CPS decided to move forward with the case, bringing an enormous sense of relief. Things then moved very quickly and on the morning of March 23, 2013, Stephen Shield was apprehended by the police in a dramatic early morning raid on the Cathedral House in Lancaster. Apparently, he was still in bed at the time.

As mentioned earlier, I had not had any contact whatsoever from Lancaster Diocese since early June 2007, almost six years previously. Now, on the very day Stephen Shield was arrested, I suddenly received an unexpected phone call from the Chair of the Lancaster Diocesan Safeguarding Commission, whom I shall refer to as [C], inquiring about how they could be of assistance to me. Did they really believe that I would be grateful? I was overwhelmed with anger and disappointment by this sudden and exceptionally false outreach. It was maddening that they had neglected to contact me for nearly six years and then only reaching out when the situation had the potential to cause them embarrassment; offering me assistance and sympathy out of convenience. I was utterly stunned and said that I needed time to think, and would he call me back; he agreed to phone me on April 3.

On the morning of April 2, I was surprised and relieved to receive a phone call from the police informing me that Stephen Shield had been charged with three counts of indecent assault. He had been released on bail, with the conditions that he would not make contact with me, either directly or indirectly, or have contact with any person under the age of eighteen. He was also scheduled to appear before the Preston Magistrates Court on Wednesday, April 17. The local newspaper, *The Lancaster Guardian* reported the arrest including news that Shield had withdrawn from the ministry pending the outcome of the court proceedings. A spokesman for the diocese said:

> In accordance with established safeguarding policies and procedures of the Catholic Church in England and Wales, Canon Stephen Shield has temporarily withdrawn from public ministry – until the matter is resolved in full. Such temporary withdrawal from public ministry does not constitute Canon Shield's

> removal from office as parish priest, nor does it in any way imply guilt on his part. For its part the diocese will work to resolve this case as expeditiously as possible and in a manner that is fair to all parties.[1]

The Bishop of Lancaster, The Rt. Rev Michael Campbell, added:

> We are committed to the protection and safety of children, young people and vulnerable adults in our care. The faithful and the clergy of the diocese join me in this pledge of prayerful support.[2]

The article concluded with:

> Shield's arrest comes just weeks after the Roman Catholic Church was rocked by the resignation of Cardinal Keith O'Brien, as Archbishop of St Andrews and Edinburgh. Cardinal O'Brien admitted sexual misconduct after resigning as Archbishop of St Andrews and Edinburgh following allegations by other priests. Other sexual abuse allegations against priests came to light in Scotland in the wake of his resignation.[3]

I was relieved to read that both the diocese, and Bishop Campbell, were taking the matter seriously and complying with existing safeguarding policies. This gave me hope. The next day, on April 3, I eagerly awaited a phone call from [C] as promised, but the call never came. Then, on Thursday morning, the police called to inform me that [C] had emailed them asking for permission to contact me about the services he could offer, making it clear that he didn't want to interfere with any ongoing matters. The police found his request to be unusual, considering that I had already agreed to speak with him and told him that it was fine for him to contact me. In spite of this, the promised call from [C] still never came, and I anxiously waited all afternoon to no avail.

The following day, I was still expecting him to call, but once again, I heard nothing. In fact, three and a half weeks passed before I heard anything. It was towards the end of April when he finally rang me, and his opening line was, "What do you want?" I was completely astonished; he was the one calling me, not the other way around. During our ten-minute conversation, it was clear that his sole intention was to gather as much information as possible about the case, while pretending that he was there to support me.

---

1. "Cathedral Priest Faces Sex Charges," para. 7–19.
2. "Cathedral Priest Faces Sex Charges," para. 10.
3. "Cathedral Priest Faces Sex Charges," para. 14.

He even assured me that he would stay in touch every couple of weeks to see how I was doing. Then, just before ending the call, he stated that he would need to report all that we had spoken of back to the Safeguarding Commission, including Bishop Campbell. I immediately expressed my displeasure, stating that he should have been transparent about this from the start, not at the conclusion of our conversation. Needless to say, he dismissed my concerns insisting that there was no cause for worry and that he would be in touch again soon.

From that day onwards, not one person, associated with the Lancaster Diocese Safeguarding Commission, contacted me ever again. It was blatantly obvious that his sole purpose in making contact was to gather information and that he never truly intended to fulfil his promise of providing support. This total lack of genuine concern left me feeling used and betrayed. Having been a lifelong member of the Church, my very identity was intertwined with being a Christian and a member of the Roman Catholic Church. It was the most powerful statement of my identity and therefore being made to feel like an outsider, unworthy of contact, left me struggling with intense feelings of loss and overwhelming uncertainty.

Following this disappointing phone call, I received a letter from the Preston Witness Care Unit, informing me that the case had been listed for a Preliminary Hearing at the Crown Court and that Stephen Shield had not yet entered a plea.

Additionally, on May 2, Michelle Blade of the *Lancaster Guardian* published an article entitled "Catholic priest to face sex charges," reporting that Shield would return to court on July 26 for a Plea and Case Management hearing, leading up to the trial date (should he plead not guilty) which had been set for November 11, 2013. The article also mentioned that the hearing would identify the witnesses who would be required to attend. Out of the twenty-two names that I had put forward I was told that only about five would actually be called to attend the trial.

The lack of support from the diocese affected me deeply and the impact was not only felt by me but also by my parents, family, and friends. The situation became even more unbearable when the Cathedral parish began holding public prayer meetings and having Masses said with the sole purpose of offering strength, comfort, and support to Stephen Shield. These events were even announced in the weekly parish newsletter, leaving no doubt that he was still being supported by the diocese. Of course, publicly they let it be known that they were also supporting me, but in reality I was just a problem that they would rather ignore and ignore me they did. My father was extremely upset by this and contacted the Cathedral clergy about the prayer meetings and Masses, but needless to say he received no response.

Consequently, he decided to address a letter directly to Bishop Campbell, who responded as follows, "I was sorry to receive your highly-charged letter and was *not* aware that your email sent to the Cathedral had been totally ignored. You should know that I have *no* access whatsoever to the Cathedral or indeed any other parish email account in the diocese. Besides, know too, that I do *not* arrange or oversee specific Prayer Meetings and Mass Intentions at the Cathedral Parish or indeed any other parish in the Diocese. Usually, Mass intentions are offered to a priest by a donor (parishioner) for a specific intention – this is the initiative of the donor."

Bishop Campbell's use of bold text conveyed an aggressive, rude, and unprofessional tone, which suggested his lack of accountability and inability to address the situation. It was surprising that, despite living in the Cathedral House alongside Stephen Shield, where the parish newsletter was printed, he felt he had no authority as bishop. Furthermore, while prayers and Masses were offered for Stephen Shield, there was not one mention of prayers for myself, his victim, which was blatantly obvious. This focus on the perpetrator and disregard for the victim's needs, including the need for acknowledgment, created a significant imbalance, leaving me, once again, deeply disappointed and hurt.

On May 15, I was invited by the police to write a Victim Personal Statement (VPS), which would allow me to express the physical, emotional, and financial impact of the crime and its ongoing effects on my life and the lives of my family and friends. I was further informed that the Judge would consider my VPS when deciding on an appropriate sentence if Stephen Shield was found guilty. I found the process to be extremely traumatic, as once again I had to contemplate and relive the distressing actions of Stephen Shield. The process took a significant emotional toll on me, but I believed that my statement would help achieve a fair outcome for everyone involved, so I did my best.

As a consequence, a few days after handing over my VPS to the police, I went to see my GP because my depression was worsening—making it difficult for me to function. My doctor was extremely sympathetic and increased my daily antidepressant dosage, giving me hope for improvement. However, this hope continued to be overshadowed by my internal struggle. On the outside I appeared to be coping; I had become a good actor, especially when around family and friends. But on the inside, I was struggling with feelings of self-hatred and bitterness, not just towards Stephen Shield, but also towards the Roman Catholic Church. I felt completely abandoned; it was as if no one cared, not even the majority of the priest friends that I had. What was even worse was that I also felt abandoned by God. It felt as if I was being unfairly blamed and shamed for the abuse I had suffered and for having the courage to report it to the police. I had broken the unspoken clerical code of silence and suddenly I was the villain. The bishop, and those in authority, would have preferred it if I had simply prayed for and forgiven Stephen Shield, even though he showed no remorse and made no effort to atone for the psychological, spiritual, and moral harm he had caused me.

Once again, the only escape I could find from the traumatic images in my head was in the numbing embrace of alcohol and the physical release of self-harm, both fueled by an overwhelming sense of anger and frustration. Over the past seven years, every time that I had turned to alcohol, it had become harder to stop. In fact, matters spiraled out of control to such an extent that, one night, I suffered a dangerous fall down the stairs, leading to hospitalization for a severe concussion. As a result, I underwent an evaluation by a liaison psychiatrist, who was focused on delivering psychiatric care to medical patients. As I look back on my life, it is clear to me now that it was the waiting that was undeniably the most excruciating part. The haunting memories of sexual abuse lingered like a relentless shadow, refusing to release their grip on my mind. They became my constant companions, making it a daily battle just to survive.

Thankfully, after what seemed like an age, Stephen Shield was summoned once again to Preston Crown Court, this time for a 'Plea and Case Management Hearing' (PCMH). Then, a few days later, on July 30, I received a letter from the Criminal Justice System Witness Care Unit. It began with, "I am writing to confirm that you are required to attend court to give your evidence as Stephen Shield has now pleaded 'not guilty.' The trial is set to begin on November 11, 2013, at the Preston Crown Court and you must attend. It is expected to last for eight days. Nearer the time of the trial date, you will be given a specific day to attend court". The letter continued with a caution, stating, "you must complete the enclosed reply form… Failure to respond may result in a visit from a police officer to secure your attendance." The warning of potential police involvement compelled me to react swiftly. Despite being advised that he might plead not guilty, the prospect of having to attend court and give evidence still weighed heavily upon me.

By early September, I was feeling very discouraged with the Catholic Church, so, without much thought, I wrote to the Abbot asking to be released from my Monastic Vows. I had just had enough, and I told him that I was considering leaving the Catholic Church altogether in order to join the Church of England. Looking back, I realize that this was just a knee jerk reaction and plea for help. I was feeling completely abandoned by my monastic community, who I never heard from, and I could no longer tolerate the frustration of dealing with the difficult and manipulative responses I had received from Church authorities since first disclosing my abuse to them.

Within a few days I received a reply saying that he had informed the Generalate (the Cistercian headquarters in Rome) to request that my petition to be released from solemn vows be presented to the Holy See. He ended the letter by saying, "As for your intention to leave the Catholic Church in order to train for Anglican ministry, I presume you have considered its significant gravity".

Under no circumstances had I fully considered the gravity of my situation; I was in a constant battle with my emotions and thoughts, feeling a deep emotional struggle and lack of compassion or support from anyone within the Roman Catholic Church. Then, in mid-September, I received another letter from the Abbot, which stated that "the Holy See is very reluctant to grant a dispensation from vows to a priest unless he has the explicit support of a bishop prepared to receive him into his diocese." He went on to say, "In your circumstances, it appears you have three options: either find a bishop who will provide the Holy See with a written promise of incardination; or produce a statement to the effect that you have no intention of exercising your priesthood and that you realize you need a bishops' explicit permission to consider ministering; or state that you intend to initiate a process of laicization".

He further advised that, after considering my options, I should write a letter to the Abbot General (the head of the Cistercian Order), the Cardinal Prefect, or the Pope, asking for a release from my religious vows. I was warned to present my reasons "clearly and respectfully" and he made it clear that expressing anger or making accusations against the Church or the Cistercian Order would not be helpful. Additionally, I was warned not to mention my thoughts about serving in the Church of England under any circumstances. In other words, I was being discouraged from being honest and telling the real reasons for my decision. Once again, I was left feeling disappointed and unsupported. The Church was 'the boss,' and I was expected to tell them what they wanted to hear rather than the truth. But there was no way that the Catholic Church was going to pressurize me ever again and so I decided not to respond, as it was clearly a waste of time.

A couple of weeks before the trial, I had the opportunity to visit Preston Crown Court to familiarize myself with the layout and environment. Since I had given consent for the prosecution to present the video of my formal interview to the court, I was informed that I wouldn't be taking the stand for cross-examination by the defense lawyer. Instead, I was advised that I would be seated in a side room and would participate in the proceedings via video link. This meant that I would only be able to see the Judge, the prosecution lawyer, the defense lawyer, and no one else. It was a great relief to learn of this in advance. With hindsight, the visit turned out to be incredibly valuable, as it gave me a sense of what to expect in a Crown Court setting, especially as I had never been in one before.

Finally, the long-awaited day of the trial arrived: Monday, November 11, 2013, a date I shall never forget. It had been eighteen grueling months since I first reached out to the police and six long years since I had disclosed my abuse to the Diocese of Lancaster. In spite of my parents' offer to accompany me, I decided to go alone, because I didn't want them to hear the distressing details of what Stephen Shield had done to me. I distinctly remember the overwhelming relief I felt as I entered the courthouse through a side door, thereby avoiding any potential encounters with Shield or anyone else from the diocese, especially the clergy.

Once inside, the Prosecutor assigned to the case introduced himself, and requested a quick interview with me. This was so he could ask me a few questions and make contact, as we had never met before. It turned out that I would be called to testify first, which I was pleased about. With the nerves that I was feeling, the prospect of having to wait around for hours to be called would have been awful.

When the case began, the Counsel for the Prosecution started by providing a detailed summary of the facts from their perspective to the jury. Following this, I was called to give evidence. I was escorted to a side room and seated in front of a large television screen set up for the video link. A court official remained present in the room throughout the proceedings. Despite being accustomed to speaking in public, I found the courtroom setting quite different and consciously tried to stay calm. After being sworn in, the Prosecution lawyer asked me many open-ended questions, allowing me to describe what had happened in my own words. However, I found giving evidence to be an incredibly isolating experience. Being asked to 'go back to that time and place' and focus on the facts of the sexual abuse I had suffered without getting an opportunity to explain the context or how this crime had impacted my life was frustrating. It felt like I was reliving the most horrendous day of my life in front of total strangers, even though I couldn't see them. I can only imagine how hard it would have been to stand in the courtroom in person.

Next, I had to undergo cross-examination by the opposing side. Though I knew this was part of the legal process, the way I was talked about and portrayed in court deeply affected me. No amount of preparation could have prepared me for the immense anguish I experienced. It felt like I was not just reliving the events but also having every aspect of my life scrutinized and judged which only served to amplify my feelings of shame and guilt. I felt as though I was being held accountable for not doing more or acting differently at the time, as if I was somehow at fault. Once the defense lawyer had finished, I felt raw and exposed, as if every facet of my life had been analyzed in a deeply personal and intrusive manner.

After enduring a lengthy interrogation, I was summoned back the next day, Tuesday. Going through the whole process again left me completely exhausted by the time the Judge excused me. The whole experience was both triggering, and nerve-wracking. I was also disappointed in myself for not presenting what I believed to be my best evidence, for becoming upset, and for being caught off guard by the defense. These emotions and the lasting impact of the case stayed with me long after it was resolved.

Later, as I was on my way to the train station, heading home, I saw a billboard outside a newsagent's shop with the headline, "Priest Denies Sex Assaults." The trial had made the front page of the county newspaper, the *Lancashire Evening Post*. To my surprise, there was a quote from me as well, in large letters, stating, "I have never felt such evil."[4] With a mixture of curiosity and discomfort I decided to buy a newspaper. Once inside the shop, I felt as though everyone knew that I was the victim, from the shopkeeper to the customers, and even later on the train, I felt like all eyes were on me, as if everyone was passing judgment. Reading my own words in the newspaper was an incredibly surreal experience, like stepping into an alternate reality. Despite not going into great detail, the article described the disturbing actions of Stephen Shield. Although I was only referred to as 'the victim,' I felt immensely exposed, like a raw nerve laid bare to the world.

I vividly remember that Tuesday evening. It had been an exceptionally long and tiring day, and I was desperate to unwind. Foolishly, I decided to have a look at the *Lancashire Evening Post* website to read the article once again before calling it a day. As I scrolled through the comments section, I encountered a wide range of reactions. While the majority offered support and understanding, there were others launching outright attacks. But what caught my attention even more was the fervent defense of Stephen Shield by a few individuals, adamantly claiming that he could never have committed the acts of which I had 'accused' him. To my surprise, among these defenders were Catholic priests, some of whom I knew personally. Their disbelief and dismissal of my story felt like personal betrayal. It was disheartening to see individuals, including those within the Church, discrediting my experience and taking the side of the accused. This experience only served to strengthen my belief that the Church prioritizes self-preservation and protecting its image above all else, even over the fundamental teachings of compassion and love that Jesus Christ preached.

---

4. Smith, "Priest Denies Sex Assaults," 1.

The following day, Wednesday, I decided to stay home for the remainder of the trial rather than attend the court in person. My mother and some incredibly supportive friends, however, chose to sit through the entire proceedings for the rest of the trial. Later that day, my friend Rachel was called to the witness box. With courage, she provided a detailed and vivid account of the evening we encountered Stephen Shield while driving in Rome, describing the late sun casting its glow on the side street and the appearance of a man—"I assumed him to be a priest"—accompanied by elderly women who looked exhausted from their day in Rome. Rachel continued to narrate how the driver interacted with Shield, who then caught sight of me, the complainant, in the bus. She shared how I had leaned over to her and whispered, "That's him," referring to the priest who had sexually abused me. Finally, she concluded by recalling our encounter with Shield at the airport, emphasizing my nervousness and fearful demeanor in his presence.

Thursday was another challenging day for me. At lunchtime, I received a troubling phone call from the police. They informed me that one of my crucial witnesses, a priest, had seemingly contradicted himself intentionally. Initially, he had corroborated my account of Shield sexually abusing me at the dinner party and even showed concern for me the next day. His supportive statement led the police to consider him a key witness.

However, when he took the stand, he completely reversed his testimony, asserting that Shield had not done anything inappropriate at the dinner party at the English Martyrs Church, which incidentally was located just half a mile from the courthouse. I felt deeply betrayed and disappointed when the police expressed their anger, saying that they would not have allowed him to testify if they had known his true intentions. I had considered this man a friend since my days in Hawkshead over twenty years earlier. He had lived in Bowness-on-Windermere, just a short distance away, and we often enjoyed spending time together on leisurely outings or evenings at the local pub. During that time, he had thought about becoming a priest and sought guidance and support from me, knowing I had spent four years in seminary, and I was happy to oblige. It was unimaginable to think of a priest holding the New Testament and solemnly swearing to tell 'the truth, the whole truth, and nothing but the truth' in a courtroom witness box and then continue to tell the courtroom the exact opposite of what he had told the police. His sudden decision to totally change his story severely shook my confidence, leaving me feeling a profound sense of loss and confusion.

Nevertheless, after speaking with the police officer on the phone, I felt somewhat encouraged, as he had said that my lawyer had done an excellent job during Shield's cross-examination that day. He told me that Shield had admitted to the first instance of sexual abuse at Castlerigg Manor. This was brilliant and so I decided to go out and buy another newspaper to read more about the day's court proceedings. As I thumbed through the newspaper, I came across a lengthy article titled "Priest tells of his 'shock' at arrest" by Stef Hall. The article described Stephen Shield's arrest by police investigating allegations of sexual assault against him. He mentioned that he was supposed to conduct a funeral service at 9:30 a.m. on the day of his arrest and was lying in bed going through the last few words of the service in his head. The article gave details about how he was dressed, his feelings about the arrest, and his experience at the police station during the interview. He confirmed that he hadn't commented during the interview and explained that he had been shocked by the arrest, making it difficult for him to think clearly. He also mentioned that he had been questioned before by 'safeguarding' staff in the Lancaster Diocese regarding the same alleged victim.[5] Before going to bed, I checked the article and comments online and found that despite Shield admitting to the first count, some priests were still calling me a troublemaker and denying any possibility of Shield being guilty.

Early Friday morning, I received another call from the police informing me that they expected the trial to conclude later that day. I was absolutely wracked with fear and paced up and down the living room all morning. I didn't dare hope that he would be found guilty, even though he had admitted one count, but I feared how I would react if he were found 'not guilty.' After all this time, and all of the stress and loss that I had already endured, I didn't know if I could take any more. The day dragged slowly on; every minute seemed like an age. Whenever the phone rang, my heart almost stopped, but it turned out to be unimportant each time. It wasn't until about 2 p.m. that I answered and it was my mum on the other end. She asked if I was okay, and by her tone of voice I began to fear the worst. Then she handed me over to a policeman standing beside her. In an emotional voice, he said, "Paul, he has been found guilty on all three charges, by a unanimous jury." I could hardly breathe, never mind reply, and as the tears ran down my face, I struggled to thank him for all he had done. I was absolutely overcome and could hardly believe what I was hearing. The relief was overwhelming, and for the first time in years, I felt an enormous weight had been lifted. Once I had regained my composure, he told me that the jury had taken three hours to find Stephen Shield guilty of three counts of indecent assault on a man aged sixteen or over. The Judge told him, "You must understand that all sentencing options, including custody, will be available to me."[6] The case was

---

5. Hall, "Priest Tells."
6. Qtd. in Smith, "Top Priest Faces Jail."

then adjourned until December 13, in order to allow reports to be prepared to help the court decide upon an appropriate sentence.

The Morecambe *Visitor* newspaper carried a piece entitled "Police Chief pleased with result of case." The Detective Chief Inspector of Lancashire Police said, "I am pleased that Mr. Shield has been convicted of these offences. The victim in this case had lived with the knowledge of Mr. Shield's offending for a long period of time; this has had a significant impact upon him. It was a difficult decision for the victim to come forward and I am pleased that he felt confident enough in the constabulary to help bring this man to justice."[7]

The day after the verdict was announced, I visited the Lancaster Diocesan Website, hoping to find some acknowledgement of the outcome. To my surprise, the only reference to Shield on the website was for a Mass being held that day for 'Canon Stephen's Intentions,' less than twenty-four hours after he had been found guilty of indecent assault. While I understand the importance of offering prayers, the public display of this Mass felt like a deliberate and hurtful gesture. The fact that there had never been a Mass said for my intentions made it even more painful. This disregard hurt me deeply, leaving me with a profound sense of disillusionment. In my naivety I believed that once Stephen Shield was found guilty the Bishop and the Diocese would reach out to me, offering the support and sympathy I so desperately needed. More fool me. Instead, Bishop Campbell made an announcement on the Diocesan website the same evening, entitled 'Media Statement from the Bishop of Lancaster.' It began by announcing the verdict and then continued, "I want to express my profound sorrow and deepest regret to the victim for the abusive behavior perpetrated by Canon Shield. It is my sincere hope that, as a result of this conviction and with the help of God, he will now be able to begin the process of healing and the rebuilding of his life. My thoughts and prayers are with him and his family and my door is most certainly open to them."

At first glance, it sounded great, but this statement was only available on the website for less than twenty-four hours before being removed. It was simply intended for journalists to use when writing their articles on the subject. Moreover, no one from the Church informed me of it, or that it would be published online, so I wouldn't have known it was there if I hadn't checked the website myself. It concluded with the usual spiel about how the Church is committed to ensuring the safety and protection of the young and vulnerable. It also stressed that Shield had not been in active ministry since his arrest. It was no more than a piece from the Diocesan Press Office

---

7. Qtd. in Blade, "Police Chief Pleased with Result of Case," 11.

intended to put the Church in a good light. In no way was it an apology to me; in fact, to this day, over a decade later, I have never received an apology or genuine offer of support from Lancaster Diocese, or anyone else in the Roman Catholic Church.

For the following few weeks, I made it a habit to check the Cathedral parish newsletter, which was posted online every week, and I even printed several of them off to keep a record for myself. On December 8, the 2nd Sunday of Advent, the evening Mass was said for 'Canon Stephen's Intentions.' I also found out, that between the conviction in November and the sentencing in December, a petition was placed at the rear of the Cathedral Church during each Sunday Mass. The petition asked parishioners, or anyone else who wanted to, to sign their name supporting Stephen Shield and stating that he was "an excellent priest," who had supported many of the parishioners through their personal triumphs and tragedies. I found this situation scandalous because it felt like yet another betrayal by the Diocese of Lancaster. Asking parishioners to sign a petition in support of a priest who had been found guilty of three counts of indecent assault, by a unanimous jury, showed absolutely no respect for the British judicial system, or for victims of clerical sexual abuse.

The origin of the petition unsurprisingly remains a mystery. With Stephen Shield, the Dean, in custody, and only the two curates left, it is unclear who initiated it. It's possible that a parishioner came up with the idea, but the bishop's potential involvement cannot be ruled out. He resided in an apartment in the Cathedral House, which is connected to the Cathedral, the same residence Shield had lived in. Additionally, there were four Sundays between the conviction and the sentencing, a significant period during which the bishop could have seen or even authorized the petition. Regardless of whether he explicitly gave permission or not, it is extremely likely that he was aware of the petition and therefore agreed to it by default.

Once again, the newsletter for the 3rd Sunday of Advent contained a notice for two masses for Stephen Shield the following week. Interestingly, one was scheduled for Thursday at 12:15 p.m., and the other for Friday the 13th at 12:15 p.m., which was the day of his sentencing. With absolutely no thought for the victim, on such a traumatic day, the Cathedral parish once more devoted its prayers and thoughts to the abuser.

As the day of sentencing dawned, I felt proud of myself. It's widely acknowledged by experts that a mere 10 percent of individuals who have suffered abuse at the hands of clergy are able to summon the courage to report it. Furthermore, of those who do come forward, only a small percentage manage to navigate the legal system to bring their abusers to court, and an even smaller fraction see them convicted. The daunting reality that I was the sole victim of Shield to speak out made the prospect of achieving justice even more challenging.

During the sentencing, the barrister representing Shield presented the petition that had been placed in the Cathedral, in support of him, to the court. It was signed by over 240 individuals and Shield's counsel made a strong case for a community service order, arguing that it would allow him to fully engage in a sex offender program. Nevertheless, the judge firmly insisted that an immediate custodial sentence was necessary and then directing his attention to Shield, he continued with his concluding remarks, "It is clear from his evidence that [the victim] felt unable to resist you because of your position as a priest and your authority over him. I am in no doubt that his experiences of those indecent assaults have had a profound effect on him. It was an abuse of power and authority over someone who was vulnerable and unable to resist you, possibly because of the hierarchal situation in the Catholic Church. I consider you targeted him."[8] Speaking of the dinner party, he said: "For a considerable period of time during the meal at the dinner table you were molesting the victim. There were others present and this must have been a humiliating and embarrassing episode."[9]

In a newspaper report from the *Lancashire Evening Post*, it was stated that "Shield's future in the clergy was yet to be determined, but the court heard that he may be stripped of his status as a priest. However, it is understood that the decision will be made in Rome."[10] At the time of writing, over a decade has passed since this statement was made in court, and Shield remains a priest. He is listed on the Lancaster Diocesan Website among the diocesan priests as "The Rev Canon S Shield, c/o The Bishop's Office, The Pastoral Centre, Balmoral Road, Lancaster."

A newspaper report that evening had a headline stating, "Sex abuse priest is jailed for one year."[11] In reality, he received different sentences for each of the three counts. He got four months for the first count at Castlerigg Manor, twelve months for the second count at the dinner party, and twelve months for the third count in the room at the English Martyrs presbytery. However, these sentences were to be served concurrently, meaning he would serve the longest sentence of twelve months. So, in essence, the legal system ensured he was jailed for one year. On top of this, he was also placed on the sex offenders' register for ten years.

8. Press Association, "Ex-Dean of Lancaster Cathedral Jailed."
9. Press Association, "Ex-Dean of Lancaster Cathedral Jailed."
10. Smith, "Sex Abuse Priest Is Jailed."
11. Smith, "Sex Abuse Priest Is Jailed."

You might think that I would have felt ecstatic that he was now in jail, but a part of me felt guilty. Initially, I had hoped the Diocese would handle the situation internally. It was only after they failed to take action that I contacted the police. That evening, there was a feature on Stephen Shields on the 6 p.m. BBC news for the Northwest of England. During the segment, they showed a photograph of him taken by the court, and he looked terrible. He looked like a man who had lost everything. The following days were difficult, but eventually my feelings shifted from guilt to gratitude. I began to reframe the messages in my head from guilt ("A priest is now in jail because I spoke up") to gratitude ("I'm grateful he's in jail so he can no longer abuse me or anyone else. I'm thankful for the healing that's begun"). It's important to note that this wasn't a one-time fix; it's something I've had to do repeatedly over the years. To remind myself that speaking up took immense courage and strength, and each time I did, it was a testament to my resilience.

Life after the trial

In the aftermath of the trial, I held on to the hope that my life would return to 'normal' and that I would one day be able to leave behind the physical, mental, and spiritual pain that I had endured. I longed for some form of communication from Bishop Campbell, or from anyone in the Roman Catholic Church; a phone call, a letter, or even a personal visit. I yearned for an apology for the actions of Stephen Shield and perhaps some support and guidance for my ongoing healing process. Unfortunately, no such communication or acknowledgment ever materialized. As both a priest and a monk, who had devoted his life to the Church, the lack of response left me feeling profoundly lonely and estranged. It was disheartening to realize that my decision to speak the truth, an action I believed to be in accordance with the highest Christian principles, had resulted in no outreach or support from the Church whatsoever. In fact, quite the opposite.

A few days after the sentencing, an article was published in both *The Morecambe Visitor* and the *Lancaster Guardian*, under the headline "Priest Victim Wins Jail Plea." It stated that:

> A priest jailed for sexual abuse could face more prison time after his victim demanded a review of his sentence. Canon Stephen Shield was found guilty last month of three counts of indecent assault following a trial at Preston Crown Court and was jailed for 12 months. But his victim says the sentence was unduly lenient and has requested a review by the Attorney General. The Attorney General's Office has until January 10 to decide whether the case should come under review. Under the pseudonym 'I care,' the victim said: "I find it belittling to the many victims of such absolutely horrific criminality that such nonsensical sentences are handed out. The Roman Catholic Church in the UK and the Criminal justice system must do a whole lot better on

this issue as survivors of abuse live with the horror every single day."[1]

I was totally stunned to read this, as I had contacted no one at all about the prison sentence. I was happy with how it was handled and contacted the police to inform them. They discovered that someone had emailed the newspaper pertaining to be me and stated what was written in the article. The Crown Prosecution Service, the body responsible for prosecuting criminal cases investigated by the police, contacted the Attorney General's Office and discovered that someone had put in a plea for the sentence to be reviewed as they believed it too lenient.

I recall experiencing a mixture of surprise, shock, and fear when I found out that someone had impersonated me. Instead of letting my emotions overwhelm me, I made a conscious decision to confront the situation head-on. My first step was to contact the newspapers to set the record straight. But, in spite of my efforts, I was disappointed to receive neither a response nor an apology. Somewhat to my surprise, however, a small note appeared in the following week's newspaper, hidden discreetly in the "Clarifications" section. It stated that "the victim of Canon Stephen Shield, who was recently jailed for indecent assault, said that he is content with the police investigation and the way it proceeded. The victim, who remains anonymous for legal reasons, is also satisfied with the sentence and clarified that it was not him who appealed to the Attorney General to have the sentence reviewed."

After the newspaper corrected their error, I felt a sense of relief, but I was still genuinely puzzled as to why someone would go to such lengths to impersonate me and falsely claim to be a victim of abuse. This was not an isolated incident. As recent as March 2024, more than a decade after the conviction of Stephen Shield, someone assumed my identity on a website overseen by Bishop Pat Buckley in Northern Ireland. This website primarily served as a platform to expose hypocrisy within the Church. In response to an article discussing the recent publication *Cardinal Sin* by Brian Devlin, an individual using the alias 'Anonymous' posted a comment that left me utterly bewildered. They wrote: "As a former RC priest who was abused by a priest when I was a seventeen-year-old seminarian on a parish placement. Then in senior seminary I was locked in a room by a fellow student for over an hour and offered money for sex." It goes on the say: "I spent five years trying to get the Church to act on the abuse I suffered, but no one really wanted to know. Eventually I went to the police and the priest who abused me ended up in prison."

1. Blade, "Priest Victim Wins Jail Plea," 1, 3.

The original piece was much longer than I have quoted above. I simply include it to illustrate that, just when you think a difficult situation is over and you are free to move on, something or someone can always pull you back. As I write now, I am still confused as to why anyone would pretend to be a victim of abuse. I can't think of anything to be gained from writing such a response to an article on abuse.

Nevertheless, back in December 2013, I encountered more distressing content on the internet. A website called *Catholic Online* posted a virtual prayer candle with the message "Canon Stephen Shield. Give him strength, hope and freedom." Whilst I have no issue with individuals offering prayers for prisoners, I found it troubling that a church website would pray for freedom for a recently convicted sexual abuser. In my opinion it demonstrates complete disregard for his victim. Although 'freedom' can have various interpretations, I firmly believe that they were praying for his physical freedom. Then, as if that wasn't enough, the Cistercian community on Caldey Island, a place I knew very well, allowed a prayer for Stephen Shield to appear on their online prayer page, causing me further emotional distress, particularly because the Abbot of Caldey had been one of my original witnesses, even though, ultimately, he wasn't called to testify.

The final straw came for me on December 22, 2013, as I read the Cathedral newsletter for Christmas week. There, in black and white, was the announcement of another Mass being offered for the 'Intentions of Canon Stephen,' only this time it was to take place on December 28th, the Feast of the Holy Innocents. The implicit association of innocence with Canon Stephen Shield was profoundly unsettling. I understand that some parishes have offered Masses for victims of clerical abuse on this feast day, which seems appropriate and respectful, but offering Mass for a convicted sexual abuser on a day dedicated to celebrating innocence is beyond belief. It felt malicious, as if the Church was proclaiming, "We don't believe you; Stephen Shield is innocent." Even writing about this, over ten years later, I am struggling to find the right words to articulate my emotions. It is true to say that the trauma I experienced at the hands of the Church was as harmful, if not more so, than the abuse I endured from Stephen Shield; yet, expressing this complexity is a challenge, even after all these years.

My parents were also deeply shocked and distressed that the Cathedral was offering a Mass for Shield on such a significant feast day. Furthermore, even a month after his conviction, he was still officially being named on the Cathedral website and the weekly newsletter as The Very Rev. Canon Stephen Shield [Cathedral Dean], because, according to Canon law and despite being in prison, he was still legally recognized as the Dean of the Cathedral.

My astonishment hit a new level. Surely, out of pastoral sensitivity, his name could have been subtly removed from the website and newsletter.

As a result of this, my father wrote to Bishop Campbell, highlighting all of the above and concluding with the hope for a better year in 2014. Bishop Campbell replied on January 6, emphasizing that Stephen Shield was still Dean according to Canon Law, and that they were awaiting word from the Holy See regarding his future as a priest and any processes that would need to be followed. He continued, "Certainly, out of pastoral sensitivity to the situation, I have now asked that the newsletter does not carry Canon Shield's name as a Mass intention. I am not entitled, however, nor is anyone else for that matter, to legislate for whom Masses are actually offered. This is the right/entitlement of the individual donor."

My hope for the bishop's genuine compassion was further dashed when, on Friday, January 24, the newsletter once again featured a Mass intention for 'Canon Stephen Shield.' Such frequent disregard for my feelings was disgusting and so I felt compelled to call the Cathedral House myself for an explanation. After several rings, the parish secretary answered, without even asking who I was. When I questioned the unchanged newsletter, still displaying the full name and title of Stephen Shield, her response was shocking, "We have been told in no uncertain terms by the Bishop's Office that we are not to update the newsletter; our hands are tied."

This, after the bishop had written to my father, informing him that he had requested the newsletter to no longer mention Canon Shield in the Mass intentions. It was abundantly clear that the bishop was telling us what he thought we wanted to hear. Luckily for me, the secretary seemed to view me as a supporter of the Bishop and the Church, since she went on to inform me that "under no circumstances did she believe that Stephen Shield was guilty" and she concluded by saying, "in fact no one at the Cathedral thinks he is guilty, and that this is the outcome that you get with a jury system."

I could hardly believe what I was hearing, but at least my suspicions were confirmed. The Diocese of Lancaster branded me as a scandalmonger and considered Stephen Shield blameless. I decided it was time to tell her that I was Stephen Shield's victim and that she ought to be very careful about what she says over the phone to people whose identity she doesn't know. Additionally, I expressed the pain of witnessing Masses being offered for my abuser every week without any acknowledgement of me or any other victims of abuse. I suggested to her the simple idea of labelling intentions as 'Private' so that only the priest conducting the Mass would know the intended recipient. However, as soon as she learned of my identity, her tone became noticeably harsher, and she promptly ended the call. My efforts it seemed, were futile as she along with the rest of the Cathedral parish, and perhaps the entire diocese, had already formed their opinions regarding Stephen Shield's innocence.

The following week I could hardly believe my eyes as I scanned the online newsletter only to discover that there were no Masses scheduled for 'Stephen Shield' and no 'Private Intentions.' It seemed like a glimmer of hope, a sign that the church authorities understood the pain that I and others were experiencing and I began to entertain the possibility that things might finally start to settle down.

However, my hopes were once again brutally dashed when I read the newsletter for February 9, which announced two Masses for the 'Special Intention of (SS)' (Stephen Shield), one to be held on Monday and another on the following Sunday. It was a real insult, as if the church was once again callously disregarding my feelings, sending the message, "We don't believe you, we don't respect you, and you are no longer one of us." Did they really believe that I wouldn't know what was meant by 'SS'?

I was struck with an overwhelming sense of abandonment. I had lost everything, my job, house, income, friends, and even the Church itself. My entire world had been upended, shaking the very core of my spirituality and mental wellbeing. I had nowhere left to turn. I had truly believed that by speaking out I was acting in the Church's best interest, striving to uncover one scandal and prevent potential future ones.

To this day, I am still deeply troubled by the apparent lack of moral outrage and the dismissive and harmful nature displayed in the reactions of bishops and priests to clerical abuse. In both my extensive reading and personal experiences, I find distressing underlying themes within their reactions, especially towards the victims who bravely come forward to inform them of sexual abuse. For example, phrases such as "He/She only did it for the money"; "Father is such a good priest, he shouldn't have to go through this"; "We should pray that this embarrassment soon passes"; "Everybody makes mistakes"; "That was a long time ago, it shouldn't be brought up now" and "That's what poor Father gets for trying to help somebody. He makes a little mistake and gets crucified." All of these are actual quotations from clergy.

Also, around this time, a close priest friend phoned me from Peru, where he was working as a missionary. We had been great friends since studying together at Ushaw College; it was he who had first mentioned Mount St. Bernard Abbey to me. During the conversation, I told him about how the recent trial had gone and how the Church had treated me poorly. I even said I was considering leaving to join the Church of England. He was absolutely horrified and couldn't believe what he was hearing, not because he understood my pain, but because I had spoken out about another priest and considered leaving the Church. Predictably, I have had no contact from him since and probably never will. Unfortunately, he was not the only one. The vast majority of my priest friends chose not to support me. Not one of them extended a hand of friendship to me during or after the trial. I have often wondered what it is that causes this astonishing reluctance in priests to condemn the behavior of perpetrators of abuse or to express any concern at all for the wellbeing of the victims.

Priests, of course, are trained to extend forgiveness and provide people with second chances. Therefore, the unity within the clergy is meant to offer a protective environment and is often referred to as safeguarding 'the Church.' However, in doing so, 'the Church' becomes an end in itself, rather than the means to an end. Preserving it at all costs becomes the priority. Thus, a priest criticizing, or even worse, *accusing* another priest, as I did, is largely seen as being disloyal to the individual, the brotherhood, and the institution. But of course, such a lack of response to wrongdoing can lead to the support of deviant behavior in others, which can also damage the reputation of the priesthood and the Church.

This unspoken code of conduct within the priesthood helps to maintain a deliberate avoidance of discussing sensitive topics such as celibacy, homosexuality, sexual relationships, and sexual abuse. This unwritten rule, which begins in the seminary, creates an atmosphere similar to that of a dysfunctional or abusive family, in which certain truths remain unspoken despite being widely acknowledged. To serve as a priest is not a right, but rather a privileged responsibility, and, to my way of thinking, if a priest finds himself unable to honor the commitments he has made, it is vital for him to either step down willingly or be relieved of his duties within the ministry. But of course, this rarely happens.

Experience has taught me that clergy sex offenders are remarkably adept at self-deception and denial, both to others and to themselves. I recall a conversation I once had with a priest who was in prison for sexual offences. He spoke of group sessions in which they worked on 'forgiving their accusers.' Of course, these so called 'accusers' were the men, women and children who they had sexually abused. Not once did they refer to them as 'victims.' In the eyes of the Church, the bishop, and the clergy of Lancaster Diocese, I was perceived as an accuser, a faultfinder, someone prepared to expose the dark side of Church culture. I was seen as a threat to the Church's reputation—instead of being acknowledged as a victim in need of support. As with tens of thousands of other victims, this greatly hindered my healing, adding significantly to my trauma and resulting in increased emotional and physiological suffering.

Then, in June 2014, just as I was beginning to believe that the diocese could cause me no more harm, I received a phone call from the police. The probation service had sought their opinion on the re-housing of Stephen Shield in Blackpool upon his release from Prison, a proposal that had come from Lancaster Diocese. Luckily, the police in their authoritative role deemed it totally unacceptable, given the fact that I was residing in the Blackpool area at the time. Needless to say, Lancaster Diocese were well aware of my address and so one more insensitive move by the Roman Catholic Church was added to my already very long list.

This marked the end of my association with the Roman Catholic Church; I had reached my limit. Earlier, I tried to convey the impact of the abuse I endured as being on a par with having my soul forcefully torn out of my body, and even though Stephen Shield was responsible for this, I firmly believe that Lancaster Diocese was equally accountable for the destruction of my faith. Betrayed by the clergy, cut off from the Church community, and left without a support system, I plunged ever deeper into despair. The absence of my once strong connection with God led to heightened levels of anxiety, depression, and hopelessness. The Church community that I was cut off from should have been my support system in this time of need, but no support ever came.

As a result, I made a rather rash decision that would shape the next decade of my life: I left the Roman Catholic Church and was received into the Church of England. My main incentive was to continue my work as a priest, but, for this to happen, I had to spend a year studying Anglican theology at Ripon College, Cuddesdon, Oxford. Once this year was over, I embarked on a five-year career as a Vicar in the Church of England, despite knowing deep down that it was not my true calling. I never felt at home there. In hindsight, the pain I was still carrying from the Roman Catholic Church should have led me to consider stepping away from organized religion altogether, rather than transferring to a different denomination. Yet, my involvement in the church had been such an integral part of my life that the thought of completely abandoning it felt impossible to me at that particular time in my life.

The aftereffects of Clergy Abuse

The awful experience of being sexually assaulted, and the subsequent betrayal by the diocese, destroyed my relationship with the Roman Catholic Church. I was left struggling to find spiritual comfort anywhere. The Church, which had once been a special place of sanctuary to me, and had given meaning to my life, now meant nothing, and this disillusionment went way beyond the institution to the very idea of a loving God. The symbols, rituals, and people that once represented spiritual security to me, had now become painful reminders of abuse and betrayal. I was left with nothing but a deep spiritual emptiness, my lifelong source of security was now a source of intense pain, which transformed into depression.

On July 27, 2014, I went to London to meet with a Consultant Psychiatrist, to try and gain a greater understanding of why I was feeling like I was, and find out what I could do about it, if anything. As I have already mentioned, I had ninety counselling sessions with the priest in Leicester, and I had also had some more counselling in the months before the trial, but in all honesty, I gained very little, and it certainly never helped with any spiritual healing. In the sixteen-page report which I received back from the psychiatrist she wrote:

> Paul fulfils the criteria for a diagnosis of Post-traumatic Stress Syndrome Disorder. He has been exposed to exceptionally threatening life events in the form of emotional and sexual abuse. He experienced reliving of this abuse in the form of intrusive memories and flashbacks, precipitated by cues which remind him of his abuse. He is avoidant and hypervigilant. His post-traumatic stress disorder is associated with significant depressive symptoms and comorbid substance abuse – harmful use of alcohol.

She also wrote that my symptoms had been exacerbated, by my original disclosure and during the trial proceedings. In fact, once it was over, and

Shield was in prison, I was engulfed in a range of emotions, starting with anger and rage directed primarily at Shield, but also at all the other seminarians and priests who had taken advantage of me over the years. I was absolutely furious with all of them, and, on some level, I still am to this day. Sometimes, I try to excuse them with thoughts about the injustices of celibacy and how, maybe, they were really struggling with it, perhaps wounded by it, but there are no excuses, and so the anger returns. It is an anger that is also directed at Church leaders, the Bishop of Lancaster, and the many hundreds of other bishops who have failed to respond compassionately to victims of abuse, and who in many cases have even enabled abusers. As a result, the struggle to forgive remains an ongoing battle.

Furthermore, it isn't helpful when people say, "You need to learn to forgive," or, "It happened so long ago, why can't you just put it behind you?" I am sure that they have my best interests at heart, but it is like them saying to someone who was bitten by a rabid dog, "If you just ignore it, it will go away." The inherent criticism of such remarks was never lost on me; they may as well have said "if you were a better, stronger, kinder, more spiritual person you would be able to forgive him." Even today, my inability to forgive can sometimes become just one more validation of my personal failings, which reinforces feelings of shame and self-blame.

In truth, forgiveness, like any other aspect of recovery, is an individual matter; it is up to me, and no one else. On many levels, I accept the idea of forgiveness, but it has to be my choice; only I can know whether or not the time is right; only then, can it be truly genuine. Anyone can say the words, but if it isn't genuine, it means nothing. It is also worth stating that forgiveness and reconciliation are not the same thing. Will I ever forgive? Possibly! Will I ever be reconciled with my abusers? Probably not! No one should ever try and push a victim of abuse to make a decision. A nun recently said to me, "Just come home Paul, come back to the Church," as if it was that simple. I don't need to be made to feel guilty, as if leaving the Roman Catholic Church was a terrible crime. In fact, what hurts me the most is the spiritual betrayal I experienced, and the resulting loss of my spiritual home and family. It is something that I still feel to this day. The Church, with its customs, devotions, absolute teachings, and regulations, exerted huge control and influence over most aspects of my life for almost five decades, and this did not evaporate as soon as I left it. Even though I wanted, so much, to leave it behind, to forget, and move on, the influence of the Roman Catholic Church reached deep into my soul, and so the anger retained a strong hold over me, even while working within the Church of England.

The psychiatrist recommended Cognitive Behavioral Therapy as the best way to deal with post-traumatic stress disorder. Unfortunately, at the time I couldn't afford it because I had no income. She emphasized that without this therapy, it would be unlikely for me to sustain a position as a vicar, as I would be at high risk of relapse. The financial strain was also taking a toll on my mental health. I don't want to go into my time in the Church of England here, as that is a whole other story. Suffice it to say that it ended with me having a complete breakdown, which led to three attempted suicides, one of which required a defibrillator, along with self-harm, and alcohol abuse. I developed a strong aversion to anything related to 'the Church,' yet I felt trapped, unable to see a way out. It was only after spending the best part of a year in rehab that I was able to find a way out and save my life.

From my lived experience, it's evident that the traditional therapeutic reactions to clerical sexual abuse often fail to address the spiritual trauma victims endure. When the Church does, on the rare occasion, extend a hand to victims, it typically offers psychological therapy, but rarely, if ever, spiritual counselling. It's surprising that in a Church where the majority of its adherents, including the clergy, have, perhaps indirectly, suffered some form of spiritual abuse, ranging from primary school 'brainwashing' to seven years in a seminary, resulting in 'enforced' celibacy, that some Church authorities would not recognize the urgent need for spiritual counselling. Sadly, and as far as I am aware, no diocese, department, or parish, has ever tried to assess the spiritual damage caused by clergy abuse.

The late Pope St. John Paul II went so far as to publicly acknowledge victims on several occasions but offered only prayer as a healing remedy. To the Bishops of Ireland, he said, "I have been close to you in suffering and prayer, commending to the 'God of all comfort' those who have been victims of sexual abuse on the part of clerics or religious."[1] I am once again reminded of the Bishop of Lancaster's media statement where he wrote, "my thoughts and prayers are with him and his family and my door is most certainly open to them," and also in a letter to my father, "I am keeping all involved in this sad and disturbing situation in my daily prayers."

However, such promises of prayer for victims are nothing but a well-practiced tactical move designed to distance the Church from the person needing help. The Bishop of Lancaster uploading a webpage for a few hours stating that his door was always open to me, was only there to impress church members and the general public. It was never intended to be a genuine offer; otherwise, he would have told me personally, but I only came across it by chance. Also, the late pope's words have provided no relief for victims in Ireland, or anywhere else, and consequently, are meaningless—just another blatant example of the Church's meaningless rhetoric.

1. John Paul II, "Address," para. 6.

After leaving the rehab in 2020, and settling in Ireland, I began to understand the true significance of the anger I had been carrying. This anger, directed at the Church and at religion in general, was, in fact, a healthy and genuine response to the abuse that I had suffered. Gradually, over time, the guilt I felt for blaming the Church and the added fear of God's disapproval began to subside and be replaced with a more accurate belief that the Church had actually served as a barrier to my relationship with God. As a Roman Catholic, the Church had always been presented to me as the only true pathway to God; all other Christian denominations, or religions, whilst having elements of the truth, did not have its fullness which was reserved for the Roman Catholic Church alone. The problem with this is that the majority of Catholics never begin to think for themselves. They are not allowed to progress beyond a level of spiritual and religious development that is early teens at best, which often leads to scruples and unfounded fears of offending God. You often hear people speak of 'Catholic guilt', which comes from the pre-conditioning that Church members go through from childhood to adulthood. Most of the guilt, shame and fear that I carried originated with a type of 'Catholic brain washing' and was therefore responsible for much of the post-abuse trauma that I suffered.

Thankfully, I have discovered over the last few years that the process of recovery from clerical sexual abuse has granted me a new opportunity to stand outside of the Church, even to stand outside of religion, and gain a fresh perspective. I firmly believe that this will provide me with the emotional security needed for whatever future choices I make about the place of religion, worship, or God, in my life. I am determined, in future, to make these choices based on what is best for me, and my healing journey, and not on what some religious institution thinks I need.

It may seem strange to read that a former Roman Catholic monk and priest, as part of his healing journey from clergy sexual abuse, is slowly discovering and accepting a new, more authentic, life-giving spirituality. A God, Creator, or Higher Power, whatever term you wish to apply, that is all-knowing and judging, for me, is becoming simply a source of love that is not confined, or defined, by human ideas. My previous 'Catholic relationship' with God was entangled in a complex web of loyalty and obedience to God's supposed earthly representatives and a monarchical church structure that bore little, if any, resemblance to the teachings of Jesus Christ. Love and the life of the spirit contain no boundaries; therefore, they do not belong to any one religious group. They are universal and all-inclusive, offering a sense of freedom and open-mindedness. You could say that they are truly catholic, with a small 'c'.

As I reflect on the numerous experiences I have had over the years as a victim of clerical abuse, it has become clear to me that most of the damage to my faith and spirituality was caused not by the original abuse, but by the duplicity and insensitivity of Church leaders. So, it comes as no surprise to me that all the bishops and religious leaders that I have encountered have been way more concerned with protecting themselves, and the institution, than with the pain and suffering of victims. Their actions have not only shattered my faith but have also left me feeling deeply betrayed and disillusioned, and this personal turmoil is only a reflection of the wider impact of the Church's actions, which have caused profound distress and disillusionment among many.

I find it heart-breaking and puzzling that the institutional Church prioritizes its own interests over genuinely addressing clerical sexual abuse and caring for the victims. Where, in any of this, is 'practicing what you preach?' Don't speak of reaching out in compassion from the pulpit only to turn your back on those who are hurting, don't claim to be celibate whilst causing sexual trauma to both children and adults, and don't profess that homosexual men cannot be ordained when possibly up to 60 percent of the clergy are gay. Jesus came to teach us how to love and speak the truth, and, in all honesty, I have seen very little evidence of love or truth in the Roman Catholic Church since I first spoke of being abused. For me, the guiding principle has always been, what would Jesus do? Protecting the reputation of the institution at the cost of human lives is something I don't believe Jesus would have done or would want his followers to do. Remember what he said to the Pharisees, "Woe to you, scribes and Pharisees, you frauds [hypocrites], because you clean the outside of the cup and the dish, but inside they are full of extortion and self-indulgence. Blind Pharisee! You should first clean the inside of the cup, so that its outside may be clean also" (Matt 23:25).

The criticism levelled against the Pharisees here could be said of all religious leaders who lose sight of their ideals. St. Matthew was not only intending to warn the Pharisees, but also his fellow followers of Jesus. He was emphasizing that living our Christianity merely as a show for others is like only polishing the outside of a cup. In contrast, if we wish to be genuine, we must first be clean on the inside, and then our external cleanliness will no longer be a sham.

I am well aware of how easy it is to place the Church and its leaders, many of whom have caused so much pain and suffering, in God's name, in the firing line, and I have often felt like being the first to throw a stone. Frustratingly, though, were this to happen, Jesus would also be standing next to the very people I would be throwing stones at. Even if I felt justified in throwing stones, they are still stones. I would be no more than a stone-thrower, throwing stones at stone-throwers.

In the eighth chapter of the Gospel of John, there is a story about a woman who was caught in adultery. Her accusers wanted to stone her to death, but Jesus, while still acknowledging the legal penalty for adultery, said that only a sinless person could throw the first stone. His actions highlighted the need for forgiveness, restoration, and hope for the woman and her accusers, and Jesus offered all three. He was consistently opposed to abuses of power, which unfortunately are still very much present in religious institutions throughout the world today. If I could say one thing to the Pope, the Bishops, and all members of the Catholic Church, it would be this:

As a community of faith, all of you must begin to care for the victim because the more you protect the institution, the more you will lose it. Following Christ's example means giving yourself away and being open and vulnerable rather than protecting yourself at the expense of abuse victims. Remember that Jesus Christ, the man you all profess to follow, was both a whistle-blower and a victim of abuse. In the Garden of Gethsemane, he prayed while awaiting the most excruciating humiliation for his rejection of an oppressive religious system. It was a system that excluded the very poorest from God's mercy and compassion by imposing financial barriers to divine mercy. It also closed the Temple door on the 'unclean,' which included lepers and, at certain times, women. Jesus always stood in solidarity with all who were and still are excluded, and this includes victims of the Church. Who are you going to side with? An oppressive religious system corrupted by power and self-preservation, or Jesus and your brothers and sisters who are hurting? Remember! If the rules of the institution stop you from living the Gospel, then change the rules.

From Victim to Survivor

> I sound unchartered oceans in the soul,
> dark seas of primal rage that storm and thrash
> through caverns of dark mind. They seethe and roll,
> they grind in anger, thunder, swirl and crash
> against the tottering ramparts of the will.
> But love hides in that cold despair,
> the night that seems the loneliness of hell,
> the wilderness of sin. Yes, love hides there.
> Past searching eye, past any sense can tell,
> he lies in ambush who is more than wise
> being wisdom's self; who knows, most thoroughly knows
> and counts and weighs each point of pain with eyes
> infallible, no grain unmeasured goes.
> Then destroy, pull down, leave not one stone in place,
> but from deep earth blast out this mass of guilt
> with fearful detonations of your grace.
> Break down in love that in strong love rebuilt,
> Walk these storm tossed-waters, ride, oh, run these waves:
> No other foot so stills, hand heals, word saves.

I wrote this poem in an attempt to communicate my own journey from victim to survivor. If one other person finds comfort and hope from it, then it will all have been worthwhile.

Part 3

Conclusion

by Debra Maria Flint

MANDATORY CELIBACY DID NOT exist at the time of Jesus or in early Christianity.

The Jewish people regarded marriage as a holy contractual bond, which fulfilled God's commands. Men and women were considered incomplete unless they married, as it was believed that a man and woman became one flesh through marriage. The concept of renouncing marriage and sexuality was completely alien to Judaism, and celibacy was seen to be incompatible with creation.

Jesus reaffirmed the Jewish idea that in marriage the two became one flesh. However, Jesus's views about celibacy were not as harsh as traditional Judaism. He saw celibacy as an acceptable form of life but only for those to whom it had been gifted (Matt 19:11). While it is highly likely that Jesus was celibate himself, there is no evidence, at all, that he expected his disciples to follow suit. Jesus almost certainly chose celibacy for himself because marriage would have been difficult to combine with his nomadic lifestyle; however, despite being celibate, he was followed by many women and formed a close spiritual friendship with Mary Magdalen. He often conversed with women in the Gospels and clearly enjoyed their company. There is also clear evidence in the New Testament that at least two of his disciples, Peter and Phillip, were married (Matt 8:14–15; Mark 1:29–31; Luke 4:38–39; Acts 21:9). Evidence of this can also be found in the second century writings of St. Clement of Alexandria.

There has been some argument that St Paul advocated universal celibacy, but I have demonstrated that this was not the case. St Paul advocated that people remain in whatever state they found themselves at the time of his preaching because he believed that the second coming of Christ and the end of the world was imminent (1 Cor 7:29; 1 Thess 4:17) and he suggested that those who were single did not marry due to his strongly held beliefs that the world was about to end. His views, however, were not shared by others and were likely to have been influenced by gnostic elements. As has already been noted, the writer of Timothy when describing the attributes for the 'overseer' (επίσκοπος) stated that he should be beyond reproach and the husband of only one wife (1 Tim 3:1–4). This would suggest that most early priests were married.

Evidence for some kind of movement towards priestly celibacy can first be seen in the early fourth century when the Synod of Elvira ruled that priests in its area should be celibate. This idea began to appear after the emergence of monasticism and was advocated later in the fifth century by St. Jerome, St. Ambrose, and St. Augustine.[1] After this time, there were more celibate priests, but they were mostly in the West, rather than the East, and were far from being a majority. Tensions began to develop between the East and the West over this, and other matters, and the question of mandatory celibacy was one of the issues that eventually resulted in the East–West Schism.

Sadly, after this schism, the West was free to enforce celibacy onto its priests, since most of the opposition had been removed. Meanwhile, in the East, priests continued to marry. In the West, Pope Gregory VII introduced mandatory celibacy and began to persecute bishops and priests who advocated the married state, and eventually, at the First Council of the Lateran in 1122, it was officially decreed that, henceforth, all priests would be celibate. Married priests were ordered to abandon their wives and children and to leave them destitute. Of course, one of the main driving factors in this movement towards priestly celibacy was the ownership of property, not holiness at all. Increasingly, however, as priests were ordered to remain celibate, a more detailed theology was developed around the practice and so, in the fourteenth century, the Dominican philosopher, St. Thomas Aquinas, argued that the clerical state was a higher, and more perfect state, than marriage. Despite this, many priests continued to break their vows and did not take mandatory celibacy seriously.

At the time of the Reformation, the issue of mandatory celibacy came up yet again in the Latin West. It is clear that celibacy was not working;

---

1. See Harrell, "Ambrose: Does Celibacy Still Have Value?"

PART 3: CONCLUSION   237

otherwise, it wouldn't have been a factor in yet another schism. Of course, in the Orthodox East, priests continued to marry. Luther, the initiator of the Reformation was an Augustinian monk who began to experience severe doubts about many of the practices of the Roman Catholic Church of the time. He eventually married a Cistercian nun, who shared his doubts, Katharina von Bora. Most protestant movements at that time eventually abolished the vow of celibacy for all their priests. The Catholic Council of Trent (1545–1563) responded to the Reformation by stating that priestly celibacy placed an 'indelible mark' on the priest's soul. The New Testament tells us that we all belong to a royal priesthood (1 Pet 2:9), but, unfortunately, the Council contradicted this by stating that the 'indelible mark' was not available to married men or women because only single men vowed to celibacy could be ordained. Sadly, one of the architects of the Council (Pope Julius III) was in an abusive sexual relationship with his underage nephew. I am therefore not sure how he possessed an 'indelible mark' on his soul.

However, the concept of the 'indelible mark' cemented the creation of an elite celibate priestly 'cult,' which had nothing whatsoever to do with the early Christian preaching of Jesus. Another consequence of the Council of Trent was to drive the human sexuality of Catholic priests 'underground,' since, prior to the council, many clerics had blatantly ignored the celibacy rule, even though the official stance in the West had been that priests should be celibate. At the time of the Reformation, many priests who were 'reluctant celibates' left the Church and, therefore, those who remained felt compelled to present an image of 'believing in' the vow. This meant that, henceforth, a large number of priests would continue to break the vow but would do so 'undercover.' Prior to the Reformation the vow had been broken more openly and honestly.

After the Council of Trent, the 'celibacy' of the Catholic priesthood became universally accepted by priests within Roman/Latin Catholicism. However, the Latin Church, instead of embracing, and Christianizing, modern learning, began to become further and further distanced from the intellectual advancement, growth, and development of the modern world. Eventually the First Vatican Council was convened in 1868. This council condemned all modern intellectual movements, such as rationalism, communism, socialism, liberalism, materialism, naturalism, pantheism, and secularism, and it also declared (in 1870) the deluded and defensive 'doctrine' of 'the infallibility of the Bishop of Rome.' As a result of this 'doctrine,' there was a further split in Catholicism, with some Catholics in the Netherlands, Germany, Austria, and Switzerland breaking away from the Roman Catholic Church. These Catholics formed the Old Catholic Church.

PART 3: CONCLUSION

After the loss of these Catholics, the Roman Catholic Church became even more entrenched in its medieval theology. Eventually, Pope John XXIII, decided that the Church needed updating, in order to connect with a more secular world, and he convened the Second Vatican Council in 1962. The prominent reform-minded theologians who attended the Council were: Marie-Dominique Chenu, OP; Henri de Lubac, SJ; Yves Congar, OP; Karl Rahner, SJ; John Courtney Murray, SJ; Bernhard Häring, CSsR; Edward Schillebeeckx, OP; Joseph Ratzinger, and Hans Kung. There were, of course, no women theologians present, or consulted, at this council, despite its advocacy of reform, and, as has been discussed, Joseph Ratzinger (who became Pope Benedict XVI) eventually 'turned-coat,' ceased to advocate reform and persecuted his previous colleagues.

However, at the time of the Second Vatican Council, many reforms were introduced, but priestly celibacy was not discussed, despite much anticipation that the celibacy mandate might be lifted. Later, after the council's closure, Pope Paul VI produced *Sacerdotalis Caelibatus* in 1967. This encyclical confirmed that celibacy would continue to be enforced on all candidates for the priesthood in the Latin rite. Since then, despite numerous requests from clergy (including archbishops, bishops, and priests) and an overwhelming vote for the removal of mandatory celibacy at the Synod of Bishops for the Pan-Amazon Region, and notwithstanding the fact that the Vatican allows Catholic priests in the East to marry, the 'powers that be' in the Vatican have stubbornly refused to make celibacy a voluntary commitment for priests of the Latin rite.

Mandatory celibacy is a breach of Article 16 of the *Universal Declaration of Human Rights*, which states:

1. Men and women of full age, without any limitation due to race, nationality or religion, have the right to marry and to found a family. They are entitled to equal rights as to marriage, during marriage and at its dissolution.

2. Marriage shall be entered into only with the free and full consent of the intending spouses.

3. The family is the natural and fundamental group unit of society and is entitled to protection by society and the State.[2]

Now, the Roman Catholic Church has tried to state that this article is not breached because no one has to become a Catholic priest, and anyone in the West who decides to follow this path knows full well that he will

---

2. United Nations, *Universal Declaration*.

be required to live a celibate life. But Jesus did not mandate celibacy and many people who experience a call to the priesthood do not feel a desire to be celibate. Fr. Peter Daly expresses that most mandated celibates do not experience celibacy as either easy, or as a 'gift.'[3] He states, "that is not how it is experienced. A gift must be freely given, not mandated. Celibacy in the Roman Catholic priesthood is a mandate. If you won't promise lifelong celibacy, the church won't ordain you. It is not experienced so much as a 'gift,' but rather as a 'price' for priesthood. For many people, the price is too high."[4] The 'price' is, of course, giving up one's own God-given sexuality and natural sexual desires. It is actually a cruel and barbaric 'price,' as it could be argued that natural sexuality is 'priceless.'

So, all Catholic priests in the Western rite continue to be forced into celibacy, but (as has been noted) there is a strong argument that mandatory celibacy causes psychological maladjustment in some priests. The psychologist, Carl Rogers, argued that psychological adjustment exists when all sensory and emotional experiences are assimilated into a consistent relationship with the person's concept of self; psychological maladjustment exists when a person suppresses their awareness of these sensory and emotional experiences, and they are not assimilated into a consistent relationship with the concept of self. When the latter situation exists, there is psychological tension, and this raises the following question concerning mandatory celibacy: has the denying, or suppressing, of sensory and emotional experiences that is brought about by the celibacy rule led to a psychological maladjustment in some Catholic priests?

A.W. Richard Sipe, who was himself both a priest and a psychotherapist, argued that obligatory celibacy, and the Church's teaching on sexuality, is at the root of the worse crisis that the Catholic Church has faced since the Reformation. He has connected mandatory celibacy to sexual abuse, stating that the Eastern Orthodox, who do not have mandatory celibacy, do not have a sexual abuse crisis. He argues that this is because mandatory celibacy limits the pool of potential candidates to the priesthood, and, also, tends to attract candidates who are sexually dysfunctional, sexually immature, or whose sexual orientation may be a motive for joining a priesthood that forbids marriage and does not include women.

The authors of this book are in no way homophobic, or 'anti-gay,' but Paul has pointed out in his own personal account of life both in the seminary and the priesthood that there is a 'gay subculture' in Catholic clerical circles. This is completely and totally wrong, not because there is anything

---

3. Daly, "Priesthood Is Being Crucified on the Cross of Celibacy," para. 31.
4. Daly, "Priesthood Is Being Crucified on the Cross of Celibacy," para. 31.

wrong with a person having a homosexual orientation, but because the Catholic priesthood should be representative of people of both heterosexual and homosexual orientations, and not just dominated by one group, in particular. The makeup of the clergy is also especially hypocritical when, on its public face, the Church has always harshly condemned homosexuality for the populace, and yet, behind the scenes, and in reality, the Roman Catholic clerical culture is predominately homosexual, and promiscuously homosexual, at that. Many homosexual lay people engage in loving, stable, long-term sexual relationships with their partners, and the Church denies these people any possibility of marriage, and yet, meanwhile, there exists within the clergy a 'gay subculture' that fosters and promotes transient promiscuous gay sexual relationships (as long as they are not discovered). How hypocritical is that?

Mandatory celibacy has not only created a 'gay subculture'; it has also created a misogynistic culture within the ranks of the clergy. It has been noted that Jesus was counter-cultural in the way he treated women; he is portrayed in the gospels as chatting with them, healing them, and allowing himself to be touched by them. He received much criticism for this. Yet, he chose Mary Magdalen as the first witness of the resurrection and, in the early church, his revolutionary attitude towards women prevailed, and women were initially ordained as both priests and deacons. There can be little doubt that the Gospel of Mary, which evidences these facts, began to be suppressed very early on, perhaps around the fourth century. In point of fact, only one incomplete copy, and hardly any fragments, have survived, unlike the so-called 'canonical' gospels. The female priesthood also began to be suppressed in the third century, and this is evidenced by the writings of Tertullian, but the female diaconate did not begin to be suppressed until the sixth century and even survived in some places in the East until the ninth century.

Of course, the initial suppression of women's ministries was largely due to the development of a patriarchal culture in Christianity, but later, after the rising of a 'pro-celibate' and 'anti-sexual' culture by the likes of St. Augustine and others, a misogynistic culture formed in the ranks of the clergy, particularly in the West. This came to a head after the East–West Schism when the First Council of the Lateran decided to mandate celibacy. At this time, priests were forced to abandon their wives and families and leave them destitute. Women were treated as if they were less than human and beyond contempt. Later, at the Second Council of the Lateran, it was decreed that nuns could not sing the Divine Office in the same choir as monks.

While both Councils of the Lateran enforced celibacy, many priests were not faithful to it, as has already been noted. At the same time, the position of women was increasingly eroded, due to it. Not only had women's ordinations been suppressed since the ninth century, but women were now, in the twelfth century, advised that they were so inferior, so much of a second sex, that they were not worthy of marrying priests. Mandatory celibacy began to create a culture that had no roots in Judaism, or in the teachings of Jesus and the structures of the early church. Women had been valued in early church traditions, and marriage had been seen as holy. In marriage, the two had become 'one flesh,' and completed one another. Now, one half of that flesh had been thrown in the gutter with her offspring, and all priests had been told that they would be better off if they denied their sexuality, regardless of their libido. This, of course, relegated many women to become mistresses, for many priests continued to have sex with women.

During, and after, the Reformation, women were further undermined by the Catholic Church. Up until the Reformation, there had always been a strong resistance by priests to mandatory celibacy but, at the time of the Reformation, those Catholic priests who had resisted mandatory celibacy left the Catholic Church of the time and joined the reformers. The result was that those who remained were, largely 'pro' mandatory celibacy, and hostile to women. The Catholic priesthood was further elevated when Council of Trent declared that the priesthood placed an 'indelible mark' on the priest's soul. Of course, this mark was accessible only to celibate men.

Since the time of the Reformation, the influence of women in the Catholic Church has been further diminished. Prior to, and during, the reformation there had been some very strong women who exercised influence. Both St. Catherine of Siena and Julian of Norwich were spiritual directors. St. Catherine of Siena advised the Pope; Julian advised eminent dignitaries and was the first English woman to write any book, yet alone a spiritual one. At the time of the Reformation, St. Teresa of Avila was part of the Counter-Reformation movement but the influence of women in the Church began to fade away after the movement ended. For example, the vocation of consecrated widow that had existed up until the Reformation completely disappeared. This was unfortunate because this ministry allowed single women to take vows while living in their own homes. As such, they exercised an autonomy that women who lived in convents did not have. After the Reformation, the only form of consecrated life open to women was that of a nun in a convent.

As has already been noted, after the Reformation the majority of priests stopped resisting mandatory celibacy, and this meant that more homosexual men were attracted to the priesthood than heterosexual men.

Unsurprisingly, over time, this led to a 'gay subculture' in the ranks of the clergy. This subculture is actually quite disturbing because it means that the Catholic priesthood is not representative of humanity. While there is absolutely nothing at all wrong with a person being gay, the vast majority of people are not gay. Gay people should certainly be represented in the priesthood, but gay priests should not be in the majority in the Church. Who is going to represent women and married heterosexual men if most priests are gay? Mandatory celibacy and its 'gay subculture' seems to have led to gay men in a predominately 'gay Vatican' influencing popes to produce encyclicals that speak for married men, women, and all lay people, without ever consulting them.

In the late twentieth, and early twenty first, centuries, several papal letters were produced without consulting women and/or married people, or which consulted them, only to disregard their views. Both *Humanae Vitae* and *Ordinatio Sacerdotalis* can be included in this list. Yet, it is not only papal letters that ignore the voices of the laity. Recently, there were two commissions set up by Pope Francis I about the ordination of women to the diaconate. The first of these was established in 2016, and the second was set up in 2020. The results of these commissions have never been made known to the wider Church, but, due to my connections, I happen to know that one of them recommended the restoration of the female diaconate. In May 2024, Pope Francis stated in a US TV interview that women deacons never existed.[5] There is irrefutable evidence to the contrary, and members of his commissions certainly thought so, too, which is probably why we have never been told what they thought. Why would Pope Francis have set up commissions to investigate the possibility of restoring the female diaconate if he believed women deacons never existed?

Furthermore, it was expected that the recent Synod on Synodality would decide whether the female diaconate should be restored but no decision was made at that Synod with the 'can being kicked down the road.' Why did the Pope originally suggest that this issue would be discussed at the Synod on Synodality and later change his mind? Personally, I think that Pope Francis I, then in his mid-eighties, and one of the very few popes who was heterosexual, was beginning to suffer from a declining mind, and to succumb to the influence of the all-male misogynistic culture of the Vatican, which took advantage of his declining health.

Finally, concerning women, it has been noted that a significant number of heterosexual clergy have had sexual relationships with women resulting in the birth of children, even though the culture of the all-male 'celibate'

---

5. Interview by O'Donnell, "Pope Francis: 60 Minutes Interview."

clergy is now predominately gay. This has been covered up for many years and has only begun to be acknowledged recently after several prominent clergymen, such as the former Bishop of Galway, Eamon Casey, have been exposed by the media for fathering children. Later, Vincent Doyle (a son of a priest who had been very close to his godfather without realizing that this man was actually his biological father) founded Coping International, an organization for the children of priests, which has demanded that the Vatican recognize and protect the rights of these children.

Doyle's organization has somewhat improved the situations of priests who father children, and the children themselves, as it has led to some changes to the guidelines concerning this issue. Priests can now get dispensations to be laicized much more quickly than before and at a much younger age. Also, the Vatican now acknowledges that these children exist. However, the guidelines continue to state that the loss of the clerical state is imposed on all priests in the Latin West who have fathered children unless, perhaps, this situation is not discovered until much later when the child is grown up as, according to the Vatican, paternal responsibilities create permanent obligations that in the Latin Church do not provide for the exercise of a priestly ministry.

Really? Why? Well, all I can say is it that it is very odd that the Vatican does not apply these rules to its Catholic priests of the Eastern rite. How is it that these priests are allowed to amalgamate their priestly ministry with the permanent obligations of fatherhood while the Catholic priests of the Latin West are not? Vincent Doyle, who founded Coping International, has welcomed the improvements to the guidelines, but continues to argue that the only real solution to this problem is to allow *all* priests in the Latin West to marry if they wish.

Moving on from the effects of mandatory celibacy on women, I have also examined if mandatory celibacy has contributed to the scale and gravity of the Catholic Church's sex abuse scandals. I conclude that it has for a number of reasons. Firstly, Catholic priests who have researched this matter, such as A.W. Richard Sipe and Peter Murnane, have argued that their statistics show that sexual abuse is higher among the Catholic clergy than in other professions and in general population. Murnane, in particular, claims that many bishops have not only tried to cover up sexual abuse but have also resisted investigating it, and, therefore, could not, and cannot, be relied on to provide accurate information concerning this matter. He has also stated that the Church always puts its own reputation above the welfare of victims and that is why it has tried to claim that sexual abuse among the Catholic Clergy is no higher than anywhere else. This tendency to 'downplay' sexual abuse among the Catholic clergy has been demonstrated again and again in this book along with the probability that it is much higher within the clerical ranks.

For example, the *New York Times* in 2003 found that the levels of sexual abuse were higher among the Catholic clergy than among lay people and other professions,[6] and the *Australian Royal Commission into Institutional Responses to Child Sex Abuse* (2013–2017) also found higher rates of sexual abuse among Catholic clergy.[7] The *Independent Inquiry into Child Sexual Abuse in England and Wales* (2020) also found that the Catholic Church had put its own reputation above the welfare of seminarians and failed to support victims.[8] In addition, Paul, who is the coauthor of this book, has himself experienced being pushed aside as a victim, in order that the interests of the Church could be protected.

Secondly, there are no women in the ranks of the Catholic clergy, and this virtually guarantees that sexual abuse will be higher in the Catholic clergy than in other professions because it has been statistically proven in most of the countries that retain data on this issue that men are much more likely to commit sexual abuse offences than women. Generally speaking, only 5 percent, or less, of sexual offenders are women,[9] and one has to wonder whether this is why the Catholic Church does not want women among its ranks: is it because they might expose the level of sexual abuse among the male clergy?

Thirdly, the enforced suppression of natural sexuality in those with a normal healthy libido can result in a culture where sexuality is seen as something to be hidden, a 'dirty secret.' Paul has stated that, in his experience, seminarians received no support in learning how to manage their sexual urges and unhealthy coping methods, such as masturbation and pornography, were used by many as a 'secret outlet.' The seminarians were (and still are to a certain extent) isolated from the real world in a comfortable little 'clerical bubble' with no real contact with women. This kind of culture creates a higher risk of sexual abuse, especially when priests are endowed with an elevated status that gives them power over others, and which makes it much harder for potential victims to resist being groomed by them.

Moreover, this kind of culture is also much more likely to attract the wrong kind of candidates to priesthood. Most people are unable to apply to the priesthood because they are either women, or men who wish to be

---

6. Goodstein, "Trail of Pain."
7. Royal Commission, *Final Report*, 31.
8. IICSA, *Investigation Report*, 95–96.
9. See, for example, UK Ministry of Justice, *Women and the Criminal Justice System 2019*, chap. 8, "Offence Analysis"; only 2 percent of British sex offenders are female.

married, and so the pool of candidates is already very thin. Then, it is very possible that a proportion of those who remain will be attracted to the priesthood for all the wrong reasons, such as misogynism or a desire to participate in gay sex, which is not a sin, in itself, but becomes one if it is either predatory or promiscuous. Whatever the reasons for joining, those who become Catholic priests will find themselves in a culture that is closed off from the rest of the world, placing them in the ranks of an elite celibate caste, due to the 'indelible mark on their soul[s]'. This is a dark, unhealthy culture and, for all the reasons above, mandatory celibacy has, and continues to have, an effect on the scale and gravity of the Catholic Church's sex abuse scandals.

In conclusion, mandatory 'celibacy' i.e., the attempt to force all members of the Catholic priesthood to abstain from sexual acts, is a sin. It is wrong because it is not biblical and has created an unnatural misogynistic culture that is not representative of humanity. It is wrong because it has perverted and twisted the Gospel. It is wrong because it has become the centerpiece of a hierarchical institution that has distorted historical facts to gain power. It is wrong because it has created an elite all-male 'celibate' hierarchy that attempts to speak for many lay people who are neither male, nor celibate. It is wrong because it has led those who perpetuate its practice to have delusions of grandeur and superiority, which stops them from respecting all members of the Church. It is wrong because it is a breach of Article 16 of *The Universal Declaration of Human Rights*. It is wrong because it has caused serious psychological damage to many priests and the lay people who have been their victims. It is wrong because it has created a profession in which sexual abuse is higher than in the rest of the populace. It is wrong because it has caused suffering to the offsprings of many priests who have grown up without a father in their lives.

Mandatory celibacy is a sin, and its impact has been to cause suffering to millions of people throughout history. We, the authors of this book, are calling this out and we are also asking for action to be taken to end this practice.

The Afterword

God is love. Whoever lives in love, lives in God, and God in them.
—1 John 4:16 (NIV)

WE ENCOUNTER THE INCARNATION of love most profoundly in relationship, above all in the union of two people who commit themselves intimately in partnership or marriage. Such a union becomes the gateway through which they discover one another's depths – their beauty and brokenness alike. In such vulnerability there is no hiding, no pretense. They are revealed to themselves and to another. They acquire a measure of divine sight.

How tragic, then, that mandatory celibacy forbids clergy this revelation—as though God demanded a cult of virginal devotees, barred from the blessing of human intimacy, and condemned instead to a sterile parody of divine union, barren of mutuality.

The roots of mandatory celibacy are entangled in themes of power, control, narcissism, patriarchy and misogyny. God has been imagined as male: the supreme authority, the giver of life and wisdom. Christ, embodied as male, was then cast as proof that men alone could be the conduits of God's presence. This patriarchal distortion fractures faith from the start, for God is beyond gender. To describe God as exclusively male risks idolatry, creating a self-serving and false narrative.

God, the Word, the Spirit, is not male, but the perfect unity of every identity. Human intimacy, where two lives learn to journey as one, becomes a living sacrament; a window through which the world can glimpse the divine.

Mandatory celibacy denies clergy this window. Instead, men are allured into the priesthood, trusting the church, only to find a life of privation, loneliness and secrecy. Spiritually castrated yet physically wired to bond, many are left frustrated, maladjusted, emotionally impoverished and desperate for touch and tenderness. The church presents them as icons of love, though they are forbidden the very experiences that reveal love's depths and terrors.

Although affected by deprivation, they remain morally responsible, and yet some have committed unthinkable acts.

The world has been shaken by reports of priests involved in sexual abuse, secret relationships, covert children and mass graves of infants at Church-run homes. These horrors are not isolated scandals but endemic, the poisoned harvest of a system that perverts the natural order.

The Church insists change is coming, pointing to safeguarding protocols. Yet it refuses to admit that its very teaching breeds abuse. Mandatory celibacy was not Christ's command, nor the apostle's practice. Peter had a wife. Many early clergy were married. Only later did the Church impose celibacy, portraying it falsely as a higher holiness. In truth, it has entrapped countless men in denial of their humanity and women in lives of exclusion.

History exposes the cruelty. At the first Council of the Lateran (1123), Pope Callixtus II decreed that clerical marriages should be dissolved. Wives were abandoned to poverty, slavery or suicide. Children were cast aside. Flint describes this as a 'wicked, cruel and ruthless affair,' but such brutality is now regarded as piety. Later, thinkers like Augustine and Aquinas deepened the misogyny. Augustine, once a lover and a father, turned to asceticism, condemning the flesh he had enjoyed. Aquinas, ignorant of biology, declared women, 'misbegotten men'—blaming their existence on weak semen or poor diet. These distortions hardened into doctrine, suffocating the Church for centuries.

Jesus was born into a patriarchal society. Religion cast Eve as the temptress, and Adam her hapless victim, endangered by the carnal fruit of desire she supposedly embodied, as though he were powerless to resist. The tale becomes the first in a long line of sacred texts that enshrine men's cruelty and violence towards women, as though divinely sanctioned, a mythology that allowed men to shield themselves against the so-called dangers of female wiles. The stories that follow are shocking. Abraham exploiting Sarah and Hagar. Lot's violation of his daughters and the erasure of his wife. Jephthah's sacrifice of his daughter. The Levite's savage abuse and dismemberment of his concubine. From the contaminated soil of such narratives mandatory celibacy would emerge, another mechanism of control, not only over women's bodies, but men's bodies too, binding sexuality in chains of fear and domination.

Given the prevailing culture, it was inevitable that Jesus would gather a group of men to support him, but the twist came when they become the agents of betrayal and women the bearers of love. When Jesus, the second

Adam, revisits Eden, he meets his Eve, Mary, on equal and respectful terms; he regards her not as a threat, but as one to whom he entrusts the good news of his resurgent love. He provides the vision of a new integrated society.

Jesus's radical vision was crushed by the men who seized the early church, reversing progress, recasting women as threats and locking power inside an all-male priesthood. The consequences have been tragic. Clergy, denied affection, companionship, and sexual fulfilment, are left wandering the frozen wastelands of solitude. Starved, many stumble into secrecy, addiction, and abuse. Their contradictory world is symbolized in their garb: men condemned to celibacy, yet enshrouded in lace-trimmed, dress-like robes, historically associated with femininity, surrogate women in a Church that simultaneously excludes women from sacramental leadership.

The hypocrisy deepens when a Church, whose rules have both enforced and blurred gender boundaries in its clergy, remains hostile to the LGBTQIA+ community.

The damage is not theoretical. Flint's searing analysis calls mandatory celibacy a 'dreadful abuse'—a human invention unsupported by Scripture or history, sustained through manipulation. She unmasks how the Church concealed the reality of married clergy in the early centuries and how its theology spawned misogyny and violence. Her words shock as she recounts the ruin of clerical families, the silencing of women, and the lifelong trauma of children deceived about their parentage.

Even in the modern era, the Church resisted new knowledge, clinging to barbaric teachings that inflicted psychological damage on its priests. It has behaved more like a cult than a community of love, breaching human rights by denying freedom of marriage and opinion. Its pretense is exposed by Coping International, where 50,000 children of Catholic priests have sought support.

And then there are the voices of survivors. Sanderson's personal account pierces through the rhetoric. Trusting the Church, he embarked on a journey of faith, only to meet systemic corruption and self-interest. Repeatedly, he forgave, he hoped, but the relentless cover-ups and collusion finally drove him out. His story, painful as it is, reflects thousands more who could tell worse. It lays bare a Church more concerned with its own survival than with God, truth, or morality.

Jesus himself condemned such hypocrisy: 'You snakes! You brood of vipers!'(Matt 23:33 NCB).

This book is therefore a cry of rage and pain—from the babies in mass graves, the children sexually abused, the abandoned partners, the fatherless children, the tormented clergy, and the countless lives twisted by a false teaching God never willed.

The evidence is overwhelming. The theology is hollow. The suffering is undeniable. Yet the Catholic Church clings still to mandatory celibacy. Its intransigence will only bring mounting shame, for to bar priests from love is to excommunicate them from the greatest sacrament of all: the Word made flesh, the incarnation of God revealed through, and in, human intimacy, and in the creation and cherishing of children.

Flint's earlier work, *No Place for a Woman*, was a groundbreaking study that exposed with unflinching clarity the Church's systematic exclusion and mistreatment of women, barring them from leadership and silencing their gifts. With 'Mandatory Celibacy' she extends this fearless enquiry, laying bare the contrived and distorted world that men have created in their covens of secrecy and collusion, fearful of the world and its complexity, terrified of women, sexuality and intimacy itself.

Unless, the Church can heed her prophetic writing, ordain women to the priesthood, and allow clergy to marry, the Church will continue to hemorrhage its people and sink further into irrelevance before an enlightened and progressive age.

Archbishop Jonathan Blake
Presiding Archbishop of the Open Episcopal Church

Bibliography

Ancrene Riwle [*The Rule for Anchoresses*]. 1225–40. *BSSWebsite*. https://www.bsswebsite.me.uk/History/AncreneRiwle/AncreneRiwle.htm/.

Apostolic Constitutions of the Holy Apostles, attributed to Clément. In *Ante-Nicene Fathers*, vol. 7, edited by Alexander Roberts, James Donaldson, and A. Cleveland Coxe, 387–508. Buffalo, NY: Christian Literature Publishing, 1886. Translated by James Donaldson. https://www.newadvent.org/fathers/0715.htm/.

Associated Press. "Belgium Prime Minister and King Blast Pope Francis for Catholic Church's Sexual Abuse Cover Up Legacy." *ABC News*. September 27, 2025. https://www.abc.net.au/news/2024-9-28/pope-francis-belgium-trip-alexander-de-croo-criticism-sex-abuse/104407796/.

———. "Pope Acknowledges Scandal of Priests Sexually Abusing Nuns." *The Guardian*, February 5, 2019. https://www.theguardian.com/world/2019/feb/05/pope-francis-acknowledges-scandal-of-priests-sexually-abusing-nuns/.

American Experience. "Dr. John Rock (1890–1984)." PBS.org. https://www.pbs.org/wgbh/americanexperience/features/pill-dr-john-rock-1890-1984/.

Anson, Peter Frederick. *Religious Orders and Congregations of Great Britain and Ireland*. Worcester, UK: Stanbrook Abbey Press, 1949.

Anson, Peter Frederick. *The Call of the Cloister*. London: SPCK, 1955.

Aquinas, Thomas. *Summa Theologica*. London: Burns, Oates & Washbourne, 1925.

Armstrong, Karen. *The Case for God*. London: Vintage, 2009.

Association of Catholic Priests. "The Children of Priests-Coping International." *ACP*, August 23, 2017. https://associationofcatholicpriests.ie/the-children-of-priests-coping-international/.

Augustine. *Against the Epistle of Manichaeus, Called Fundamental*. Savage, MN: Lighthouse Christian Publishing, 2017.

Ballano, Vivencio. O. *Celibacy, Seminary Formation and Catholic Clerical Sex Abuse*. London: Routledge, 2024.

Beck, George A. *The English Catholics (1850 – 1950)*. London: Burnes & Oates, 1950.

Bede. *Ecclesiastical History of the English People (673–735)*. Revised edition. London: Penguin Classics, 1990.

Blackstock, Gordon. "Gay Mafia Book Claim, Priest Accuses Church of Bullying." *BBC News*, February 12, 2024. https://www.bbc.co.uk/news/uk-scotland-glasgow-west-68254498/.

Blade, Michelle. "Catholic Priest to Face Sex Charges." *Lancaster Guardian*, May 2, 2013.

———. "Police Chief Pleased with Result of Case." *The Morecambe Visitor,* November 19, 2013: 11.

———. "Priest Victim Wins Jail Plea." *The Morecambe Visitor,* December 17, 2013: Front cover, 3.

Boff, Leonardo. *Church: Charism and Power: Liberation Theology and the Institutional Church.* Translated by John W. Diercksmeier. New York: Crossroad, 1985.

Boorstein, Michelle. "Catholic Seminarians Are Newly Speaking Out About Sexual Misconduct—And Being Shunned as a Result." *The Washington Post,* October 4, 2019. https://www.washingtonpost.com/local/social-issues/some-catholic-seminarians-are-speaking-out-about-sexual-misconduct—and-being-shunned-as-a-result/2019/10/03/be6f1184-d8b9-11e9-ac63-3016711543fe_story.html/.

Brady, Seán. *Statement by Cardinal Seán Brady on the Report of the Commission to Inquire into Child Abuse.* Archdiocese of Armagh, May 20, 2009. https://www.armagharchdiocese.org/statement-by-cardinal-sean-brady-on-the-report-of-the-commission-to-inquire-into-child-abuse/.

Braiden, Gerry. "Priest to Sue Fellow Cleric After Sexual Bullying Book Allegations." *The Scottish Herald,* June 12, 2013. https://www.heraldscotland.com/news/13109036.priest-sue-fellow-cleric-sexual-bullying-book-allegations/.

Brody, Stuart. "The Relative Health Benefits of Different Sexual Activities." *The Journal of Sexual Medicine* 7.4 (2010) 1336–1361.

Brown, Andrew. "Celibacy and Child Abuse." *The Guardian,* March 19, 2010. https://www.guardian.co.uk/commentisfree/andrewbrown/2010/mar/19/religion-catholicism-celibacy-ireland/.

Brown, Raymond. *The Community of the Beloved Disciple.* New York: Paulist Press, 1978.

Bruni, Frank. "The Wages of Celibacy." *New York Times,* February 25, 2013. https://www.nytimes.com/2013/02/26/opinion/bruni-the-wages-of-celibacy.html/.

Bunting, Madeleine. "An Abuse Too Far by the Catholic Church." *The Guardian,* May 21, 2009. https://www.theguardian.com/commentisfree/belief/2009/may/21/catholic-abuse-ireland-ryan/.

Byrne, Lavinia. *Woman at the Altar: The Ordination of Women in the Roman Catholic Church.* London: Continuum, 1994.

Canadian Conference of Catholic Bishops. *Canadian Bishops' Statement on the Encyclical 'Humanae Vitae.'* ["The Winnipeg Statement"]. Encyclical letter, September 27, 1968. https://www.scribd.com/document/145198871/Winnipeg-Statement/.

Caputo, Nina. *Nahmanides in Medieval Catalonia: History, Community and Messianism.* Notre Dame, IN: University of Notre Dame Press, 2008.

"Cardinal Keith O'Brien: Allow Priests to Marry." BBC News, February 22, 2013, https://www.bbc.co.uk/news/uk-scotland-21552628/.

"Cardinal Ricard Among 11 French Bishops Accused of Abuse." BBC News. November 7, 2022. https://www.bbc.co.uk/news/world-europe-63545586/.

Carlson-Ghost, Mark. "Phillips Daughter's 'Great Lights' of the Early Church." *Mark Carlson-Ghost: Celebrating diversity in culture, myth and history,* September 16, 2016. https://www.markcarlson-ghost.com/index.php/2016/09/17/philips-daughters-prophets-names/.

Catechism of the Catholic Church. Dublin: Veritas, 1994.

"Cathedral Priest Faces Sex Charges." *Lancaster Guardian,* April 4, 2013. *Bishopaccountability.org.* https://www.bishop-accountability.org/news2013/03_04/2013_04_04_LancasterGuardian_CathedralPriest.htm/.

Cernuzio, Salvatore. "Synod Report: A Church That Involves Everyone and Is Too Close to World's Wounds." *Vatican News,* October 28, 2023. https://www.vaticannews.va/en/vatican-city/news/2023-10/the-synod-report-a-church-that-involves-everyone.html/.

Chan, T. H. "Why More Sex May Lower Prostate Cancer Risk." *Harvard T.H. Chan School of Public Health,* March 23, 2022. https://hsph.harvard.edu/news/why-more-sex-may-lower-prostate-cancer-risk/.

Charnetski Carl J., and Francis X. Brennan. "Sexual Frequency and Salivary Immunoglobulin A (IgA)." *Psychological Reports* 94, no. 3 (2004): 839–44.

Clapham, Andrew. *Human Rights: A very short introduction.* Oxford: Oxford University Press, 2016.

"Clarifications." *The Morecambe Visitor.* December 24, 2013.

Clement of Alexandria. *The Stromata.* In *Alexandrian Christianity: Selected Translations of Clement and Origen with Introduction and Notes,* edited by John Ernest Leonard Oulton and Henry Chadwick, 57–148. Vol. 2 of *The Library of Christian Classics.* Philadelphia: Westminster, 1954.

Code of Canon Law, English translation. https://www.vatican.va/archive/cod-iuris-canonici/cic_index_en.html./

Commission to Inquire into Child Abuse. *Report of the Commission to Inquire into Child Abuse.* Dublin: Ryan Monitoring Group, 2009.

Congregation for Catholic Education. *Instruction Concerning the Criteria for the Discernment of Vocations with Regard to Persons with Homosexual Tendencies in View of Their Admission to the Seminary and to Holy Orders.* November 4, 2005. https://www.vatican.va/roman_curia/congregations/ccatheduc/documents/rc_con_ccatheduc_doc_20051104_istruzione_en.html/.

Congregation for the Doctrine of the Faith. *Dominus Iesus: Declaration on the Unicity and Salvific Universality of Jesus Christ and the Church.* August 6, 2000. https://www.vatican.va/roman_curia/congregations/cfaith/documents/rc_con_cfaith_doc_20000806_dominus-iesus_en.html/.

Congregation of the Holy Office. *Crimen Sollicitationis: Instruction on the Manner of Proceeding in Causes Involving the Crime of Solicitation.* Vatican Polyglot Press, 1962. https://www.vatican.va/resources/resources_crimen-sollicitationis-1962_en.html/.

Congregatio Pro Clericis. "Vatican Guidelines." *Coping International Ltd.* https://www.copinginternational.com/vaticanguidelines/.

Cook, Alison. "My Ordeal with a Sex Monster Monk." *The Irish Sunday People,* November 12, 2000.

Council of Laodicea. *Canons of the Synod of Laodicea (4th Century).* In *Nicene and Post-Nicene Fathers,* 2nd ser., vol. 14, *The Seven Ecumenical Councils,* edited by Philip Schaff Repr., Peabody, MA: Hendrickson, 1994. https://www.newadvent.org/fathers/3806.htm/.

Cozzens, Donald. *The Changing Face of the Priesthood: A Reflection on the Priest's Crisis of Soul.* Collegeville, MN: Liturgical Press, 2017.

Crawford, Siobhán. "Father Michael Higginbottom Sentenced for Child Abuse at Upholland College." *BoltBurdenKemp,* May 13, 2017. https://www.

boltburdonkemp.co.uk/our-insights/posts/father-michael-higginbottom-sentenced-child-abuse-upholland-college/.

Curry, Jan. "The Law of Celibacy Must Change." *Journal of the Catholic Women's Network* 54 (1998) 6–7.

Daly, Peter. "The Priesthood Is Being Crucified on the Cross of Celibacy." *National Catholic Reporter*, July 15, 2019. https://www.ncronline.org/news/priestly-diary/priesthood-being-crucified-cross-celibacy/.

Danaher, Dan. "Clare Bishop of Ferns Says He Is in Favor of Women Priests." *Clare Champion*, June 19, 2021. https://clarechampion.ie/clare-bishop-of-ferns-says-he-is-in-favour-of-women-priests/.

Daniëls, Ibbe, and Ingrid Schildermans, dir. *Godvergeten [Godforsaken]*. Zaventem, Belgium: De Mensen. Aired on VRT Canvas September 2023. Documentary series, 4 × 50 minutes (Dutch language).

Degeorge, Gail. "Women Religious Leaders Call for 'Decisive Action' on Abuse." *Global Sisters Report: A Project of the National Catholic Reporter*, February 7, 2019. https://www.globalsistersreport.org/news/trends/women-religious-leaders-call-decisive-action-abuse-55851./

Dennis, George T. *The Apostolic Origins of Priestly Celibacy*. San Francisco: Ignatius, 1991.

Devlin, Brian. *Cardinal Sin*. Dublin: Columba Books, 2021.

The Didache. Translated by M. B. Riddle, in *The AnteNicene Fathers*, vol. 7, edited by Alexander Roberts, James Donaldson, and A. Cleveland Coxe. Buffalo, NY: Christian Literature Publishing, 1886. Revised and edited for New Advent by Kevin Knight. https://www.newadvent.org/fathers/0714.htm/.

"Disgraced Priest Is Released from Prison." *The Impartial Reporter: Fermanagh and South Tyrone News*, December 17, 2009. https://www.impartialreporter.com/news/13851898.disgraced-priest-is-released-from-prison/.

Encyclopedia Britannica. "Council of Elvira." Last modified January 10, 2023. https://www.britannica.com/event/Council-of-Elvira/.

———. "East-West Schism: Summary, History, & Effects." Last updated April 4, 2019. https://www.britannica.com/event/East-West-Schism-1054/.

———. "Second Lateran Council." Last modified January 20, 2023. https://www.britannica.com/event/Lateran-Council-Second-1139/.

"Father Higginbottom, Former Priest of Darlington St Augustine's, Is Jailed." *The Northern Echo*, July 30, 2019. https://www.thenorthernecho.co.uk/news/17804386.father-higginbottom-former-priest-darlington-st-augustines-jailed/.

Farrell, Derek Patrick. "An Historical Viewpoint of Sexual Abuse Perpetrated by Clergy and Religious." *Journal of Religion & Abuse* 6, no. 2 (2004): 41–80, http://doi.org/10.1300/JI54n02_04/.

Fisher, Helen. E "The Biology of Attraction." *Psychology Today*, April 1, 1993. https://www.psychologytoday.com/gb/articles/199304/the-biology-of-attraction/.

Flannery, Tony. "The Story of Lavinia Byrne and the CDF." *Tony Flannery: Priest and Writer*, January 20, 2024. https://www.tonyflannery.com/the-story-of-lavinia-byrne-and-the-cdf/.

Flint, Debra. "East and West: Understanding the History of the Female Diaconate." *The Tablet*, December 16, 2024.

Flint, Debra Maria. *No Place for a Woman: The Spiritual and Political Power Abuse of Women within Catholicism*. Woodstock, NY: Lantern Publishing, 2024.

Fox, Thomas C. "Hans Kung on John Paul II Beatification," *National Catholic Reporter*, May 2, 2011. https://www.ncronline.org/blogs/ncr-today/hans-kung-john-paul-ii-beatification/.

Francis. *Querida Amazonia: Post-Synodal Apostolic Exhortation to the People of God and to All Persons of Good Will*. Vatican City: Libreria Editrice Vaticana, 2020. https://www.vatican.va/content/francesco/en/apost_exhortations/documents/papa-francesco_esortazione-ap_20200202_querida-amazonia.html/.

Freeman, Charles. *The Closing of the Western Mind*. Evansville, IN: Vintage, 2002.

Freud, Sigmund. *Three Essays on the Theory of Sexuality (1905)*. London: Verso, 2016.

Gledhill, Ruth. "Doomed Love Affair Led Priest to Suicide." *The Times*, November 4, 1993, https://womenpriests.org/john-wijngaards/seddon-doomed-love-affair-led-priest-to-suicide/.

Gnostic Society Library. "Gnostic Scriptures and Fragments: The Gospel According to Mary Magdalene." Modified November 4, 2022. http://www.gnosis.org/library/marygosp.htm.

Goodstein, Laurie. "Decades of Damage: Trail of Pain in Church Crisis Leads to Nearly Every Diocese." *The New York Times*, January 12, 2003. https://www.nytimes.com/2003/01/12/us/decades-of-damage-trail-of-pain-in-church-crisis-leads-to-nearly-every-diocese.html/.

The Gospel of Mary. A new translation by David Curtis, third draft, last modified August 7, 2025. https://www.thegospelofmary.org/the-gospel/.

The Gospel of Philip. Translated by Willis Barnstone. In *The Nag Hammadi Library*. The Gnostic Society Library. https://www.gnosis.org/naghamm/gop.htm.

Gutiérrez, Gustavo. *A Theology of Liberation: 50th Anniversary Edition*. Translated, with a new Introduction, by Michael E. Lee. Maryknoll, NY: Orbis, 2023.

Haines, Michael. "New Irish Bishop Calls for Women Priests, Then Changes Tune." *Lifesite News*, June 25, 2021. https://www.lifesitenews.com/news/new-irish-bishop-calls-for-women-priests-then-changes-tune/.

Hall, Stef. "Priest Tells of His 'Shock' at Arrest." *Lancashire Evening Post*, November 14, 2013.

Harlan, Chico. "Ex-Cardinal McCarrick Defrocked by Vatican for Sexual Abuse." *The Washington Post*, February 16, 2019. https://www.washingtonpost.com/world/europe/ex-cardinal-mccarrick-defrocked-by-vatican-for-sexual-abuse/2019/02/16/0aa365d4-2e2c-11e9-8ad3-9a5b113ecd3c_story.htm.

Harrell, Daniel. "Ambrose: Does Celibacy Still Have Value?" *Patheos*, November 22, 2010. https://www.patheos.com/resources/additional-resources/2010/11/ambrose-celibacy-still-have-value/.

Holland, Joe. *The Cruel Eleventh Century Imposition of Western Clerical Celibacy*. Washington: Pacem In Terris Press, 2017.

Horrowitz, Jason, and Elisabetta Povoledo. "Vatican's Secret Rules for Priests Who Have Children." *New York Times*, February 18, 2019. https://www.nytimes.com/2019/02/18/world/europe/priests-children-vatican-rules-celibacy.html/.

Hyer, Margorie. "Priest Agrees to Stop Teaching Spirituality, Blasts Vatican." *The Washington Post*, October 21, 1988. https://www.washingtonpost.com/archive/local/1988/10/22/priest-agrees-to-stop-teaching-spirituality-blasts-vatican/dfc84875-2e0e-48f2-935e-af7d7278df33/.

Ignatius of Antioch. *The Epistle of Ignatius to the Antiochians*. https://catholiclibrary.org/library/view?docId=/Fathers-EN/anf.000016.Ignatius.EpistletotheAntiochians.html&chunk.id=00000003./

Independent Inquiry into Child Sexual Abuse (ILSA). *Safeguarding in the Roman Catholic Church in England and Wales*. London: Crown Copyright, 2022.

Jacobson, David. "Is Being Single Acceptable in the Jewish Community?" *Jewish Insider*, February 5, 2015, https://ejewishphilanthropy.com/is-being-single-acceptable-in-the-jewish-community/.

"Jesus' Teachings Include Women." *Theology of Work Project*. Adapted April 5, 2017. https://www.theologyofwork.org/key-topics/women-workers-in-the-new-testament/jesus-teachings-include-women/.

Jewish Virtual Library. "Celibacy." Last modified November 25, 2022. https://www.jewishvirtuallibrary.org/celibacy/.

John Jay College of Criminal Justice. *The Nature and Scope of Sexual Abuse of Minors by Catholic Priests and Deacons in the United States, 1950–2002*. Washington, DC: United States Conference of Catholic Bishops, 2004.

John Paul II. "Address of Pope John Paul II to the Bishops of Ireland on Their 'Ad Limina' Visit." August 27, 1987. https://www.vatican.va/content/john-paul-ii/en/speeches/1987/august/documents/hf_jp-ii_spe_19870827_bishops-ireland.htm

———. *Ordinatio Sacerdotalis* [Apostolic Letter on Reserving Priestly Ordination to Men Alone], May 22, 1994. *Acta Apostolicae Sedis* 86 (1994) 545–48. https://www.vatican.va/content/john-paul-ii/en/apost_letters/1994/documents/hf_jp-ii_apl_19940522_ordinatio-sacerdotalis.html/.

———. *Pastores dabo vobis*: Apostolic Exhortation on the Formation of Priests in the Circumstances of the Present Day. March 25, 1992. Boston: Saint Paul Books and Media, 1992. https://www.vatican.va/content/john-paul-ii/en/apost_exhortations/documents/hf_jp-ii_exh_25031992_pastores-dabo-vobis.html/.

Jones, Ruadlan. "New Bishop of Ferns 'Daunted' but Eager to Get Started." *The Irish Catholic*, June 4, 2021. https://www.irishcatholic.com/new-bishop-of-ferns-daunted-but-eager-to-get-started/.

Julian of Norwich. *Revelations of Divine Love*. Oxford: Oxford World Classics, 2015.

Jurgens, William. *The Faith of the Early Fathers, Volume 1*. Collegeville, MN: Liturgical Press, 1970.

———. *The Faith of the Early Fathers, Volume 2*. Collegeville, MN: Liturgical Press, 1979.

Keeler, Bob. "The New Shepherd: A Form Hand for LI Flock." *Newsday*, February 21, 1999. *Bishopaccountability.org*. https://www.bishop-accountability.org/news/1999_02_21_Keeler_TheNew.htm/.

Keenan, Marie. *Child Sexual Abuse and the Catholic Church*. Oxford: Oxford University Press, 2013.

Kempe, Margery. *The Book of Margery Kempe*. London: Penguin, 1985.

Kenny, John. "Saturday 28th December." *The Venerable* 28.4 (1986) 72.

King, Karen L. *The Gospel of Mary of Magdala: Jesus and the First Woman Apostle*. Santa Rosa, CA: Polebridge, 2003.

Lea, Henry Charles. *An Historical Sketch of Sacerdotal Celibacy in the Christian Church*. Philadelphia: J. B. Lippincott & Co., 1867. https://name.umdl.umich.edu/aga4909.0001.001/.

Lefevere, Patricia. "Children of Priests: An Invisible Legion of Secrecy and Neglect." *National Catholic Reporter*. August 21, 2017. www.ncronline.org/news/children-priests—invisible-legion-secrecy-and-neglect/.

Leo XIII. *Rerum Novarum* [Of New Things], May 15, 1891. https://www.vatican.va/content/leo-xiii/en/encyclicals/documents/hf_l-xiii_enc_15051891_rerum-novarum.html/.

Lotty, Sian, dir. *Abused: Breaking the Silence*. London: BBC One, 2011.

Louf, André. *The Cistercian Alternative*. Dublin: Gill and Macmillan, 1983.

Mac Donald, Sarah. "252 Abuse Allegations Made Against Members of Catholic Church in Ireland over Past Year." *Irish Independent*. June 12, 2024. https://www.independent.ie/irish-news/252-abuse-allegations-made-against-members-of-catholic-church-in-ireland-over-past-year-new-report/a581907821.html/.

Maslow, Abraham. *A Theory of Human Motivation*. New Delhi: General Press, 2021.

———. *Motivation and Personality*. Harlow, England: Pearson, 1997.

Matranga, Anna. "Saint John Paul II Accused of Protecting Pedophiles, Fueling Debate over Pope's 'Fast-Track' to Sainthood." *CBSNews,* March 10, 2023. https://www.cbsnews.com/news/john-paul-ii-former-pope-sainthood-debate-accusations-protecting-pedophiles-poland/.

McAleese, Martin, chair. *Report of the Inter-Departmental Committee to Establish the Facts of State Involvement with the Magdalen Laundries*. Dublin: Department of Justice and Equality, 2013.

McDonald, Marie. "The Problem of the Sexual Abuse of African Religious in Africa and in Rome." *NCR Online,* November 20, 1998. https://natcath.org/NCR_Online?documents/McDonaldAFRICAreport.html/.

McDonald, Sarah. "Priest Who Leaves Ministry After Fathering a Child Must Be Financially Supported." *The Tablet*, March 30, 2022. https://corpus-blog.blogspot.com/2022/03/priest-who-leaves-ministry-after.html/.

McGarry, Patsy. "Irish Figures for Mass Attendance Approaching 'Normal' World Level." *The Irish Times*, September 20, 2002. https://www.irishtimes.com/news/irish-figures-for-mass-attendance-approaching-normal-world-level-/.

McGarry, Patsy, and Ronan McGreevy. "Blackrock College: Who Were the Priests Accused of Abuse?" *The Irish Times*, November 13, 2022. https://www.irishtimes.com/ireland/social-affairs/2022/11/13/blackrock-college-who-were-the-priests-accused-of-abuse/.

McLaughlin, Martyn. "Catholic Priest Dismissed over Abuse Claims." *The Scotsman*, September 8, 2013. https://www.scotsman.com/news/catholic-priest-dismissed-over-abuse-claims-1562023/.

McManus, Michael J. "Catholic Priests Seek End to Celibacy." *The Royal Gazette*, February 4, 2011. https://www.royalgazette.com/religion/lifestyle/article/20110204/catholic-priests-seek-end-to-celibacy/

Mears, Tyler. "Priest's Suicide After Being Arrested of Suspicion of Historic Sex Abuse." *WalesOnline*, June 9, 2016. https://www.walesonline.co.uk/news/wales-news/priests-suicide-after-being-arrested-11446490/.

Meek, James. "Nun Quits over Ordination of Women." *The Guardian*, January 12, 2000. https://www.theguardian.com/world/2000/jan/12/religion.uk1.

Miller, Lisa, and Bronwen Reed. "The 'Hidden Children' of the Catholic Church Are Refusing to Live in Secrecy Anymore." *ABC News*, September 14, 2019. https://

www.abc.net.au/news/2019-9-24/children-of-priests-connect-through-coping-international/11532668/.

Ministry of Justice. *Statistics on Women and the Criminal Justice System 2019*. Chapter 8, "Offence Analysis." December 2019. https://assets.publishing.service.gov.uk/media/5fbe7396d3bf7f5739417e31/statistics-on-women-and-the-criminal-justice-system-2019.pdf/.

Murphy, Annie, with Peter DeRosa. *Forbidden Fruit: The True Story of My Secret Love Affair with Ireland's Most Powerful Bishop*. Boston: Little, Brown, 1993.

Murnane, Peter. *Clerical Errors*. Eugene, OR: Resource, 2022.

"No Charges, but Priest Still Told to Stay Away from Parish." *Darlington & Stockton Times*, December 11, 2007. https://www.darlingtonandstocktontimes.co.uk/news/1896990.no-charges-but-priest-still-told-to-stay-away-from-parish/.

The New Testament in the Original Greek: Byzantine. Edited by Maurice A. Robinson and William G. Pierpont. Textform 2005/2010. Chilton, GA: Original Word, 2005.

Oakley, Lisa. "Understanding Spiritual Abuse." *Church Times*, February 16, 2018.

O'Donnell, Norah. "Pope Francis: The 60 Minutes Interview." *60 Minutes*. CBS News. Aired May 19, 2024. https://www.cbsnews.com/video/pope-francis-the-first-with-norah-odonnell/.

O'Loughlin, Thomas. "Celibacy in the Catholic Church: A Brief History." *History Ireland* 3.4 (1995) 41–44.

O'Fatharta, Conall. "Ryan Report That Shocked Nation Offers Much but Gaps in Detail Still Remain." *Irish Examiner*, May 19, 2019. https://www.irishexaminer.com/lifestyle/arid-30925312/.

Office for National Statistics. "Child Sexual Abuse in England and Wales." March 2019. https://www.ons.gov.uk/peoplepopulationandcommunity/crimeandjustice/articles/childsexualabuseinenglandandwales/yearendingmarch2019/.

Otterman, Sharon. "A.W. Sipe, a Leading Voice on Clergy Sex Abuse, Dies at 85." *New York Times*, August 9, 2018. https:www.nytimes.com/2018/08/09nyregion/aw-richard-sipe-a-leading-voice-on-clergy-sex-abuse-dies-at-85.html/.

PA Reporter. "Ex-Dean of Lancaster Cathedral Jailed over Assaults." *The Guardian*, September 14, 2013.

———. "Priest Who Abused Schoolboys at Seminary Jailed for 18 Years." *The Scotsman*, July 30, 2019. https://www.scotsman.com/news/crime/priest-who-abused-schoolboys-at-seminary-jailed-for-18-years-1412109/.

"Pat Lawson Was Removed from His Parishes." *The Herald*, April 19, 2015. https://www.heraldscotland.com/news/13210378.pat-lawson-removed-parishes-not-neglectful-caring-people-blew-whistle-child-abuse-much-meets-eye-story-one-priests-fight-justice/.

Paul VI. *Humanae Vitae* [Of Human Life]. Encyclical letter, July 25, 1968. https://www.vatican.va/content/paul-vi/en/encyclicals/documents/hf_p-vi_enc_25071968_humanae-vitae.html/.

———. *Sacerdotalis Caelibatus* [Priestly Celibacy]. Encyclical letter, June 24, 1967. https://www.vatican.va/content/paul-vi/en/encyclicals/documents/hf_p-vi_enc_24061967_sacerdotalis.html/.

Paulson, Michael. "World Doesn't Share US View of Scandal." *The Boston Globe: Spotlight Investigation*. April 8, 2002. https://graphics.boston.com/globe/spotlight/abuse/stories/040802_world.htm/.

Pepinster, Catherine. "Laicized Friend of Former Hexham and Newcastle Bishop Jailed." *The Tablet,* March 14, 2025. https://www.thetablet.co.uk/news/laicised-friend-of-former-hexham-and-newcastle-bishop-jailed/.
Peters, Edward N. *The 1917 or Pio-Benedictine Code of Canon Law.* San Francisco: Ignatian, 2021.
Pius IX. *Decrees of the First Vatican Council.* Papal Encyclicals Online. https://www.papalencyclicals.net/councils/ecum20.htm/.
Plant, Thomas. G. "Separating Facts About Clergy Abuse from Fiction." *Psychology Today,* August 2018. https://www.psychologytoday.com/gb/blog/do-the-right-thing/201808/separating-facts-about-clergy-abuse-fiction/.
"Pope's Celibacy Rule: How Abstinence Affects Priest's Psychological Health." *Medical Daily,* March 20, 2013. htpps:/www.medicaldaily.com/popes-celibacy-rule-how-abstinence-affects-priests-psychological-health-244715/.
Prone, Terry. "Eamonn Casey: Man of the People with Life of Lies and Sex Crimes." *Irish Examiner,* July 21, 2024. https://www.bishop-accountability.org/2024/07/eamonn-casey-man-of-the-people-with-life-of-lies-and-sex-crimes/
Rahner, Karl. *Theological Investigations.* Vol. 6: *Concerning Vatican Council II.* Translated by KarlH. Kruger and Boniface Kruger. London: Darton, Longman & Todd, 1969.
Ramsey, Michael. *The Gospel and the Catholic Church.* Peabody, MA: Hendrickson, 2009.
Ratzinger, Joseph, and Peter Seewald. *Salt of the Earth: The Church at the End of the Millennium.* Translated by Aidan Walker. San Francisco: Ignatius, 1997.
Reisinger, Doris. "Reproductive Abuse in the Context of Clergy Sexual Abuse in the Catholic Church." *Religions* 13.3 (2022) 198. https://www.mdpi.com/2077-1444/13/3/198.
Reese, Thomas. "Synod on Synodality Report Is Disappointing, but Not Surprising." *National Catholic Reporter,* November 3, 2023. https://www.ncronline.org/opinion/guest-voices/synod-synodality-report-disappointing-not-surprising/.
Rigoni, Alexander. *The Gospel of Mary Magdalene: Lost Apocryphal Gospels: Jesus and the First Woman Apostle.* London: History Academy, 2021.
Robertson, Geoffrey. *The Case of the Pope.* London: Penguin, 2010.
Rogers, Carl. *On Becoming a Person: A Therapist's View of Psychotherapy.* London: Constable, 1961.
Rodricks, Dan. "From 'Spotlight' to 'Keepers,' Richard Sipe Sees Celibate Priesthood as Problem for the Catholic Church." *Survivors Network of those Abused by Priests.* May 26, 2017. https://www.snapnetwork.org/from_spotlight_to_keepers_richard_sipe_sees_celibate_priesthood_as_problem_for_the_catholic_church/.
Royal Commission into Institutional Responses to Child Sexual Abuse. *Final Report: Volume 16, Religious Institutions.* Sydney: Commonwealth of Australia, 2017.
Rutherford, Adrian. "Devastating Account of Abuse Inflicted on Children." *Belfast Telegraph,* March 18, 2010. https://www.belfasttelegraph.co.uk/news/devastating-account-of-abuse-inflicted-on-children/28524526.html/.
Santana, Edward. *Jung and Sex.* London: Routledge, 2016.
Scott, Marion, and Stacey Mullon. "Investigation: Church Files Reveal Scots Catholic Priests Have Been Accused of Abuse 126 Times but Never Reported." *The Sunday Post,* January 13, 2019. https://www.sundaypost.com/fp/investigation-scale-of-allegations-against-churchmen-is-exposed-as-campaigners-call-for-scotland-

to-follow-america-and-name-themsuffer-the-little-children-church-files-reveal-scot/.
Schillebeeckx, Edward. *Jesus: An Experiment in Christology*. Translated by Hubert Hoskins. London: Collins, 1979.
———. *Ministry: Leadership in the Community of Jesus Christ*. Translated by John Bowden. New York: Crossroad, 1981.
———. *The Church with a Human Face: A New and Expanded Theology of Ministry*. Translated by John Bowden. New York: Crossroad, 1985.
Second Vatican Council. *Presbyterorum Ordinis: Decree on the Ministry and Life of Priests*. Promulgated by Pope Paul VI, December 7, 1965. Vatican City: Libreria Editrice Vaticana. https://www.vatican.va/archive/hist_councils/ii_vatican_council/documents/vat-ii_decree_19651207_presbyterorum-ordinis_en.html./
Shield, Stephen. "The Traditional Latin Rite in the Church Today." Talk at the Latin Mass Society's First Northern Conference, English Martyrs Parish, Preston. Published September 2016. *Una Voce Canada*. https://unavocecanada.org/wp-content/uploads/2016/09/The-Traditional-Latin-Rite-in-the-Church-Today.pdf./.
Sipe, A.W. Richard. *Celibacy in Crisis: A Secret World Revisited*. New York: Brunner-Routledge, 2003.
———. *Sex, Priests and Power: Anatomy of a Crisis*. New York: Brunner-Routledge, 1996.
Smith, Rachel. "Priest Denies Sex Assaults." *Lancashire Evening Post*, November 12, 2013: front page, 7.
———. "Sex Abuse Priest Is Jailed for One Year." *Lancashire Evening Post*, December 14, 2013.
———. "Top Priest Faces Jail After Sex Trail." *Lancashire Evening Post*, November 16, 2013.
Smith, Suzanne. "Hidden Children." *ABC News*, August 12, 2023. https://www.abc.net.au/news/2023-8-13/children-catholic-priests-search-truth-justice-secrets/102706050/.
Tertullian. *The Prescription Against Heretics (De Praescriptione Haereticorum)*. Translated by Peter Holmes. In *Ante-Nicene Fathers*, vol. III: *Latin Christianity: Its Founder, Tertullian*, edited by Alexander Roberts, James Donaldson, and A. Cleveland Coxe, 243–67. Grand Rapids, MI: Eerdmans, 1980.
Thavis, John. "Legion of Christ Acknowledge Founder Abused Seminarians." *National Catholic Reporter*, March 26, 2010. https://www.ncronline.org/news/accountability/legion-christ-acknowledge-founder-abused-seminarians/.
"Thomas Aquinas and Women's Ordination." *Women's Ordination Worldwide*. Last modified February 22, 2023. https://womensordinationcampaign.org/thomas-aquinas-and-womens-ordination.
Tracy, James D. *Erasmus of the Low Countries*. Oakland: University of California Press, 1996.
United Nations. *Universal Declaration of Human Rights*. December 10, 1948. https://www.un.org/en/about-us/universal-declaration-of-human-rights/.
Wang, Stephen. "Why I Choose to Live a Celibate Life." *BBC News Magazine*, April 26, 2010. https://news.bbc.co.uk/2/hi/uk_news/magazine/8644214.stm/.
Watkins, Brendan. "For 30 Years, My Mum Lied to Me About Who My Dad Was. Then She Made a Confession." *Mamamia*, September 4, 2023. https://www.mamamia.com.au/brendan-watkins-story/.

Watson, John, ed. *The Canterbury Dictionary of Hymnology*. https://hymnology.hymnsam.co.uk/e/ernest-sands/.

Wikipedia. "John Jay Report." Last modified February 18, 2004. https://en.wikipedia.org/wiki/John_Jay_Report.

Winfield, Nicole, and Rodney Muhumuza. "After Decades of Silence, Nuns Talk About Abuse by Priests." *AP News*, July 27, 2018. https://apnews.com/general-news-f7ec3cec9a4b46868aa584fe1c94fb28/.

———. "Vatican Meets #MeToo: Nuns Denounce Their Abuse by Priests." *AP News*, July 28, 2018. https://apnews.com/article/96ecb00927ba4433824f74ba51d9c5e0/.

Wright, Louisa. "Study Links Catholic Church, Celibacy and Child Sex Abuse." *DW.com*, December 15, 2017. https://www.dw.com/en/australia-child-sex-abuse-study-notes-catholic-church-mandatory-celibacy-as-cause/a-41817456/.

Zoll, Rachel. "More Than 1,200 Priests Accused of Abuse." *The Irish Examiner*, January 13, 2003. https://www.irishexaminer.com/world/arid-10087689.html/.

www.ingramcontent.com/pod-product-compliance
Lightning Source LLC
Chambersburg PA
CBHW050842230426

43667CB00012B/2112